Chicken Soup for the Soul®

Moms & Sons

Our **101** BEST STORIES

Chicken Soup for the Soul® Our 101 Best Stories:
Moms & Sons; Stories by Mothers and Sons, in Appreciation of Each Other
by Jack Canfield, Mark Victor Hansen & Amy Newmark

Published by Chicken Soup for the Soul Publishing, LLC   www.chickensoup.com

The publisher gratefully acknowledges the many publishers and individuals who granted Chicken Soup for the Soul permission to reprint the cited material.

Cover photos courtesy of Getty Images/© Kieth Brofsky; and Photos.com. Interior illustration courtesy of iStockPhoto.com/©OlgaTelnova[Tolchik]

Cover and Interior Design & Layout by Pneuma Books, LLC
For more info on Pneuma Books, visit www.pneumabooks.com

Distributed to the booktrade by Simon & Schuster. SAN: 200-2442

Publisher's Cataloging-in-Publication Data
(Prepared by The Donohue Group)

Chicken soup for the soul. Selections.
    Chicken soup for the soul : moms & sons : stories by mothers and sons, in appreciation of each other / [compiled by] Jack Canfield [and] Mark Victor Hansen ; [edited by] Amy Newmark.

    p. ; cm. — (Our 101 best stories)

    ISBN-13: 978-1-935096-16-0
    ISBN-10: 1-935096-16-8

1. Mothers and sons--Literary collections. 2. Mothers--Literary collections. 3. Sons--Literary collections. 4. Mothers and sons--Conduct of life--Anecdotes. I. Canfield, Jack, 1944- II. Hansen, Mark Victor. III. Newmark, Amy. IV. Title.

PN6071.M7 C484 2008
810.8/03520431   2008931088

PRINTED IN THE UNITED STATES OF AMERICA
on acid∞free paper
16 15 14 13 12 11 10 09   03 04 05 06 07 08

Chicken Soup for the Soul Moms & Sons

Our 101 BEST STORIES

Stories by Mothers and Sons,
in Appreciation of
Each Other

Jack Canfield
Mark Victor Hansen
Amy Newmark

Chicken Soup for the Soul Publishing, LLC
Cos Cob, CT

Chicken Soup for the Soul

Contents

❶
~Raising Boys~

❷
~Being a Sport~

❸
~Thanks Mom~

❹

~Grieving and Peace~

❺

~Single-Minded Devotion~

❻

~I Choose You as My Son~

❼
~Raising Wonderful Men~

❽
~Special Moments~

❾
~Love through the Generations~

❿
~Through the Eyes of a Child~

⓫
~Courage and Persistence~

⓬
~Making a Difference~

⓭

~Gratitude~

⓮

~Learning from Each Other~

Chicken Soup for the Soul

A Special Foreword

by Jack and Mark

or us, 101 has always been a magical number. It was the number of stories in the first *Chicken Soup for the Soul* book, and it is the number of stories and poems we have always aimed for in our books. We love the number 101 because it signifies a beginning, not an end. After 100, we start anew with 101.

We hope that when you finish reading one of our books, it is only a beginning for you too—a new outlook on life, a renewed sense of purpose, a strengthened resolve to deal with an issue that has been bothering you. Perhaps you will pick up the phone and share one of the stories with a friend or a loved one. Perhaps you will turn to your keyboard and express yourself by writing a Chicken Soup story of your own, to share with other readers who are just like you.

This volume contains our 101 best stories and poems about mothers and sons. We share this with you at a very special time for us, the fifteenth anniversary of our *Chicken Soup for the Soul* series. When we published our first book in 1993, we never dreamed that we had started what became a publishing phenomenon, one of the best-selling series of books in history.

We did not set out to sell more than one hundred million books, or to publish more than 150 titles. We set out to touch the heart of one person at a time, hoping that person would in turn touch another person, and so on down the line. Fifteen years later, we know that it has worked. Your letters and stories have poured in by the hundreds of thousands, affirming our life's work, and inspiring us to continue to make a difference in your lives.

On our fifteenth anniversary, we have new energy, new resolve, and new dreams. We have recommitted to our goal of 101 stories or poems per book, we have refreshed our cover designs and our interior layouts, and we have grown the Chicken Soup for the Soul team, with new friends and partners across the country in New England.

This new volume includes our 101 best stories and poems about mothers and sons from our rich fifteen year history. We chose heartfelt and loving stories written by mothers, sons, and grandmothers celebrating the special bond between mothers and their male offspring. Some will make you laugh and some will make you cry, but they all should warm your heart.

We hope that you will enjoy reading these stories as much as we enjoyed selecting them for you, and that you will share them with your families and friends. We have identified the 43 *Chicken Soup for the Soul* books in which the stories originally appeared, in case you would like to continue reading about motherhood and families among our other titles. We hope you will also enjoy the additional titles about families, parenting, and women in "Our 101 Best Stories" series.

With our love, our thanks, and our respect,
~*Jack Canfield and Mark Victor Hansen*

Moms & Sons

Raising Boys

*Boys are beyond the range
of anyone's sure understanding,
at least when they are between the ages of
18 months and 90 years.*
~James Thurber

Don't Blink

The future destiny of the child is always the work of the mother.
~Napoleon Bonaparte

To prepare for motherhood, I read all the current books by Dr. Spock, Penelope Leach and T. Berry Brazelton. I spoke to new and "seasoned" mothers and received a wealth of information and parenting tips. But one piece of advice I wish I had received was, "Don't blink."

One morning I was delighting in listening to my toddler son's chatter as we talked on his Fisher-Price telephone—I blinked—and one afternoon I called home to realize the deep voice saying "Hello" was my son.

I helped him when my preschooler begged me to turn on Sesame Street—I blinked—and my teenage son was the only one who could operate the multiplying number of remote controls for the TV/DVD/Cable/PlayStation/Stereo system.

I gave my son colorful Playskool keys to play with on our way to the grocery store, the park and the zoo—I blinked—and our Toyota car keys were taking him places to explore on his own.

I spent wonderful hours helping him learn the alphabet—I blinked—and in high school he learned new and frightening combinations of those letters—SAT, GPA and AP.

Many a day I commiserated as my little boy complained that there was no one to play with since only the girls in our neighborhood were home—I blinked—and he was asking for my advice on finding the best dozen roses to send his sweetheart for Valentine's Day.

On the first day of kindergarten, I dropped him off and worried for three hours until I could rush back to pick him up—I blinked—and I was dropping him off at college, knowing I wouldn't see him for three months.

When he was in first grade, I packed a bag for him to take to a sleepover two houses down—I blinked—and he was packing his own luggage to spend six months studying halfway across the world.

On a spring day I took the training wheels off the shiny new bike for my determined four-year-old—I blinked—and an even more determined young man had saved enough money to buy his own shiny new car.

Surely it was only last night that I was tucking him in and heading for bed myself at 10:00 P.M.—I blinked—and my bedtime now coincides with the hour he's heading out the door for a night out with his friends.

I photographed his adorable end-of-preschool pageant when he donned his paper-plate mortarboard and proudly accepted his graduation certificate—I blinked—and he was striding confidently to shake hands with the university president and accept his college diploma.

I always bent down to give my son a bear hug and smother him with kisses—I blinked—and now I reach up to show this young man my love.

I relented when, as a sophomore in high school, my son made an impressive case for why he absolutely had to have a cell phone—I blinked—and as a sophomore in college he was the first family member whose cell phone finally reached me on 9/11 to be sure I had made it out of the World Trade Center. "Mom! Are you okay?"

So to all the new mothers, take it from this seasoned one. Don't blink.

~Pamela Hackett Hobson
Chicken Soup for the Mother and Son Soul

Back from the Heights

Think left and think right and think low and think high.
Oh, the thinks you can think up if only you try!
~Dr. Seuss

On the day my son Alex was born, if you let him hold onto
your little fingers he would stand up. I didn't realize how
unusual that was until years later, when my scrawny little
teenager wanted to pack his harness, his shoes, his chalk and ropes,
and go climb an Alp.

Every time Alex went to the climbing gym, I thought he'd get
tired of it. I secretly hoped something would deter him, but I couldn't
say no because it was the only thing he loved to do. I couldn't say no
to the look in his eyes, and I couldn't refuse when he pleaded with
me to let him accept his buddy Pierre's invitation to visit the Swiss
Alps. Not even when I knew it meant he would be invited to climb
with Pierre's father, Philippe. How could I tell Alex that the sole, driving passion of his life happened to terrify his mother?

If I had seen the "rock" they were going to climb that sunny day,
I never would have agreed. Philippe had assured me it was within my
son's ability.

The Monolith (how could I not have wondered why it was called
that?) rose straight up from the floor of the National Park of Haute
Savoie, cleaving the sky like a skyscraper—a three-hundred-foot
vertical sword of pale granite.

I gasped. "That?" I pointed as all my rock-climbing fears

coalesced into one giant, monolithic terror. They couldn't be up there—Alex would never do anything so foolhardy. There was no way that this—this giant—was within my son's ability.

"Regardez!" Shouts of, "Look!" People milling about at the foot of the mountain had noticed two climbers clinging to its side, moving very slowly, barely visible. A crowd began to form as I walked farther around the base of the rock, my neck already sore from looking up.

"People way up there!" someone commented in French, pointing skyward. Expecting the worst, I felt a stab of guilt. I should have known where they were going. I should have stood my ground and said "No." Now my folly could cost my son and his friend's father their lives.

In the still Alpine air, we could hear the smallest sounds clearly. Alex's voice sounded so small, so unsure, as he responded to Philippe's directions. Although Alex's French was fine, Philippe was speaking English to him just to be on the safe side. The safe side! This irony wasn't lost on me as I clenched and unclenched my fists and tried to breathe slowly.

A murmur surged through the now sizable crowd. "Ce n'est pas des Français, ça. "They aren't French," someone said. "They're speaking English." More mumbling, then a group of heads nodded in mutual judgment: "Those English are crazy!"

English or not, the crazy pair continued slowly, haltingly, up the sheer side of the rock. Why would anyone want to hang onto the side of a slippery wall of stone like that?

But Alex wasn't looking down; he was looking up at Philippe who was shouting directions down to him as my son followed him skyward.

Voices were building again—someone had made another discovery.

"There's a little boy up there." That revelation seemed to touch a chord among all the adults, and heads were shaking vigorously as voices grew more adamant.

"Where is that boy's mother?" said one observer. "How could she let him do such a thing?"

How, indeed, I thought, hoping the nausea would pass.

The silence that followed made me aware that the onlookers had shifted their focus away from the thousand-foot-high rock. Someone had noticed I was lingering nearby, not joining in. Others had come and gone, but I had stayed, alone and silent, staring at the tiny figures. They were looking at me, the lone suspect, the bad mother. A few dared to smile in sympathy or amusement. I smiled back.

"C'est mon fils," I finally admitted. "That's my son." When I explained in French why the climbers were speaking English, heads bobbed silently. "Ah, Americans." That, apparently, explained everything.

There was something else in their eyes, in their stance, in the way they glanced upward as we spoke. Their accusations, uttered before they had known I was present, spoke of good sense and caution and caring, but now their smiles, their wistful peering up the side of the monolith, whispered something louder than our fears.

I squinted upward and felt my smile return, my heart begin to calm. That was my son up there, the one everyone was watching, the one doing what we earthbound beings feared, or perhaps never dared to dream—following his passion to the heavens.

At last, when he and Philippe, in rope-bound slow motion, landed safely back on earth at the foot of that granite monster, the crowd erupted with applause for the little boy who had conquered it. The tears I brushed away before greeting the triumphant climbers were not from fear. I was proud of him—of his courage and what he'd done.

Alex's smile was unlike any I'd ever seen. It radiated a quiet pride that came from his supreme accomplishment. Not an accomplishment I wished for him, but one he had chosen for himself. He had set his own hurdle and overcome it. Wasn't that the true measure of success?

At home, Alex still couldn't seem to pick up his socks, remember to put his dirty clothes in the hamper or clean up his kitchen clutter. But here, on his own sacred ground, fighting the battle he'd chosen for himself, he had mastered the mountain and found the measure of himself.

I can't promise I will never again worry about his safety. What mother could? But from that day on, those feelings lessened as I conquered my own fears at the base of le Monolithe.

~Dierdre W. Honnold
Chicken Soup to Inspire the Body & Soul

A Cup for the Coach

Every survival kit should include a sense of humor.
~Author Unknown

Our next-door neighbor was the coach of my oldest son's team. He frequently took the team "back to the field for practices." On one such occasion it was a warm spring day, and the boys were at practice. I was busy doing my "motherly chores" when I heard a knock at the back door. Upon answering the door I found two boys from the team. They said Mr. P., the coach, needed a cup. I immediately went to one of my boys' rooms and got a cup. The boys ran back to the field with it. A few minutes later and another knock at the back door. The same players were there. I opened the door and the boys proclaimed Mr. P. didn't need an athletic cup, he needed a drinking cup! Oh the mindset of the mother of boys!

~Joanne P. Brady
Chicken Soup for the Baseball Lover's Soul

Brian

The best portion of a good person's life —
his little, nameless, unremembered acts of kindness and love.
~William Wordsworth

Brian is seven. He's a dreamer and drives his teacher crazy. She's stiff as taffy in December.

One day Brian got to school an hour late. His teacher stormed from the classroom, down to the office, and called Brian's mother. "Brian was an hour late today," his teacher said. "I've just about had it!"

Brian's mother worried all day. Finally, Brian got home.

"Brian, what happened at school?"

"I was late. My teacher got mad."

"I know, Brian. She called me. What happened?"

"Well," Brian started, "it must have rained. There were worms all over the sidewalk." He paused a while and went on. "I knew the kids would step on them, so I tried to put them back in the holes."

He looked up at his mother. "It took a long time because they didn't want to go."

His mother hugged him. "I love you, Brian," she said.

~Jay O'Callahan
Chicken Soup for the Gardener's Soul

A Little League Mom

The other sports are just sports. Baseball is a love.
~Bryant Gumbel

While raising our first three sons, my wife had put aside her dislike of sports and served as a Little League mother. Now, eight years after the birth of our last son, she was about to have a fourth child.

After the baby arrived, the nurse came out to the hospital waiting room to get me. My wife was on a stretcher being wheeled back to her room when I caught up with her. "Your husband doesn't know what you had," the nurse said, prompting her.

My wife looked up with a drowsy smile and answered, "Another four years of Little League — that's what I had."

~Harry Del Grande
Chicken Soup for the Baseball Lover's Soul

Rites of Passage

Everyone is the age of their heart.
~Guatemalan Proverb

For some time, my fourteen-year-old son Tyler had been acting more responsibly: doing his chores without having to be told, keeping his room organized, keeping his word. I knew he was making his transition into manhood.

Memories of other turning points flooded my mind. I remembered breathing in Tyler's scent as a baby, and then one day noticing that scent had shifted, changed—my baby had become a little boy. Then I recalled the day the training wheels came off his bicycle. Another time, I'd watched wistfully as he had thrown out all of his toys, only saving a stuffed gorilla that my mother had given him when she was alive. Now another, bigger change was brewing. So, with tears welling up inside, I began to plan a rite-of-passage day for my son.

Tyler's special day began with breakfast at a restaurant. It was just Tyler, his father, stepmother, stepfather and me—no other children. He seemed so happy being with us all together for the first time by himself.

After breakfast, we all went to a heavily wooded park outside of town. I gave him a special journal created just for the day. In the weeks before the ceremony, I had written numerous questions in the journal for him to think about and answer. Questions like: Who was his hero and why? When did he feel the deepest connection to God? What gift in his life had been his favorite and why?

He had chosen several adults who were important in his life, and I had arranged for each of them to come and walk with him for about an hour over the course of the day. The adults were told that this was Tyler's time to "pick their brain," and they were asked to be as open and candid as they comfortably could.

His school principal, whom Tyler had invited to walk with him, shared his favorite prayer—the St. Francis prayer—with Tyler. This had special meaning for my son as it is the same prayer my mother read every morning of her life. She and Tyler were very close, and later he told me it almost felt as if she were there reading it to him.

As dusk began to settle, family and friends gathered for a ceremony on a dock by a lake. A brief rain had freshened the air, which held a fall chill. A tape of Indian flute music played as we sat around a dancing fire. During the ceremony, Tyler shared his intentions about his responsibility to the planet, guests publicly blessed him and we, his parents, made a verbal commitment that—from that moment on—we would hold him as a man in our hearts.

The guests had been instructed to bring nonmonetary gifts to share with Tyler. He received a box of "What I Love About Tyler" notes filled out by the guests, an acorn of a mighty oak tree, handmade pouches and more. One man read a poem aloud that he had written about his father.

During the ceremony and in the weeks following, numerous people came up to me and said, "I would be a different person today if my parents had given me the gift of a rite-of-passage ceremony." Never in my wildest dreams as a mother could I have anticipated the feelings and sacredness that my son and I experienced that day.

Things are different in our house now; there is a deeper, richer feeling of respect for each other. Frequently, before I speak to Tyler, I ask myself, "How would I say this to a man?" And Tyler seems less self-absorbed and more sensitive to how others feel.

This was clearly demonstrated several months later, when our family was planning a fun outing. It was a cold rainy day, and everyone wanted to go to play games at the arcade—except for me. I had made some feeble attempts to recommend something different, but their enthusiasm won out. I did not have the energy to stick up for myself that day.

We were walking out the door when Tyler, now a head taller than I was, came over and put his arm around my shoulders and said, "I can see that you don't really want to go to the arcade. Let's sit down and decide on something we ALL want to do. 'Cause I'm not going anywhere unless you're happy, too."

I was so surprised, I burst into tears, but they were tears of happiness. It felt wonderful to be cared for and to know that my son would be a loving husband and father to his own family someday. Yes, Tyler had become a man—a good man.

~Kathryn Kvols
Chicken Soup for the Mother's Soul 2

The Mother's Day Note

As a single mom, my treasures consist of things my sons, Luc and Sam, have said or written. My most recent treasure came from Luc on Mother's Day.

I felt doubly blessed, sandwiched between both teenagers in church that morning, listening to our pastor speak about families rather than just mothers. His message was encouraging and uplifting, with instruction directed to both parents and kids about showing your love for each other.

During the sermon, Luc scribbled on a piece of paper and handed it to me. My heart swelled as I began unfolding his written declaration of love. I hoped I wouldn't cry in public, as I anticipated his declaration that I was the best mom in the world. I bit my lip to contain my emotion as I read, "Watch the Lakers game today for me while I'm at work."

~Jeri Chrysong
Chicken Soup for the Mother and Son Soul

Moms & Sons

Being a Sport

*October is not only a beautiful month
but marks the precious yet fleeting overlap
of hockey, baseball, basketball, and football.*
~Jason Love

One of the Boys

Laughter is an instant vacation.
~Milton Berle

"Who's better?" I asked my bridegroom of several weeks, "Cassius Clay or Muhammad Ali?"

My new husband looked at me with wide-eyed terror.

"You're kidding, aren't you?"

I shook my head meekly, wondering what was wrong with my question.

"They're the same person," he said, bursting with laughter as he buried his head back in the sports page.

As a young bride, I was simply trying to acclimate myself to my husband's world of sports. My father and two brothers enjoyed sports, but their interest was nothing compared with my bridegroom's obsession. He watched all the games, knew all the statistics, analyzed all the coaches and listened to all the sports talk shows on the radio.

He tried his best to draw me into his sporting world. "Watch this replay!" he would shout from the TV room.

Dropping what I was doing, I'd dash through the house to catch sight of yet another spectacular catch, block, putt, run or leap. Although it was great stuff, the action didn't grab my attention like a good book, a long walk, stars on a clear night or a Monet on a museum wall.

As our marriage moved through the game plan of life, three sons were born to us. Unwittingly, I had chanced upon the perfect team for a pickup game of pitcher, catcher and batter. While my friends with daughters got all dolled up for outings of lunch and shopping, I threw on my jeans for hours of fielding, refereeing and yelling, "Run! You can make it!"

"Aren't you just a little bit disappointed you don't have a girl?" friends often asked.

"Not at all," I answered truthfully.

"Well, there's a special place in heaven for mothers of three boys," they replied, quoting from a popular parenting guide.

So as each young son grew and took his section of the sports page at the breakfast table, I refused to be benched on the sidelines. So what if I didn't have long hair to braid, sweet dresses to iron or ballet shoes to buy? I wasn't going to be left in the dugout. It didn't take long to figure out I could be the ball girl, or I could step up to bat.

In short order, I became one of the boys. I pitched, I putted, I fished. And a whole new world opened up to me. Activities I never would have chosen turned into wondrous adventures.

As pitcher for the neighborhood pickup game, I discovered the joy of a well-hit ball as well as the earthy smell of trampled grass on a hot summer afternoon.

As driver to the putting green, I marveled at the exactness of nailing a four-foot putt as well as the birdsong that serenaded us from a nearby oak tree.

As threader of worms, I caught the excitement of a fish tugging on a line as well as the shade-shifting brilliance of a setting sun.

Just about the time I grew accustomed to these activities, the boys moved into their teenage years, and I found myself thrown into a whole new realm of challenges. Because I was often involved in getting the guys where they wanted to go, I decided there was no point in just sitting and waiting for them to finish. Against my better judgment, I joined the action.

I've spent hours on a cold, overcast day climbing up a forty-foot pine tree, swinging from a rope and yelling "Tarzan" before plunging into the cold waters of a North Woods lake. I rode the fastest, steepest roller coasters of a theme park screaming my head off, and attended years of baseball conventions, running with a crush of fans for auto-graphs from players I didn't even know. I found myself at the top of a snow-covered mountain peak as a novice skier on too steep a slope, simply because my sons knew I would like the view.

"Go for it, Mom," they said. "You can do it!"

And I did.

The highlights of my sporting career came, however, when my sons crossed over into my playing field.

I knew I'd scored when my eighteen-year-old returned from the city and described the personal tour of the art museum he gave his friends, when my sixteen-year-old discussed the contrasting novels of a popular author, and when my thirteen-year-old spotted sparkling Orion in the velvet dark-ness of the sky and announced that it was his favorite constellation.

Not long ago, as we rode home from dropping off my oldest son at college, my younger sons and husband joined in a spirited game of sports trivia.

"Name three pro basketball teams that don't end in 's.'"

"Who holds the record for most home runs by a catcher?"

I listened vaguely as I watched the silver-beamed headlights of farmers' tractors glide down rows of moonlit cornfields. Breathing in the sweet scent of the summer harvest, I noticed a sudden halt in their questioning. I seized the moment.

"Who was better," I asked, "Muhammad Ali or Cassius Clay?"

Stunned silence.

"Muhammad Ali," answered one.

"Cassius Clay?" guessed the other.

Their father burst out laughing. "They're the same person!" he explained.

"Hey, that's a cool trick question, Mom!" said one son.

"Let's try it on Billy and Greg when we get home," said the other.

Twenty-five years later, I had redeemed myself. Just don't ask me the score.

~Marnie O. Mamminga
Chicken Soup for the Mother's Soul 2

Simple Pleasures

As an adult, it's sometimes easy to become jaded about life and miss seeing the joy in small events. I think that's why God allows us to be parents. Living the joy that my ten-year-old feels about racing has softened my heart and given me new perspective.

Such was the case when we traveled to the inaugural race at Kansas City to see the NASCAR Busch and Winston Cup races. Though I'd been to races before, this was the first for my son, Colby, and he was thrilled to be at the first race of a new track, but even more thrilled with the lineup of plans I'd made. Not being much of a navigator, I seemed to get lost every time we went out. But rather than become frustrated, I was able to laugh that each time we did get lost, we happened upon another show car. We saw Jeff Gordon's car, my son's favorite, while looking for Wendy's to have lunch. We saw the Tide car ride simulator at a grocery store while driving ten miles out of our way looking for an interstate on-ramp. We chanced into seeing the M&Ms car as it was being unloaded (what a thrill that sound is!) when we were lost in the same place on a different day (although I decided it didn't count as being lost since I'd been there before).

Our first night in town, I'd planned to go to a fan celebration at a local fairground where many drivers were scheduled to appear. Hoping for an autograph, we soon realized that the line had formed even before we arrived, and so we stood and waited. Our target this time was Rusty Wallace. The adult in me might have been leaning toward wondering how long this wait would be, but my son's joy and anticipation eclipsed any skepticism I might have otherwise felt. He would run from place to place taking picture after picture, and then report back to me, the designated line-stander.

His first (and maybe best) thrill came when Mark Martin was up on the stage talking to the people gathered. Ten-year-old Colby, seemingly without any inhibitions, walked up to the stage and stood just six feet from Mark Martin, pointing a camera in his direction. Not settling for one quick shot, he stood. And he stared. I don't know if Mark felt that feeling we all get when we know someone is staring, but soon he looked down and made eye contact with an admiring young fan. Mark smiled at the boy, and then went on talking to the crowd. Colby's next report back to me was to report this "thrill of my lifetime," as he called it.

When at last we made it to the front of the line to meet Rusty Wallace, Colby wanted a picture. This would be tricky, since the line must keep moving, and nobody else was taking pictures. We hatched a plan that would need to be executed perfectly, as we'd have but one chance.

With precision choreography, Colby jumped up on the platform where Rusty sat. There was no more than half an inch on which to balance himself, so he grabbed the table for dear life. Rusty, upon hearing his name shrieked by a giddy mom (that would be me), looked up and obliged us with a smile. We moved along with our autographs, high-fiving one another at what we'd accomplished.

Race day might have paled in comparison to seeing the drivers we root for week after week, up close and personal. Still, my son pressed his little body against the fence to get as close as he could to Jeff Gordon after his introduction, and snapped picture after picture of his favorite driver as he drove by waving to the crowd.

Jeff went on to win that day, and although I was tired with aching feet, suffering the effects of sleep deprivation and a weekend of junk food, I smile whenever I hear Colby tell people about his race experience. He always says the same thing: "I met Rusty Wallace, Mark Martin smiled at me, and Jeff Gordon WON!"

There you have it, the perfect weekend for any ten-year-old race fan. I was just lucky enough to share the joy.

~Carol Einarsson
Chicken Soup for the NASCAR Soul

Youthful Promises

They say that age is all in your mind.
The trick is keeping it from creeping down into your body.
~Author Unknown

The water sparkles below me. Breezes blow through my hair. I am feeling young. The titillating promise of excitement, fun and more youthful feelings is only a ski-length away.

While on vacation with my husband and two sons, I wanted to rent a ski boat and make a day of it. I thought it was a grand idea. I was imagining myself actually being an active participant in this family experience instead of the same, tired old cheerleader Mom. Since hitting midlife, I sporadically become delusional. So it was I who shamed my reluctant husband into renting the boat, by calling him a middle-aged grouch with no sense of adventure and precious little time to still assert his male athletic prowess. That seemed to do it.

I was feeling unusually frisky and daring that morning as I tugged on the old swimsuit, not standing in front of a mirror, of course. I recalled the young girl of my early twenties. Ah, I was so cute, so tan, so skinny. I had once skied on a clear blue lake in Colorado. The sky so blue, the air so clean as I skimmed effortlessly along the surface of the water. I had the world at my feet. I was in control. I could do anything!

The flood of exciting memories was quickly taking hold, smothering that one little nagging doubt. The doubt that whispered, "You only did this once?" But who cares for caution when the lure of the ski is calling? I was pumped! I was revved! I was ready! My husband could see the gleam in my eye, the determination to ski toward my youth. He knew there was nothing he could say to dissuade me. He only stood there slowly shaking his head.

The first minor detail to attend to is finding the right size life vest. After rummaging around the boat and trying on three or four, which were, of course, made for big strong men (who know how to ski), I finally found a cute little red vest that I thought looked pretty good on me, especially since it hid most of my body.

Next comes the part where I jump, however awkwardly, off the boat and into the water. This was my only moment of slight hesitation as I remembered the swarm of nasty-looking fish by the dock. I had more pressing things to think about at the moment though. The boys were throwing skis at me. I began struggling to get those slender, very long skis on my feet, not an easy task when you're in the water with your cute little life vest having swollen up around your neck and continuously making you roll on your back. After accomplishing that unlady-like task, I was feeling pretty damn good about myself, feeling a little more empowered—a little more cocky, a little more back-to-the-middle of middle age.

Meanwhile, the guys are circling around me in the boat. Over the hum of the engine, I think I hear words. "Row-row!" Row? Why do they want me to row? I begin to move my arms in some sort of circular motion when my son leans way over the boat and screams "Rope!" Oh yes! The rope! Grab the rope as it comes around. I knew that. All I need to do is to find the rope that is floating out there somewhere in all that water. I don't see it, but the guys are yelling and pointing so I guess it's out there. I keep searching, searching. Paddling this way, paddling that way, spinning in circles looking for the rope. "Right there, Mom! Right there!" "Right where—WHERE?" Finally the boys throw the rope out where I can see it. I'm wondering why they didn't just do that in the first place.

Rope in hand, skis in a semi-upward direction, I nod my head like a professional, signaling "Good to go!" I'm sure I can do this. I did it once before, didn't I? The engine revs up, the propeller begins spinning. My husband, behind the wheel, full of trepidation, pulls back on the throttle and takes the boat slowly forward, his head bowed, in what I think is prayer.

We start slowly. I feel the rushing of the water against my skin, surfacing the memories of yesteryear. Aaah, yes. I'm beginning to relax into this when the boat starts speeding up. I grip the rope a little tighter, remembering that I still need to get up out of the water. Suddenly we begin going very fast... faster... and now way too fast! I don't know what happened, but without warning, this sleek, shiny new ski boat has turned into a rip-roaring monster, twisting and turning, blazing through the water at breakneck speed. My mind is a complete blank. What am I supposed to do? There's no time to think. I just keep gripping the rope even as my arms are being ripped apart from the rest of my body! I do remember I'm supposed to keep my legs together—but, oh, the water. There's so much water! I don't remember this much water. Coming at me with the force of steel. I'm using every single muscle in these fifty-year-old legs, struggling to keep them together. Trying to maintain my balance, as well as a little dignity, I begin to come up-up—just a little more—and then... in a nanosecond I feel it! Oh my God! My legs are actually coming apart—it's happening—it's—it's the splits!

The rope tears itself out of my clutches as if to say, "I've had enough of you," and leaves me to slam face down into what feels like a brick wall. Water immediately rushes up my nose and into my mouth. I think I may be drowning! Am I drowning? Is this it? Will this be in my obituary: "Drowned by splitting"? But then, I feel myself being buoyed up and rolled over on my back—Oh my dear, dear little red life vest!

Dazed and sputtering, I surface to find my family circling back towards me. They beg me to get back on the boat, which would have been the intelligent thing to do. But I couldn't let go of the dream just yet. After two more attempts, which were exact replicas of the first, I finally succumb to defeat. With resignation weighing heavy in my mind and heavier still in my body, I clumsily climb back on board, hitting my ankle on the propeller—the last humiliation. The monster's final way of saying, "Gotcha!"

While riding back to middle age, I look behind me, knowing I left my youth somewhere out there in the wide expanse of blue water. A tear forms and rolls down my sunburned (slightly wrinkled) cheek. My mind knows it is time to say goodbye. My heart, well, my heart is heavy and sad.

My boys are already scrambling to jump in and begin their amazing acrobatics. As I watch them, I feel my sad and heavy heart begin its slow and healing journey. It will take time, but somehow this cushy seat makes it a little more tolerable. I feel my bones relaxing and my skin soaking up the sun. Maybe, just maybe, there are a few perks that come with my much-resisted promotion. I may not have to struggle so hard anymore. Perhaps the hard raw action of youth is giving way to a softer, gentler gesture of age. I am being carried along by the waves of time and with that thought I collapse into an exhausted and most welcomed sleep.

~Denise Fleming
Chicken Soup to Inspire a Woman's Soul

11

First Day Fishing

The greatest part of our happiness
depends on our dispositions, not our circumstances.
~Martha Washington

All summer, our six-year-old son Chris had been begging his dad to take him on his first fishing trip. Tomorrow was the big day, but now Ron had to work and the day was ruined. I could see the disappointment in our son's eyes. Choking back the tears, he turned to walk away.

"Wait a minute, Chris," I heard myself say. "Can I take you fishing?"

"Well, uh, okay, Mom," he answered as if he wasn't sure he'd heard me correctly.

"We'll get up at five o'clock in the morning. Is that all right?"

"Sure," he said with a smile quickly replacing his tears.

I should have thought it through more clearly before I had spoken; I hadn't been fishing before either.

The alarm buzzed at 5 A.M. I couldn't remember the last time I'd been up that early. After eating a quick bowl of cereal, we hoisted the ice chest into the car. It was loaded with sandwiches, lots of drinks and plenty of ice to pack all the fish we were going to catch. With a list of things we needed, we headed for the nearest bait and tackle shop to buy a pole, line, hooks and some worms. Then we were off to the lake.

It was a typical August morning with the sun already scorching. We trudged along the rocky shore carrying our gear and finally settled under a "wannabe" tree. I explained to Chris that a wannabe tree is a want-to-be tree, because the trees here in Arizona don't grow very big due to the extreme heat and lack of rain. He agreed that the small amount of shade was better than none at all.

I attached the line to the pole and secured the hook with a knot that would have held Moby Dick.

I was dreading the next step.

"Mom, can you put a worm on my hook for me?"

"Okay, but you'd better learn quick. This is my first and last time."

All right, I can do this, I thought as I scrunched my eyes shut and quickly grabbed the first worm that unwittingly wriggled between my thumb and forefinger. The next chore was putting the worm on the hook. I didn't know worms came in different sizes; this one was really skinny. Chris stood back, partly because of the look on my face and partly because it amazed him that I'd even dare touch a worm. Chris must have been reading my mind as I wondered how this worm was going to stay on the hook.

"It doesn't want to stay on the hook," he murmured as the worm kept falling off.

Suddenly, quite by accident, I stabbed the worm. There it hung mortally wounded and writhing in pain. "Quick, throw the line into the water!" I screamed. There was no way that Chris was going to be able to skewer these skinny worms onto a hook without hooking himself. The realization that I was going to have to put the rest of these wriggling, slimy little crawlers on the hook for Chris didn't thrill me, but I soon became quite the expert at "accidentally" attaching worms to the hook.

Three hours later and with three small bluegill neatly lined up in the corner of our ice chest, we decided to head for home. The fish had given up trying to make a meal from our "slim" offerings, and the glaring sun had sent them for deeper, cooler water.

Ron was still at work when we arrived home. I was relieved because I was sweaty, smelled of fish, and our meager catch didn't qualify for bragging rights.

"Mom, are we gonna cook 'em?"

"I suppose we could," I grimaced. The thought hadn't even entered my mind. The fish were so puny that we'd be lucky to get more than two small bites out of each one. Nevertheless, I popped them into the pan, and within minutes they were ready to eat. I put all three fish on Chris' plate.

"No, you get one too, Mom," he insisted.

My plan hadn't worked; I was going to have to eat one. Chris took the first bite and didn't spit it out, so I tried a bite too. It tasted just like the fishy lake water, but I forced it down. Ron walked in just as I was taking my last bite.

"Well, how was your trip?" he asked.

Chris began talking before I could swallow my last mouthful.

"It was great, Dad! The water was so clear and smooth, and the sky was really blue. There were no boats when we first got there so it was real quiet. We could hear the birds singing. Mom and I sat on a rock and watched a duck swim and make a trail in the water. It was really fun and Mom was the best!" He then told Ron all about wannabe trees. When he had finished talking, Chris turned and hugged me.

Was the sky that blue? What singing birds? And I hadn't even seen the duck. I had been too engrossed putting the worms on the hook to appreciate the beauty, but Chris had taken it all in.

"Thanks, Mom. Let's go back to our wannabe spot again real soon," he said, his eyes sparkling.

How could I refuse his irresistible offer?

"Yes, we'll go again soon."

~Tanya Breed
Chicken Soup for the Fisherman's Soul

12

Mom Has a Wicked Curveball

No man stands so straight as when he stoops to help a boy.
~Knights of Pythagoras

The boys of summer are full swing into their season. After watching a major-league baseball game on TV, my son, Daniel, digs into the closet for his plastic bat, ball and miniature baseball glove.

"Come on, Mom," he says, "let's go play ball."

I know I won't get any peace until I go to the nearby ball field with him to play his unstructured, invigorating version of baseball, so I throw on my well-worn New York Mets cap, grab my own battered glove and we're off.

On the way to the park, it strikes me as singularly sad that this little boy has to play baseball with his mother. Not that I'm a slouch; after all, I was a softball star in high school and college, and I'm still a mainstay on my church and work softball teams. And it's not that I don't love baseball, because I do. It's just that sometimes I wish my son had someone else to play ball with him. Someone male.

Being the single mother of a growing boy is one of the most difficult things I have ever done in my life. There is only so much that I, as a woman, can teach my son. I can sit beside him in the bleachers at the ballpark and describe the action on the diamond with good authority. I can teach him how to pitch, how to get the flowing rhythm of the wind-up, stretch and delivery beautifully and gracefully in sync. I can show him how to bat: "Keep your stick off your shoulder! Raise that back elbow! Choke up! Step into the pitch and follow through!" I can show him how to hit first base with his outside foot, so he can have a straight path to second without going too far out of the baseline. I can show him how to scrabble sideways, glove low, limbs loose, in pursuit of a hard grounder hit to him at second base. I can teach him the duties of a good catcher, including how to block the plate with his body so a run won't score, taking the jarring impact without a murmur. This is the way I play ball myself. I can coach him well, and he will be a good player.

But there are so many things I can't teach him. While I can tell him how he should act as a young man, injecting a womanly wish of how men should behave, I can't tell him how to be a man. I don't know anything about the subtleties and secrets of manhood. I can play at men's games all I want, and play them convincingly, and my son will learn something. But it won't be the same as having a man in his life, someone he can admire, relate to and learn from.

I search out role models for him, but it's easier said than done. I'm choosy—I have to be. I want Daniel to become a good, brave man who respects women, loves equality and diversity, and is strong and sure of himself. Although all these qualities may not be embodied in only one of the men who take it upon themselves to be part of my son's life in the absence of a full-time father, there are enough men around who, together, give my son an excellent overview of the man he has the potential to become.

I want my son to have Frank's social conscience, Alan's sense of humor, Darren's work ethic and Steve's gentleness. I want him to have Phil's love for his mother, David's devotion to church and family, Tony's eagerness for education and Ted's spirit of fun. I want him to have Larry's quiet calmness, Levon's friendliness, Bill's helpfulness and Ben's sense of adventure. I want all these attributes for Daniel and something more. I want him to take everything he learns from these men and, one day, pass it on to another boy—making a connection that continues unbroken.

I hope my son gets to play baseball someday soon with someone who, during the game, will also teach him about some of life's nuances. Someone who will talk to him in a way that I can't—as a man to a boy, with a man's point of view and a masculine sort of love. My son will be very lucky to meet a person like that.

Meanwhile, I have this quiet little fantasy:

The World Series has just ended. My son, the Series' Most Valuable Player, has led his team to victory by pitching a perfect game: no runs, no hits, no errors, no walks. It awes everyone that someone so young can pitch so flawlessly.

"Who taught you to pitch like that?" a reporter asks.

My son smiles. "My mother," he says. "Mom has a wicked curveball."

~Tanya J. Tyler
Chicken Soup for the Single Parent's Soul

Mom Hits the Links

The mind can have tremendous control of the body; very few ailments can defeat focused energy and a determined spirit.
~Katherine Lambert-Scronce

I talked to my mother on the phone one night. She had just returned from her first golf school, which also happened to be her first golf game.

"I sure do love this game," she gushed.

You see, my brother and sister and girlfriend and myself had purchased a starter set of clubs for Mom last Christmas. She runs her own business, in the sports insurance and benefits arena, and over the years her travels to meetings had taken her to places like Doral and Pebble Beach. But she was the only member of the family who didn't play golf. So the rest of us would hear: "Well, I could have played a round there if I played golf. But I did enjoy riding around the course in a cart. You know how I love the sound of the ocean."

Naturally, there was only so much of this we muni hacks in the family could take. So we took a chance and surprised her with the clubs. We figured she'd be decent because we'd seen her take a few swings one time at a driving range. Although she's a southpaw she seemed comfortable swinging right-handed, and she had whacked the heck out of the ball. Plus, it seemed like a good mode of exercise for her as she moved into a different phase of her life.

She was very excited, but knew so little about the game and how to play it that she feared embarrassment.

"Just go to the range for a while, Mom. Then you can try playing a few holes, and gradually work your way up to a full round," I counseled.

Those first few months, she went to the range just a couple of times. But it was exciting to buy the clothes.

"I got myself a new golf outfit today. And I now have golf shoes."

"How about your swing—have you hit any balls lately?"

"No, but I'm going to be all ready when it's time for golf camp!"

We siblings conferred and separately advised her to start some simple stretching and exercises a few weeks before going to Pine Needles. Then we sat back and waited.

I didn't hear from her the entire week. The day I knew the school ended I called her not long after she arrived home.

"Oh, we had so much fun," she said again. "And you know what? Yesterday I played my first round."

"Wow, a full eighteen?"

"Well, it was a nine-hole round. And my team won! It was what they call 'best ball.' And on one hole I drove it all the way to the green and we used my ball."

"What do you mean—was it a par-3 or a par-4?"

"Oh, I don't know."

"I love that kind of attitude, Mom." I really did.

"All I know to do is try and get the ball into the hole in as few strokes as possible," she continued succinctly. "The other ladies' shots were back a ways, and one of them said, 'Oh my gosh, Sally's ball is on the green.'"

I could tell that this was one of those watershed conversations, the kind you only have once.

"So I played another nine holes later, and guess what? I shot a 46."

"Holy cow," I said, stunned, "you must have even had a par in there somewhere."

"Oh yes, I had a couple of those, and also did one of the holes under par."

"A birdie?" I said, sitting down. "That's incredible! What was it, a par-5?"

"I don't remember. When I told the bartender what I had shot, he was surprised, and said, 'Sally, do you realize that if you doubled that score for a full eighteen, you'd break 100? That's fantastic.' But I thought it wasn't that great, since it was over par."

I paused to let that settle in.

"Thank you again for the clubs, Adam. Oh, you know what? I need to find out where you got them, so I can get a sand wedge and pitching wedge."

"Oh yeah," I said sheepishly, "we only got you the starter set. I suppose you'll need some even-numbered clubs too."

"Oh, heavens no. Not yet. But I did learn about what to hit what distances. Of course, I'll probably fall back some now, but I sure love this game!"

It was a wry turning of the tables, as I, the son, pondered the wonderful, fleeting innocence of my mother's introduction to golf. There she was, discovering the pleasures of the game, apparently still whacking the heck out of the ball and enjoying the very act. The experiment had succeeded, and she was launched on a late-blooming golf career. Perhaps she will never pay attention to the score... until she reaches par that is.

For me, and anybody else who is unlearning the techniques and visualizations and just learning to hit the darned ball, it is a lesson in rediscovery. Chances are we sure do love this game too. And I, for the thousandth and not the final time, get to say... thanks, Mom.

~Adam Bruns
Chicken Soup for the Golfer's Soul

Moms & Sons

Chapter 3

Thanks Mom

All mothers are working mothers.
~Author Unknown

About the Doubt

*H*e cried for the first time at eleven o'clock one February morning. It would not be the last time, but it would be the best time. I had given birth to my soul and did not even know it.

An enthusiastic young nurse, not yet used to the arrival of new life, grinned at me and said from beneath her garishly flowered surgical cap, "You have a beautiful baby boy! Do you want to see him?" "No," was my flat reply. She giggled and brought him to me from behind the drapery.

"Oh... he's so ugly," I said. And he was—bald except for a fringe of shoulder-length, stringy brown hair, and covered in blood and some sort of let's-not-talk-about-what-it-is goo. I was drugged, but I remember asking myself, *What's the matter with you? You aren't supposed to think or act like this!*

That was Thursday. By the following Thursday, we were home, and I was waiting for that "mother love" thing to kick in. I nursed him, I held him, I changed him, I bathed him, I this'ed him and I that'ed him... and I waited.

So I can't tell you if it was while I was winding the swing or cleaning up something better left to the imagination, but there it was—a moment when my heart felt as though it were stuck on the upside of a beat so powerful that had it burst free from my chest it would certainly have ended up orbiting Venus.

The years passed. I had some doubts about this love that felt so powerful. Doubts as profound as the love I had for my son colored every moment of the next twenty years. His childhood was destined to be fraught with struggle. There was never enough money. There would be no Prince Charming to come along and save us from the poverty I fought to overcome. Positive male role models for my son were nonexistent. The men I attracted were not interested in signing up for the family plan, and any less than that was simply not an option.

Try as I might, underemployment became my principal career. I went back to school with dreams of becoming an educator. When day care was not available, I dragged Matt to class with me, where he sat through long lectures without complaint. Four hundred and sixty-four dollars a month meant tough choices on a regular basis, and we visited the food banks more than once, not just for food, but clothing as well. Many a meal consisted of nothing more than boiled potatoes. My meager credit rating deteriorated to horrendous as rent took precedence over luxuries like a telephone and credit cards. I finally got my bachelor's degree, but my dream would not be realized because graduate school proved too great a challenge for this single mother.

I had failed.

What kind of role model was I? Should I have kept him? Should I have given him up to a family who would have provided for him much better than I ever could? These doubts recurred with every layoff and corporate downsizing to which I fell victim.

One doubt that I never had was my love for and responsibility to him. He inspired me when there was no inspiration to be found. I watched him grow and his dreams grew right along with him. We rarely traded a cross word. He grew up long before he should have. When worry consumed me, he comforted me, soothing away the tears that flowed, despite my efforts to control them. This loving, wonderful child deserved so much better. By being his mother, I could not let go of the feeling that I had done him some great disservice.

Yes, I doubted myself, but never doubted for a moment this one mission in my life. We spoke openly of anything about which he was curious. I answered his questions to the best of my ability and admitted my limitations when I simply did not know. But this I did know: he was never bad, just sometimes did things that were not good. It was my belief that love without condition was not love without responsibility. On the few occasions when he got into trouble, he was expected to face the consequences of his actions; but I was, and always will be, there.

In spite of the challenges, we persevered, and we laughed far more often than we cried. Matt and I were a team.

Disruption and upheaval were regular parts of his existence. Money issues dictated that we move a lot. He attended no fewer than seven different elementary schools. Every move was either an attempt to improve our situation or simply save us from homelessness. There were only two constants in those days: our love and my doubts. By the time he got to middle school, it was clear he was someone special. Repeated displacement had robbed him of opportunities he would surely have been offered under more stable circumstances. Yet Matt had shone like a beacon in every school that he attended. His hard work, resultant scholarships and financial aid made it possible for him to go to college.

We continued to speak regularly about anything and everything that was going on in his life. Memorial Day weekend of his sophomore year he came home for a visit. I can't recall how the conversation started, but he talked about one of his roommates whose father was the CEO of a major international corporation. John had grown up not wanting for anything but had told Matt that he would trade it all for the kind of relationship that Matt had with me.

Then Matt said to me, "Mom, I want you to know that despite being dirt poor and never knowing where the next meal was coming from, my childhood was the happiest time of my life. I would not trade having had you for a mother for anything in the world. You gave me a sense of self that tells me that I can accomplish anything if I set my mind to it. You taught me values that I cannot find fault with, and I learned by your example what true love is. I could not have created a better parent if I had been able to custom order you. I feel incredibly lucky to have had you for my mother. Thank you for giving me life." With those words, my choice was finally vindicated.

Matt graduated from college with honors. He managed to study abroad for a year and is now in California pursuing an acting career. I don't worry anymore about whether I did the right thing. His life, his courage and his determination reassure me daily that he is the best person he can be, and I take pride in the fact that I had a hand in that.

~Wanda Simpson
Chicken Soup for the Single Parent's Soul

The "No Hug" Rule

There's nothing like a mama-hug.
~Adabella Radici

The first day of kindergarten
He hurried to the door
Shrugging off his mother's hugs
He didn't need them anymore
For he was all grown up now
Too big for all that stuff
Instead he waved a quick goodbye
Hoping that would be enough
When he came home from school that day
She asked what he had done
He handed her a paper
With a big round yellow sun
A picture quite imperfect
For he'd messed up here and there
But she didn't seem to notice
Or she didn't seem to care
The first day of junior high
He hurried to the door
Running from his mother's hugs
He didn't want them anymore
He ignored her calling out to him
As he hurried down the street
Near the intersection

Where his friends had planned to meet
He hoped that she would understand
Why he had to walk to school
Riding with his mother
Just wouldn't have been cool
And when he came home from school
She asked what he had done
He handed her some papers
With Xs marked on more than one
The teacher clearly pointing out
The wrong answers here and there
But his mother didn't seem to notice
Or she didn't seem to care
The first day of senior high
He hurried out the door
Jumped into the driver's seat
Of his jacked-up shiny Ford
He left without his breakfast
He left without a word
But he turned and looked back
Before pulling from the curb
He saw her waving frantically
As he drove away
He tapped his horn just once
To brighten up her day
He saw a smile cross her face
And then he drove from sight
Onward to a different world
A new exciting life
And at his graduation
As tears shone in her eyes
He knew the time had come
To bid his mom goodbye
For he was off to college
Off to better days

No more rules to abide
Alone to find his way
Suitcases filled the trunk
Of his dirty beat-up Ford
He couldn't wait to get to school
To check out his room and dorm
She opened up his car door
Closed it when he got in
Then smiled proudly at her son
As tears dropped from her chin
She reached through the open window
Wished him luck in school
And then she pulled him close to her
And broke the "no hug" rule
He felt the freedom greet him
As he pulled out on the interstate
At last his life was his alone
He anticipated fate
College life was more challenging
Than he ever could have hoped
There was no time to respond to letters
His mother often wrote
He was a grown adult now
Too old for all that stuff
His visits during holidays
Would have to be enough
Besides, midterms were quickly coming
The pressure was immense
He studied late into the night
His need to pass intense
He wondered how he'd manage
How he'd ever cope
What if he failed his tests?
Would there be no hope?
As if he had a calling

He headed down the interstate
Driving at full speed
The hour getting late
He pulled up to the curb
Where once he used to roam
And went through the open door
Of his mother's home
She was sitting at the table
With a drawing in a frame
Memories from the past
That brought both joy and pain
She didn't need to ask
Why he was home from school
Because she knew the answer
When he broke the "no hug" rule
His arms around her tightly
Peering at the drawing he had done
Lots of trees, imperfect branches
And a big round yellow sun
She smiled a knowing smile
And then she spoke aloud
"Son you always did
And you always will make me very proud
For look how far you've traveled
From that little boy so brave
Heading off to kindergarten
Your hand up in a wave
And through the years you've made mistakes
But son I've made them, too
Being perfect is not an option in life
Simply do the best you can do
And don't expect more than that
For life is supposed to be fun
You've only got one to live
Do what is best for you son"

Sitting in his dorm room
When the pressure seems too much
And all that he is striving for
Seems completely out of touch
He peers at the drawing
Of a big round yellow sun
And then he is reminded
Of just how far he's come
From childhood to manhood
Fighting back many a fear
Through trials and tribulations
Holding back many a tear
Knowing that being successful
Isn't passing every test
And the only way to falter in life
Is by failing to do his best
And the biggest lesson he's learned
One he did not learn in school....
That it's okay, for even a man
To break the "no hug" rule

~Cheryl Costello-Forshey
Chicken Soup for the College Soul

P.K.'s Mission

P.K. was the center of his mother Talia's universe, and she was very happy to spend what little free time she had with her beautiful boy. P.K. was the youngest of three children and the last one to live at home. P.K. didn't know his father. When the other children in his neighborhood asked him about his father, he explained that his father was not around, but his mother was happy having him all to herself.

P.K.'s neighborhood was crowded and dangerous, plagued by unemployment, poverty and violence. From a very young age, P.K. was taught to avoid trouble, and he was good at it—most of the time. P.K.'s uncle, who until recently had lived two blocks away, often took P.K. along on his bread-delivery route during the summer. P.K. absorbed the words of wisdom his uncle judiciously dispensed between deliveries—much of it focused on how to stay out of trouble and how to pick friends. To P.K., his uncle was much larger than his 150-pound frame. P.K. looked forward to being a few years older so that he could go on all-night catfishing adventures with his uncle on the river that bordered the city.

A good student, P.K. paid attention in school. His mother checked his homework every night. P.K. heeded his uncle's words about choosing friends and avoiding fights. Also, P.K. was a good friend; all the other third-graders knew that they could count on P.K.

One warm October afternoon, P.K.'s mother walked six blocks to pick him up after school. A new job and a bigger paycheck prompted a sense of hope in P.K.'s mother. Her steps were light and brisk. She anticipated P.K.'s surprise and pride at her coming to pick him up after school. On the way home, the two would buy the school supplies that most students brought with them on the first day of school, but which Talia could not afford until now because of her new job. A slice of pizza and an ice cream cone would celebrate the paycheck and guarantee a memorable day together.

Heading for the store, P.K. and his mother rounded the corner to head up Mill Street. P.K. felt his mother's hand grab his shoulder tightly as his slight torso was drawn to hers. Their feet stopped so abruptly that they leaned forward, off balance. At the end of the block, two groups of young men were screaming threats at one another. Shots were fired, the sound of them bouncing sharply off the hard, graffiti-covered factories and storefronts. Tires squealed and cars dashed through stoplights to get away from the area. The noise stopped as abruptly as it had begun. The young men disappeared into the crevices of the city. Sirens interrupted the interminable, numbing silence.

P.K.'s mother lay bleeding at his feet, her eyes staring blankly upward. The ambulance came, but it was too late: Talia was dead.

When the funeral was over, P.K. was shuttled among relatives and friends—a month with his aunt and uncle, a couple of weeks with his mother's best friend, a month with his older sister and her family—the length of his stay determined by the available room and resources. P.K. shared beds and slept on couches; often, he slept on the floor.

P.K. was quiet in school. He stared blankly as his teacher's explanations and assignments went unheard. His grades dropped, and P.K. found himself drifting further and further from his friends. Gradually, his friends tired of encouraging and consoling P.K., whose once-familiar laugh became a distant memory. And as the weeks and months dragged by, the reassuring words of relatives and his minister became hollow. Anger and despair competed for P.K.'s attention.

One day, a woman visited P.K.'s school and spoke to his class about starting a peer-mediation program. P.K. came to life, bouncing in his seat and waving his arms to ask questions. He waited until she finished her presentation about peer mediation, then bolted to the front of the room to sign up for training.

"Are you sure, P.K.? You have seen so much conflict and violence. I am afraid that mediation will make you think about your mother," his teacher cautioned.

"Yes, I'm sure about the training," he answered. "And yes, I'm thinking about my mother. This is exactly who she would want me to be."

~Roberta Anna Heydenberk, Ed.D.
and Warren Robert Heydenberk, Ed.D.
Chicken Soup for the Soul: Stories for a Better World

A Worthy Investment

My mother had a slender, small body, but a large heart—a heart so large
that everybody's joys found welcome in it, and hospitable accommodation.
~Mark Twain

When we were growing up, we always suspected our mother was a little bit crazy. One day in particular stands out in my mind. It was a Saturday afternoon in the fall, and Mom had been running errands all day. We five kids were raking leaves in the front yard when Mom pulled into the driveway. She was driving our beat-up old pickup truck. (It still amazes me that she wasn't embarrassed to be seen in that thing.)

"Hey kids, come see what I got!" Mom yelled excitedly, and we rushed over to investigate. We never knew what Mom would be up to. She climbed up into the back of the truck, flung her arms open wide, and cried, "Ta-daa! Can you believe it was free?" She wore an enormous smile of anticipation.

Climbing into the pickup to join her, we saw the ugliest couch in the world. It had once been blue and red plaid, but now it was faded, stained and the stuffing was coming out in spots.

"Mother, please tell me you're not putting this in the living room!" I groaned, dreading the embarrassment of explaining this monstrosity to my friends. Teenage boys were supposed to pull stunts like this, not mothers! Sometimes, I thought, Mom was just nuts.

"Of course not!" Mom laughed. "I'm going to put it in the garage. You see, I had this idea that we could clean out the garage a little bit and make it into a kids' hangout room. Mr. Larson down the street said we could have his old ping pong table for only ten dollars if we wanted it, and we'll set that up in there, too. Then, when friends come over you can hang out in the garage, stay up late and not bother anybody! So what do you think?"

I looked at my brothers and sisters, who were obviously excited by the idea. "Hooray!" Chris yelled. "It can be a guys-only hangout. No girls allowed. Right, John?" John was quick to agree, but Mom interrupted as my sisters and I began to protest.

"We'll all share it. You know that's how we do things around here! But before we do anything else, we've got to get that garage cleaned out. Let's go!" Rakes and leaf piles were deserted as we followed Mom to the garage. I had to admit, as crazy as Mom was to bring home a nasty couch, the idea of a hangout room was starting to grow on me. There was already a basketball hoop and a dartboard outside the garage. This could actually become a pretty cool place to hang out. I wasn't so sure my girlfriends were into ping pong, but at least we could sit on the couch (once I found a clean blanket to cover those spots) and talk.

Our garage quickly became a neighborhood favorite where kids in the neighborhood could hang out and relax. Mom couldn't have been happier. She loved having lots of young people around the house. They all loved her, too, and treated her like one of the gang. Sometimes I would come home at night with friends and end up going to bed while Mom and my friends were still sitting up chatting! Everyone considered her their friend, and I was secretly very proud of having a "cool" mom.

Mom made our house a place that was always open to our friends, no matter who they were or what their background and reputation were. Our parents were always very strict about our going out at night to parties and on dates, but Mom was always quick to remind us that she was glad to have all our friends come to our house. We could always bring the party home!

Her real concern was that we were safe. She was much happier knowing that the party was going on downstairs instead of somewhere else! I think that Mom and Dad probably passed many sleepless hours, while ping pong games and basketball tournaments went on outside their bedroom window at all hours of the night. But we never once heard them complain. To them, it was a worthwhile sacrifice.

Mom wasn't the kind of mother who always had cookies and milk waiting for us and our friends. Instead she had refrigerated cookie dough, brownie mixes and microwave popcorn available twenty-four hours a day. Even now, when my husband and I come to visit my parents, we can count on seeing my brothers and sisters and friends there in the kitchen. Sometimes, even when my siblings aren't there, their friends are! Mom has so endeared herself to them by her open heart and open house policy, they know they can count on her to listen when no one else will.

We still have that old couch in the garage. Although it's pretty much destroyed, no one wants to part with it. For us, it's a very special monument to Mom's investment in our lives and our relationships.

~Allison Yates Gaskins
Chicken Soup for the Mother's Soul 2

A Mother's Love

There came a time when the risk to remain tight in the bud
was more painful than the risk it took to blossom.
~Anaïs Nin

Think back to the early '90s, before Ellen "came out" and *Will & Grace* was not yet all over prime-time television. Before Matthew Shepard received national attention, and being gay got the public support it has today. Imagine a nineteen-year-old Mexican son coming out to his mother and seeing the heartbreak in her eyes. Picture her heart breaking into pieces so small they could fit through the eye of a sewing needle.

Living in Texas, growing up Catholic with a strong Mexican ancestry and influence, it was difficult coming to terms with my own homosexuality. I can remember many nights when I prayed the entire rosary and begged God to change me. As the years pushed on, I gradually accepted who I was and learned to love myself despite my machismo-rich heritage. However, that was only the first step.

All Latinos know how important family is, and I am not any different. Accepting my sexuality was a big move for me on my journey to self-discovery. Yet, the burning question was, would my family accept me as well? The thought of losing them and being disowned frightened me more than death.

In our culture, we are taught that family is everything. I could gladly meet any of life's challenges as long as I had my family by my side to face them head-on. Nonetheless, the time had come, and I needed to be honest with them.

Easing into the task, I came out to my younger brother first. Surprisingly, his reaction was good and more or less indifferent. He was of the mind-set that I was his brother, and my sexual orientation was not important. Feeling particularly confident about the experience, I decided to come out to my mother.

It was October 11, 1994, National Coming Out Day. She cried, yelled, screamed and ultimately blamed herself. It was a nightmare. By the end of the night, our eyes were red and puffy from all the crying, and our noses dripped with mocos. We were exhausted and retired to our respective rooms without saying good night. I never expected her to react the way she had, and I worried that our relationship was forever damaged.

That night I lay in bed and thought about a TV talk show that I had seen earlier that day. The focus of the show was National Coming Out Day, and the guests were a variety of non-Latinos coming out to their families. Their experiences on the show were much better than mine that night, and I could not comprehend why my mother had reacted so awfully. For the next few days, the house was covered with a blanket of awkwardness.

The next day I came out to my sister, and a month later I came out to my dad. I was able to delay telling my father as my parents divorced when I was in middle school. I could not bear another episode like the one I experienced with Mom. Nevertheless, their reaction to my news was much like my younger brother's, and I was very much surprised by my father's kind words. He said, "You're my son, and I'll always love you no matter what."

I wish I could write that my mother soon thereafter came to her senses and we promptly mended our relationship. The truth of the matter is, the road to her acceptance and understanding was a long one. In the months that followed, we had many emotional discussions, and she had several questions. She was determined to figure out what went wrong. Mom would encourage me to continue to pray, and I know that HIV and AIDS were huge concerns for her. A lot of people, especially at that time, believed that being gay was equivalent to an AIDS death sentence.

Today, eight years later and thanks to a lot of determination and persistence, my mother and I have a very healthy and open relationship. In a lot of ways, she is my best friend. Recently, we've watched movies with gay themes as she tries to gain a better understanding of my life. Her favorite is *The Broken Hearts Club*.

As far as my seemingly open-minded brother, sister and father and our relationship today, they have adopted the philosophy, "Don't ask, don't tell." We are all still close, and I now have a sister-in-law, a three-year-old niece and one-year-old nephew. But they turn a blind eye and deaf ear to those things they choose not to know. Unfortunately, that means there are parts of me missing from their lives. My mother and I had a rough start as 1994 came to an end, but today she is the only one in my family who knows me completely.

My Mexican-proud mom had survived an impoverished childhood on the north side of town, coupled with years of adolescence tormented by Texas-style bigotry and hatred for our race. And just when she probably thought she was in the clear, her first-born son professes he is gay. But falling back on our faith and cultural importance of family, that no longer matters to her. Come what may, we promise to be there for one another and to stand together.

People's reactions vary when I come out to them today, but as long as I have my mother supporting me, I am happy. What more could a son ask from his mother than her continued support and love? Nothing can compare to a mother's love, and being a mama's boy is a good thing. My mom has been the rock in my life, y no puedo imaginar mi vida sin ella.

¡Gracias a Dios por ti mamá, gracias por quererme sin límites!

~Johnny N. Ortez, Jr.
Chicken Soup for the Latino Soul

Against the Odds

It was the summer of 1942. I was nineteen years old and a signalman third class on the USS Astoria stationed in the South Pacific.

One hot night in August, we found ourselves skirmishing with the Japanese for control of Guadalcanal, gearing up for the bloody battle that soon followed. At midnight, I finished my duty on watch. Still wearing my work detail uniform of dungarees and a T-shirt, and only pausing long enough to unstrap my standard-issue life belt and lay it beside me, I fell into an exhausted sleep.

Two hours later, I was awakened abruptly by the sound of an explosion. I jumped to my feet, my heart pounding. Without thinking, I grabbed my life belt and strapped it on. In the ensuing chaos, I focused on dodging the rain of enemy shells that were inflicting death and destruction all around me. I took some shrapnel in my right shoulder and leg, but by some miracle, I avoided being killed.

That first battle of Savo Island lasted for twenty minutes. After the enemy fire ceased, the men left standing helped with the wounded, while others manned the guns.

I was making my way toward a gun turret when suddenly, the deck disappeared. My legs windmilled beneath me as I realized that an explosion had blasted me off the deck. My shock was immediately replaced by a stomach-clenching fear as I fell like a stone — thirty feet into the dark, shark-infested water below.

I immediately inflated my life belt, weak with relief that I'd somehow remembered to put it on. I noticed between ten and thirty men bobbing in the water in the area, but we were too far away from each other to communicate.

I began treading water, trying to stay calm as I felt things brushing against my legs, knowing that if a shark attacked me, any moment could be my last. And the sharks weren't the only danger: The powerful current threatened to sweep me out to sea.

Four agonizing hours passed this way. It was getting light when I saw a ship—an American destroyer—approaching. The sailors on board threw me a line and hauled me aboard.

Once on the ship, my legs buckled and I slid to the deck, unable to stand. I was fed and allowed to rest briefly. Then I was transported back to the Astoria, which, though disabled, was still afloat. The captain was attempting to beach the ship in order to make the necessary repairs.

Back on board the Astoria, I spent the next six hours preparing the dead for burial at sea. As the hours passed, it became clear our vessel was damaged beyond help. The ship was taking on water and finally, around twelve hundred hours, the Astoria began to roll and go under.

The last thing I wanted to do was to go into that water again, but I knew I had to. Filled with dread, I jumped off the high side of the sinking ship and began swimming. Although I still had my life belt on, it couldn't be inflated a second time. Luckily, I was soon picked up by another destroyer and transferred to the USS Jackson.

Against all the odds, I had made it—one of the lucky men to survive the battle of Savo Island. We were issued Marine uniforms, and I spent my time, in between visits to the ship's doctors for treatment of my wounds, sitting on the deck of the Jackson, waiting for our transport to San Francisco's Treasure Island and the leave that would follow.

Though it felt odd to wear the unfamiliar uniform, I wasn't sad to lose my old dungarees and T-shirt. The one thing I found I didn't want to give up was my life belt. I hung on to the khaki cloth-covered rubber belt, studying it sometimes as I sat around on the Marine ship.

The label on the belt said it had been manufactured by Firestone Tire and Rubber Company of Akron, Ohio, which was my hometown. I decided to keep the belt as a souvenir, a reminder of how lucky I'd been.

When I finally took my thirty-day leave, I went home to my family in Ohio. After a quietly emotional welcome, I sat with my mother in our kitchen, telling her about my recent ordeal and hearing what had happened at home since I went away. My mother informed me that "to do her part," she had taken a wartime job at the Firestone plant. Surprised, I jumped up and grabbed my life belt from my duffel bag, putting it on the table in front of her.

"Take a look at that, Mom," I said. "It was made right here in Akron at your plant."

She leaned forward and, taking the rubber belt in her hands, she read the label. She had just heard the story and knew that in the darkness of that terrible night, it was this one piece of rubber that had saved my life. When she looked up at me, her mouth and her eyes were open wide with surprise. "Son, I'm an inspector at Firestone. This is my inspector number," she said, her voice hardly above a whisper.

We stared at each other, too stunned to speak. Then I stood up, walked around the table and pulled her up from her chair. We held each other in a tight embrace, saying nothing. My mother was not a demonstrative woman, but the significance of this amazing coincidence overcame her usual reserve. We hugged each other for a long, long time, feeling the bond between us. My mother had put her arms halfway around the world to save me.

~Elgin Staples
Chicken Soup for the Veteran's Soul

Mason's Sacrifice

You don't raise heroes, you raise sons. And if you treat them like sons,
they'll turn out to be heroes, even if it's just in your own eyes.
~Walter M. Schirra, Sr.

*I*t was Christmas morning the year that my only son, Mason, was thirteen years old. I had been raising him alone for ten years now. My husband had been diagnosed with cancer when Mason was two, and he passed away when Mason was only three. The years had been tough, but my son and I had a very special bond. We were best friends, and my son was the most thoughtful and caring person I knew.

At thirteen, Mason got a weekly allowance of five dollars for keeping his room clean and doing odd chores around the house. Each payday, Mason would jump on his bike and ride to the nearby drugstore to buy some candy or the latest magazine. He just couldn't seem to save his money, and so by the time Christmas rolled around, he had nothing to spend on gifts for others. I had never gotten a gift from him that was not homemade, so this year I expected nothing different.

After Mason finished opening all his gifts, he thanked me, kissed me and then slid off into his room. I wondered why he didn't seem to want to spend any time playing with the new stuff he had gotten. Caught in my thoughts, I was startled by Mason, who was now standing in front of me holding a nicely wrapped gift. I assumed that it was a project he had made at school, and I was looking forward to seeing what he had created this time. I cherished all of his gifts, just as I cherished him.

Inside the box was a brand-new pair of expensive black leather gloves, price tag still attached. The shock on my face was very apparent. As tears welled in my eyes, I asked him where he had gotten them. "At the store, Mom, where else?" he simply said.

I looked confused, as I knew that he didn't have that much money. I asked if someone had helped him purchase them, and he shook his head, held it high and said he had bought them all by himself.

After figuring out just the right questions to ask, I got him to reveal to me how he was able to buy the beautiful gloves. He had sold his brand-new bike to a friend at school, the one he had just gotten for his birthday two months earlier.

I cried just thinking about his sacrifice. Through my tears I told him that this was the most thoughtful thing he's ever done for me, but that I wanted to get his bike back for him.

He simply said, "No, Mom, please don't. Because Dad isn't here anymore, you never get a nice gift at Christmas, and you never buy yourself nice things. I wanted to get this for you. My old bike is still perfectly fine, really. Please, Mom, keep the gloves and know I love you every time you wear them."

We hung out for hours that morning, and I never removed the gloves. From that day on, I put them on so often that, eventually, I wore holes in them. But I still have them, tucked in a drawer in my closet. Once in a while, I come across them and am reminded of Mason's sacrifice. I immediately become filled with the gift of love that they represented that Christmas morning—the kind of gift that can never wear out.

~Veneta Leonard
Chicken Soup for the Soul Christmas Treasury for Kids

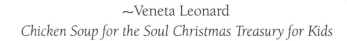

Angel

Most of all the other beautiful things in life come by twos and threes,
by dozens and hundreds. Plenty of roses, stars, sunsets, rainbows,
brothers and sisters, aunts and cousins, comrades and friends—
but only one mother in the whole world.
~Kate Douglas Wiggin

I just sit here, watching the funny looking bird through the window. It is washing itself in the driveway, which is full of rain from last night's shower. I think, What if I were a bird? Where would I go? What would I do? Of course, I know that is not possible, especially now. I'm just sitting here, watching my life pass by, second by second, minute by minute. I know I should do something productive, like homework, but I just feel like it's my job to watch the funny looking bird. Then the bird flies away, and I turn on the TV and watch a show about buffalo.

School's almost out, but I'm not there. I have to be sick, stuck inside with the flu, stuck inside underneath this blanket.

It's such a beautiful day outside, and I feel so sick. I feel like I am falling up (which just isn't possible, but I still feel like it). My head is spinning, almost as if I am in a daze. My brain starts pounding, like someone is hitting my skull with a hammer. The sun is shining, which doesn't help; it just makes it worse. I hide under the covers. This is the one time I feel like the sun is a bad thing.

Now my stomach starts to ache, so I move from the couch to my room to lie on my bed. Even though my brain hurts, I start to think. I let my imagination go.

I think about how much easier it is to tap your foot to a country song than to a rock song. I think about how long a day seems when you're bored, but when you do something fun the time flies by. I think about how they make us go to school for seven hours, then expect us to do three hours of homework every night and endure a big test in science or history the next day.

I start to dream, daydream that is, even more. I wander even further into my imagination. Somehow the thought of an angel comes into my head. What do they look like? Do they have golden wings? Do they live in the moment, rather than the past or the future? Are they light?

For some reason I can't stop wondering about them. Can a human being become an angel after life? My friends tell me no, but I think my grandpa is my grandma's guardian angel. I take out a piece of paper and start drawing what I think an angel looks like. In the finished drawing, the angel has golden hair as rich as the sun and gold wings that stretch from her body so that she can touch everyone's heart. She is wearing a smile and a pure white robe. A golden halo of stars floats atop her head.

The drawing makes me smile, and I feel a little better. Tomorrow will be a better day, I think. At that, I fall asleep.

"Anyone home?" greets me as I awaken.

"Hi, Mom," I reply.

"How are you feeling?" she asks.

"Better."

She insists on making me some chicken noodle soup anyway. Mom sure know how to make me feel better when I'm sick. Seems like she would take my sickness away from me in a second and give it to herself if she could. That's what moms are for, always there for you. Mothers hate to see their children suffer, even if it's just a little flu bug.

I don't need to know what an angel looks like, I think, I already know. An angel is a mom, my Mom. Her smile is that light that fills the room when it's dark. And her thoughtfulness touches my heart. My mom is an angel, watching over me. Thanks, Mom.

~Nathen Cantwell
Chicken Soup for the Teenage Soul III

Moms & Sons

Grieving and Peace

He spake well who said that graves are the footprints of angels.
~Henry Wadsworth Longfellow

22

Remembering Eric

I'm sure he never expected to see me there. He froze right in his tracks. His big green eyes looked like they might pop out of his head!

There he was—my eleven-year-old son Eric, standing among the crowd of children entering the cafeteria at his school. It was lunchtime. From a distance, I waved. I summoned him out of the lunch line, shaking the familiar fast-food bag I held in my hand. As he eagerly ran toward me with a huge grin on his face, I knew this would be a special time for us. As it turns out, it was one of the most rewarding experiences I remember with my son.

It was a Wednesday morning and probably one of the most hectic days in my office. The telephone was ringing off the hook; there were numerous reports due at the end of the day, and an important meeting to prepare for that afternoon. I had not yet had my first cup of coffee. As I reached into my pocket, searching for my favorite mint, I found a pink paper with a list of things I intended to buy at the grocery store during my lunch hour. There were several more items to add.

I turned it over and discovered it was actually a flyer inviting parents to come to the school and have lunch with their child. How could something like this have slipped my mind? I guess I hadn't paid much attention to the flyer because my son wasn't fond of things like that.

But for some reason, I couldn't seem to get that invitation off my mind. Eric was a fifth-grader and would be graduating and going to middle school the next year. This would probably be my last opportunity to have lunch with my son. I checked my watch. There was time. I could still make it. Forty-five minutes before the scheduled lunch, I shut down my computer, locked the file cabinets and dashed out to fetch Eric's favorite double cheeseburger and fries.

The shock on Eric's face mirrored my own. This was not the same child I had sent to school that morning. The son I dropped off wore clean, starched, navy blue slacks and a spotless, button-up white cotton dress shirt. The child before me sported a white mesh football jersey (with no shirt underneath), navy blue fleece shorts (three sizes too big), and a very nice and rather large gold hoop earring. Around his neck was a fancy gold chain with the initial "A" dangling from it. (I only hoped that it was for the grades he intended to earn.) As it turned out, the necklace belonged to a little girl named Ashanti.

As we both recovered, we slowly made our way to the lunch benches to begin our midday meal. Prior to arriving, I feared he would be too embarrassed to have lunch with his mother. After all, it had only been three years earlier when he had adamantly refused to take a picture with me at school in front of his buddies. I prepared myself. I knew he wouldn't be rude to me, but I thought he might eat as quickly and quietly as possible, and then run off to play with his friends.

But Eric began to tell me what he did in class that day. He told me a story he had read in his social studies book and described in detail a film he watched about Indians. Funny, he didn't tell me how or when he had changed his clothes. I was enjoying his company so much that I chose not to bring it up.

As he talked, he became the little boy who always drew a picture in preschool to show me. He was the small child who wanted me to kneel at his bedside at night and pray with him. He was my young son yelling in triumph while I clapped my hands as he rode down the street for the first time on his two-wheeler.

As he spoke, ketchup ran down the side of his mouth and proceeded to drip onto his white mesh football jersey. He seemed to neither notice nor care. Young girls passed slowly, at first trying to get his attention, and then to whisper and giggle as they watched him talk at full speed, so unlike the cool jock they all adored.

Although I hated for the lunch to end, we began to gather our trash. He would go back to the playground to finish recess with his classmates. I would go back to my office, this time in much better spirits. Eric actually wanted me there. My son was enjoying my company as much as I was enjoying his. He began a joke but fell out laughing hysterically before he could finish it. His laughter was so contagious I, too, doubled over with giggles, and we laughed so long and so hard I thought we would both lose our lunches.

It really didn't matter whether or not he finished the joke or even if it was funny. All that mattered was that for twenty minutes, on a Wednesday afternoon, we tuned out the entire world, my son and I, and no one else existed but us. We had made magic memories on the elementary school lunch benches with a $2.99 burger special.

Two weeks after our luncheon together, the child I had prayed for, loved, treasured and adored, died during the night, without warning, suddenly and silently of a massive seizure.

There are no more funny stories. There are no more opportunities for me to hug him tightly and kiss his forehead. There will be no new photographs.

Even as I watch his friends grow up, he will always remain that eleven-year-old boy. I still talk to him. I think of him constantly. I miss him terribly. His memory is so precious to me. We shared many things in the short time we had together. But I'll always be thankful I took the time for that schoolyard lunch we shared; it was one of the most rewarding experiences in my life.

~Tracy Clausell-Alexander
Chicken Soup for the African American Soul

23

The Joy of Easter

*E*ight years have passed since the day I pulled into the driveway of our family home to find my life forever changed. I looked up to see our seventeen-year-old son writhing in excruciating pain in our front yard. He was so incapacitated, he was unable to tell me what was the matter.

Once at the hospital, he was diagnosed with an extremely rare and deadly cancer called Burkitt's Lymphoma. Arrangements were quickly made to fly him south to Vancouver General Hospital where he could receive the care he needed. On Thanksgiving Day, our family gathered together and prayed in the hospital chapel for courage and strength.

Later that night, my son and I boarded the air ambulance. Looking out the small window, I could see the darkening blue sky. For a moment the beauty spared me from the fear and pain I was feeling. Then the darkness of the night sky was upon us, and everything was suddenly silent. I remembered Father Forde once saying that we could find God in nature, and at that moment I experienced just that. I felt God's presence. It was at that moment that I was able to surrender our difficult journey into God's hands.

When we arrived, the medical staff were ready and waiting, and within minutes I was told that he would not live to see the morning. I asked them to please do what they could for his pain, then I softly said, "Only God knows when someone is going to die." Judging from the looks on their faces, I was sure they all thought I was some religious nut.

Morning arrived, and he had made it through the night. Days and then weeks of radiation and chemotherapy followed. Gradually, the cancer was forced into remission. A bone-marrow transplant was his only hope, and miraculously both his older sister and younger brother were perfect matches. Soon healthy bone marrow was flowing into his depleted body.

The transplant was only a temporary success, however, and all too soon the cancer came back with deadly force. Once again, we were told that there was no chance of survival, and this time we knew it was true.

That evening, in the darkness of his hospital room, my son bravely asked, "What will it be like to be dead?" I didn't know what to say. I felt so unsure. I tried to be honest and tell him what I felt or believed. I told him how each day I was glad to be alive, that I always looked forward to going to heaven, and now he would be there to greet me when I arrived. We could not talk anymore. Our words were choked by sobbing tears, but words weren't really necessary. Death was no longer our enemy. After talking about it and praying, it all took on a different meaning. It was the start of a new journey, from life to death, to eternity and to God.

The following days were spent planning his funeral, which he called his "going-away party." He had very specific requests for this event, down to wanting balloons at his funeral. I told him that I had my doubts as to balloons, but he said, "Ask Father Forde. He'll let us have them."

He wanted to be cremated and have his ashes scattered at his favorite places. He wanted a small wooden cross overlooking the ocean at his grandparents' home in Nova Scotia that said, "Peace is seeing a sunset and knowing who to thank." I had my misgivings, but he said, "Mom, just do it. God will understand."

He was quickly slipping away from us. He had been fed by IV for months now and had waited patiently for the day that he could eat pizza again. I lost control and screamed that even the worst criminal on death row gets his choice of a last meal, and my son couldn't even have pizza! I heard his soft voice say, "Mom, I had

Holy Communion this morning. I have all the food I need." I knew at that moment that all our prayers were being heard. He was no longer afraid to die, and I was no longer afraid to let him go. He had surrendered himself to God.

He died in my arms on Ash Wednesday. His last words were, "Mom, it is a beautiful day to die."

His funeral was a celebration of life. The church was full of his friends holding balloons that were to be released with prayers inside them. His ashes were scattered as he had asked. His grandfather lovingly made a wooden cross that stands facing the sea.

A few years passed before I was to visit his cross again. Walking across the moors toward the sea, I saw a man and his two small children placing wildflowers on the cross. As I approached he looked up. "Did you know the family?" he asked. My reply was joyous as I said, "This boy was my son."

I stayed for a while as we all silently watched the sun set into a crimson sky.

My eyes turned toward the engraved cross, and I took in the meaning of the words as if for the first time. My heart was full, and the moment brought tears to my eyes. It was clear to all of us who to thank for this moment, and I could hear my son saying, "God will understand."

~Marion Blanchard
Chicken Soup for the Christian Teenage Soul

24

Music-Loving Tabby

Music was my refuge. I could crawl into the space
between the notes and curl my back to loneliness.
~Maya Angelou, Gather Together in My Name

In July 1999, our world changed forever when five little words were delivered to my husband during a telephone call that woke us in the wee hours of the morning: "Your son did not survive."

Our son, Don Jr., was living in North Carolina and working toward achieving his doctorate in classical guitar so that he could one day teach. He had already received his Master of Music Performance degree from Southern Methodist University in Texas. On July 17, he fell asleep at the wheel of his car and hit a bridge abutment. He was killed instantly.

With Donnie gone, we inherited his cat, Audrey. He had only brought her to our home for a few visits over the years, and she had spent each visit hiding under a bed. She was skittish and shy, a gray feline beauty whom he had acquired from a shelter when he lived in Memphis, Tennessee. He called Audrey a "prissy-miss" and said she only tolerated petting on her own terms—when she was in the mood for it!

Audrey arrived in our home just a month after we had adopted MoJo, a stray from our local shelter. Audrey spent all her time hiding under a bed or sofa. MoJo, being a domineering male, stalked her constantly. I wanted so much for Audrey to get to know us, but she was wary of coming out for longer than it took to gulp down her morning meal.

One thing I noticed about Audrey was that she loved music. Whenever music played, she would poke her head out and look around as if she wanted somehow to be a part of it.

"Just think of all the music she has been exposed to," I said to my husband. "It must comfort her because the sound is so familiar."

My son had loved music of all kinds. Not only did he play guitar every day, he also had friends over to play different musical instruments. I know that he had many CDs—everything from classical to bluegrass. He and I shared a love of good acoustical bluegrass music.

Audrey had been with us approximately three weeks when a good friend of mine lost the little dog she'd had for years. I offered to give her MoJo, knowing that it would help her with her grief. I knew I would miss MoJo, but also knew that his absence would permit Audrey to come out from hiding and get to know us a little better. I wanted so much for her to feel at home with us—and for us to love her openly and have her give back that love.

Then it happened. One evening, after MoJo was gone from the house and I had been attempting for a few hours to coax Audrey out of hiding, I had an idea. I pulled out one of Donnie's recital CDs and began to play it on our CD player. My husband had spent many hours transferring all of Donnie's guitar recitals from tape to CDs so that we would always have his music with us.

The music began playing, and my eyes filled with tears as I imagined my son seated before me with his guitar. He was never happier than when performing. His head would sometimes fall and rise to emphasize a note, and, in my mind's eye, I saw him with a glint of sunlight accentuating the blond hair that tumbled over his forehead. I turned up the volume, letting the music swell louder and fill my soul.

Within minutes, I felt it—Audrey rubbing on my leg and purring! Then she walked in circles around the room as if on a search mission. Where was her beloved Donnie? She heard him and she remembered him—I just knew she did!

I walked gingerly by her so I would not frighten her into hiding again, and I retrieved his quilt from the closet. It was a quilt I had made him and he had slept on, using it as a sheet on the mattress in his apartment. I had not washed it. I carefully spread the quilt out on the floor and called to my husband to come see what was transpiring. By this time, tears were rolling down my face, and I felt my son was with us as never before.

Audrey walked on the quilt and suddenly dropped and rolled. She rolled over and over, rubbing the side of her face into the quilt repeatedly, as if to say, "Hey, I loved your son; now, I love you, too." Happy tears were shed that day—the day that Audrey accepted the love we wanted so desperately to show her. I truly believe she grieved his absence in her own way and, suddenly, realized the connection we had to this wonderful young man when she once again heard him perform on his guitar.

Our music-loving tabby blesses our lives each day. She and I now share that "bluegrass connection." When I put my favorite bluegrass CDs on, she comes running to purr and rub her love all over me while the songs are playing! It is amazing to witness the actions of this cat who is undeniably stirred by music. She can also sense when I am sad and thinking about how much I miss my son. Certain pieces of music still bring him to mind, and she will come to me and glide against me, extending her soul in comfort. The tears roll down my cheeks as I feel my son near me through his cat. I know she is in my life for a reason—to continue to comfort me and bond me to him with her love.

~Beverly F. Walker
Chicken Soup for the Cat Lover's Soul

25

I Still Choose "Mom"

You cannot do a kindness too soon,
for you never know how soon it will be too late.
~Ralph Waldo Emerson

I watched through blurred vision as my husband, Chuck, walked away with his ex-wife.

The heaviness in all our hearts was almost unbearable. Turning back to my stepson's casket, I somehow helped my children pluck a rose from the brother spray to press in their Bibles. With tears streaming down my face, I rested my hand on the son spray. I no longer knew my place.

God, I silently screamed, how did I fit in Conan's life?

From the moment I'd met my stepson, I was in awe of this angelic little boy whose bright, blond hair seemed to glow with a heavenly radiance. At only a year and a half, he was built like a three-year-old. Solid and stocky, sleeping curled in my lap, his tiny heart beat against mine, and a maternal bonding began stirring inside me.

Within a year, I became a stepmother to Conan and his older sister, Lori. Soon after that, a visit to the doctor revealed some disheartening news.

"You have an infertility disease," the doctor had said. "You might not ever have children of your own."

At twenty-two, that news was shattering. I had always wanted to be a mother. Suddenly, I realized being a stepmother might be as close as I would get, and I became even more involved in their lives.

But thankfully, four years later we joyfully discovered I was pregnant. Chase was born; then two years later we were blessed with our daughter, Chelsea.

I loved being both a mom and a stepmother, but as in any blended family, it had its ups and downs. Chuck's ex-wife had custody of his kids and gave them more freedom than we gave our children. Needing to be consistent with our rules, I'm certain we appeared overly strict to his kids. On their weekend visitations, I usually felt like an old nag.

As a second wife, I was jealous of my stepchildren's mother. I complained about her and her husband within earshot of my stepkids, and even grumbled about buying my stepchildren extras on top of paying child support. Somehow I overlooked the important fact that my stepchildren were the innocent ones thrust into a blended family.

Then one day at a gathering of my own family, I watched as my mother went up to my stepmother and gave her a hug. I turned and saw my father and stepfather laughing together. Having always appreciated the cooperative relationship my parents and stepparents had, it occurred to me that Chuck's children longed for the same. So Chuck and I decided to work hard at bridging gaps instead of creating them.

It wasn't easy, and changes didn't come overnight, but they did come. By the time Conan was fifteen, a peace had settled between parents and stepparents. Instead of griping about child-support payments, we voluntarily increased them. And finally Conan's mom gave us copies of his report cards and football schedules.

I was proud of my kids and stepkids. After graduation, my stepdaughter married, and she and her husband built a house together. At seventeen, Conan had become a sensible, intelligent young man. With rugged good looks and a deep, baritone voice, I wondered what fortunate girl would snatch him up.

But then came that phone call, changing our lives forever—Conan was killed instantly by a drunk driver.

Over the years we'd been married, Chuck had reassured me that I was a parent to his children, too. He sought my opinion in matters concerning them and relied on me to make their Christmases and birthdays special. I enjoyed doing those things and looked upon myself as their second mother.

But in his grief immediately upon Conan's death, Chuck suddenly stopped seeking my opinion and began turning to his ex-wife. I knew they had to make many final decisions together, and I realized later that he was trying to spare me from the gruesome details, but for the first time, I began to feel like an outsider instead of a parent.

I also knew the driver responsible for the accident had to be prosecuted, which meant Chuck and his ex-wife would have to stay in contact. Those ugly jealousies from the past began to resurface when, night after night, he talked to her, seldom discussing their conversations with me.

And it stung when friends inquired only about Chuck's coping, or sent sympathy cards addressed just to him, forgetting about me and even our two children. Some belittled my grieving because I was "just" a stepparent. Did anyone realize my loss and pain? I'd had strong maternal feelings for Conan; he considered me his second mother—or did he? As the weeks turned into months, that question haunted me, dominating my thoughts. I became driven to understand just what my role had been.

I rummaged through boxes of photos and dug out old journals, searching the house for mementos, even Christmas ornaments he had made.

There were several comforting journal excerpts, one describing Mother's Day phone calls from Conan to me, and a beautiful white poinsettia he gave me at Christmas. And I cherished the memories old photos brought back—his loving bear hugs after cooking his favorite meal—or a kiss for simply doing his laundry. As comforting as these things were, they still weren't enough.

One beautiful spring day, almost a year after he died, I was lovingly caressing the pressed rose from his grave that I kept in my Bible. Suddenly, I felt compelled to visit his grave alone. I had never done that before, but I desperately needed some answers.

Arriving at the gravesite, I remembered Chuck mentioning

that the permanent headstone had recently arrived. Chuck had told Conan's mom to select what she wanted. As I looked down on the shiny marble surface, I noticed she had chosen a bronze sports emblem, along with a picture of Conan that had been permanently embedded under a thick layer of glass.

I bent down and lovingly ran my fingers over his engraved name and the dates commemorating his short life. Through a mist of tears, memories of a rambunctious, fun-loving little boy filled my heart. The child I'd mothered part-time for so many years may not have come through my body, but I had been chosen by God to provide a maternal influence in his life. Not to take his mother's place, but to be just a "step" away. I suddenly felt very honored to have been chosen.

"It was a privilege to be your stepmother," I whispered out loud, bending to kiss his picture.

Finally, a sense of peace was beginning. With a heavy sigh, I got up to leave. But as I turned to walk away, the sun glistened on the border of the headstone, causing me to look back.

"Oh my gosh! How could I have not noticed it before?"

The entire border of the headstone was trimmed in gold shafts of wheat... exactly like a gold shaft-of-wheat pin Conan had given me years ago. Chills ran up and down my spine. I hadn't seen that pin in years.

Somehow, I just knew it was the missing link. I had to find that pin.

The ride home was a blur. I was so excited. Finally, I was upstairs in my bedroom tearing apart my jewelry box. Where was it? Dumping the contents on the bed, I frantically tossed earrings and pins to and fro.

Nothing.

God, this is important. Please help me find it, I prayed.

Turning from the bed I felt compelled to search my dresser. Rummaging through drawer after drawer proved futile, until finally, in the last drawer, clear in the back, I felt it. It was a small, white box with my name scribbled on top in a child's handwriting. Prying it open, I was instantly transported back in time.

Conan had been about ten years old, and it was the night before going on vacation to Florida. He was going with us, and I was packing in my room when I heard a knock on my door. Conan stood there, his eyes downcast and his hands behind his back.

"What is it, son?" I asked, concerned by this unexpected visit.

Shuffling his feet, he quickly mumbled, "I don't know why I don't call you 'Mom' very often, even though I call my stepdad 'Dad.'"

I hugged him and reassured him he was free to call me whatever he was comfortable with. Then suddenly, with a wry smile on his pudgy face, he handed me the small, white box.

"You choose," he said, and darted from the room.

Assuming I'd find two items inside the box, I opened it. Instead, I found the single gold wheat pin he'd bought at a garage sale with his own money.

Scribbled inside the lid of the box were the words, "I Love You. To Mom or Connie."

That had been almost a decade ago, yet as I pushed the spilled contents of my jewelry box aside and slowly sat down on the edge of the bed, it felt like yesterday.

Thank you, God, for finding this pin, and for the closure that comes with it.

Wiping the tears from my face, I reflected on an angelic little boy whose heart beat close to mine.

I still choose "Mom."

~Connie Sturm Cameron
Chicken Soup for the Grieving Soul

26

Reaching for Peace

*P*aul was dead. My delightful twenty-one-year-old son was murdered in a carjacking attempt, and my world collapsed. The bullet that ripped through his heart shattered mine, destroying my peaceful world forever.

Just as it seemed things would be easier for us, his life was taken senselessly, and now, mine had no meaning. I raised Paul as a single parent, and we were so very protective of each other. He was a senior in college, planning to marry a wonderful young woman, and my life would be moving into another dimension. I would no longer need to send a check each month to help with his college expenses. We chatted the evening before he was murdered about what I would do with all the money I wouldn't be spending after his graduation.

There are no words to describe the rage I felt toward the seventeen-year-old who asked Paul for a ride, then killed him in cold blood. So many times in my life I had wanted to be taller than my five feet, two inches, for it seems that power comes with height. I sat in the Austin courtroom looking at a young man, over six feet tall. If looks could kill, he would have met his doom, for nothing came from me but utter hatred.

Charles White received a forty-year prison sentence, and again I was enraged! Paul was dead, and a worthless, hardened criminal was allowed to live. My taxes would feed him, pay for his guards and furnish him with clothes to wear and food to eat. Paul is dead. That was all I could think of. It gave me no peace to know that the murderer would serve thirteen years of "flat time" for Paul's murder. Paul would never be alive again, not in thirteen, twenty-three or thirty-three years!

Every three months I sent a scathing letter to the Board of Pardons and Paroles, pouring out my great anguish and pain from the depths of my soul. How I wanted to know that someone would read those words and know the continuous, overwhelming pain that results from the murder of a loved one. Two times a year, on February 18th (the date Paul was murdered) and again each August, I made a personal trip to Austin to speak with a staff member and get an update on Charles's actions in prison. I was elated when he got in trouble and "lost good time." That proved that he was a really bad guy.

Years passed, thirteen to be exact, and I had no peace. I continued my letters and personal visits of protest and lived to hate the murderer of my precious Paul. One day, as I opened the mail at my office, I received a letter from the parole board informing me that my son's killer was being considered for parole. I became physically ill and had to leave the office. My staff did not know what was wrong, but they knew something drastic had happened. How could they even think of allowing him to go free? Paul was still dead, and I felt so overwhelmed with helplessness. Through the years, I was told, "He won't be released," but after reading the letter I knew that I had to take immediate action: I would go talk with my son's murderer.

The state of Texas has a program that allows victims to meet with perpetrators, and I made the dreaded call and received confirmation that I could participate in the program. Even greater anger consumed me, for it was my responsibility to pay for my trips to Austin to work through the program. Charles, on the other hand, languished in prison, and my taxes paid for the mediator to help prepare him to meet with me.

The meeting was scheduled for June 9, 1998. Again, I paid for a trip to Austin, but was taken to the prison site in a state vehicle. Though I had been in numerous prisons as a speaker for the victim impact programs, it felt different when I went inside that prison. HE IS HERE! This is HIS prison! My heart beat frantically, and I did not know if I could go through with the meeting.

In preparation for the time we would spend together, I had

meticulously decided what I should have with me for this momentous meeting; I was ready! I sincerely hoped to shatter any shred of peace he felt. When I left, he would know that he had destroyed my world with a single bullet.

To say that the meeting was awkward is putting it lightly. Everyone in the room, including the guards, was deathly quiet, and frequently my soft voice was barely audible. I had not slept at all the night before; I paced the floor in the tiny hotel room, alone with my thoughts and questions. I had been instructed to write out the questions that I wanted to ask Paul's murderer and have them in order so that the meeting could progress in an organized manner. Of the seventy-seven questions I had written down, the one I asked first was simple: WHY?

The young man, who did not look much different from when I last saw him thirteen years earlier, had no answer for me other than to shake his head and say, "It was just a stupid thing to do. Stupid, just stupid, stupid, stupid...."

I felt no pity for him; he senselessly murdered my son. I wanted him to squirm and feel my pain. Tears streamed down my face as I spoke of Paul, and I said to him, "If you knew how much I loved him, you would not have killed him." He sat across the table from me, showing no emotion.

For this meeting, I had Paul's photos enlarged to fourteen by eighteen inches. I wanted him to know Paul as a real person, not as "him, the dude, the kid," as he referred to Paul in his writings to the mediator. He said he didn't even remember what Paul looked like, and I wanted to scream, "How can you not remember him? You killed him!"

I became pensive and, as if to myself, I began to talk of how Paul would call to see if my car was okay. If I thought it sounded funny, he would tell me that he was coming home over the weekend to take care of it for me. I spoke of how he would ask about our yard, telling me that he'd come home because I was "too little to mow the lawn."

Something touched Charles at that point. I could not believe the tears that streamed down the face of the man across the table from me. What was going on? Charles put his head in his hands and sobbed. Without thinking, I pulled a tissue from the box on the table, handed it to him and said, "Here." Those tears of shame and remorse touched me deeply. The tone of the meeting changed; suddenly, the mother and the murderer began to connect. I listened to how Charles was raised in extreme poverty, one of several children, living mostly in the streets. Paul, by contrast, was an only child and knew only love and all the security I could provide.

For the very first time, I really looked into the eyes of my son's murderer and was amazed that I felt no hate. I encouraged him to stop being violent in prison. I asked that he attend classes and get a GED. He looked at me in disbelief, for he seemed to realize that my rage was gone. The meeting ended with him agreeing to attend classes and stop his violence. I thanked him for meeting with me, folded my hands and closed my eyes. I felt a great need to put my hand across the table and take his, but I dared not do that. He had murdered my son. If I did that, I would be reaching out to the hand that held the pistol that killed Paul. Again, I felt that I should reach out to the killer across from me. No, I just couldn't do it.

Then, almost against my will, my hand reached across the table to grasp the hand of my son's killer. A great cry of anguish was released from the depths of my soul as I felt him take my hand. He covered my hand with both of his, and his tears of remorse washed over them. The same hand that, thirteen years earlier, had held a pistol and pulled the trigger, releasing the shot that shattered my peace, now clung to mine as if I were his lifeline. Though Charles never said, "I am sorry, please forgive me," and I never said the words, "I forgive you," we came to our place of peace. Our communication continues to this day.

~Thomas Ann Hines
Chicken Soup for the Soul Stories for a Better World

27

I'll Make You a Rainbow

There are things that we don't want to happen but have to accept,
things we don't want to know but have to learn,
and people we can't live without but have to let go.
~Author Unknown

Looking back, I've often thought the doctors should have written a death certificate for me as well as my son, for when he died, a part of me died, too.

Andy was almost twelve. For over three years he had been battling cancer. He'd gone through radiation and chemotherapy; he'd gone into remission and come out again, not once but several times. I was amazed at his resiliency; he just kept getting up each time the cancer knocked him flat. Perhaps it was his pluckiness and grit that shaped my own attitude about Andy's future, or maybe I was simply afraid to face the possibility of his death. Whatever the cause, I always thought Andy would make it. He would be the kid who beat the odds.

For three summers, Andy had gone to a camp for kids with cancer. He loved it and seemed to relish the week he could forget about hospitals and sickness and just be a kid again. The day after he returned from his third camp adventure, we went to the clinic for a routine checkup. The news was bad. The doctor scheduled a bone-marrow transplant two days later in a hospital three hundred miles from our home. The next day we threw our things in a suitcase and left.

One of the things I tossed into my suitcase was the present Andy had brought me from camp—a plastic sun catcher shaped like a rainbow with a suction cup to attach it to a window. Like most mothers, I considered any present from my child a treasure and wanted it with me.

We arrived at the hospital and began the grueling ordeal the doctors said was my son's only chance. We spent seven weeks there. They turned out to be the last seven weeks of Andy's life.

We never talked about dying—except once. Andy was worn out and must have known he was losing ground. He tried to clue me in. Nauseous and weak after one of the many difficult procedures he regularly endured, he turned to me and asked, "Does it hurt to die?"

I was shocked, but answered truthfully, "I don't know. But I don't want to talk about death, because you are not going to die, Andy."

He took my hand and said, "Not yet, but I'm getting very tired."

I knew what he was telling me, but I tried hard to ignore it and keep the awful thought from entering my mind.

I spent a lot of my days watching Andy sleep. Sometimes I went to the gift shop to buy cards and notepaper. I had very little money, barely enough to survive. The nurses knew our situation and turned a blind eye when I slept in Andy's room and ate the extra food we ordered from Andy's tray. But I always managed to scrape a bit together for the paper and cards because Andy loved getting mail so much.

The bone-marrow transplant was a terrible ordeal. Andy couldn't have any visitors because his immune system was so compromised. I could tell that he felt more isolated than ever. Determined to do something to make it easier for him, I began approaching total strangers in the waiting rooms and asking them, "Would you write my son a card?" I'd explain his situation and offer them a card or some paper to write on. With surprised expressions on their faces, they did it. No one refused me. They took one look at me and saw a mother in pain.

It amazed me that these kind people, who were dealing with their own worries, made the time to write Andy. Some would just sign a card with a little get-well message. Others wrote real letters: "Hi, I'm from Idaho visiting my grandmother here in the hospital..." and they'd fill a page or two with their story, sometimes inviting Andy to visit their homes when he was better. Once a woman flagged me down and said, "You asked me to write your son a couple of weeks ago. Can I write him again?" I mailed all these letters to Andy and watched happily as he read them. Andy had a steady stream of mail right up until the day he died.

One day, I went to the gift store to buy more cards and saw a rainbow prism for sale. Remembering the rainbow sun catcher Andy had given me, I felt I had to buy it for him. It was a lot of money to spend, but I handed over the cash and hurried back to Andy's room to show him.

He was lying in his bed, too weak to even raise his head. The blinds were almost shut, but a crack of sunlight slanted across the bed. I put the prism in his hand and said, "Andy, make me a rainbow." But Andy couldn't. He tried to hold his arm up, but it was too much for him.

He turned his face to me and said, "Mom, as soon as I'm better, I'll make you a rainbow you'll never forget."

That was one of the last things Andy said to me. Just a few hours later, he went to sleep and during the night, slipped into a coma. I stayed with him in the intensive care unit, massaging him, talking to him and reading him his mail, but he never stirred. The only sound was the constant drone and beepings of the life-support machines surrounding his bed. I was looking death straight in the face, but still I thought there'd be a last-minute save, a miracle that would bring my son back to me.

After five days, the doctors told me his brain had stopped functioning, and it was time to disconnect him from the machines keeping his body alive.

I asked if I could hold him. Just after dawn, they brought a rocking chair into the room, and after I settled myself in the chair, they turned off the machines and lifted him from the bed to place him in my arms. As they raised him from the bed, his leg made an involuntary movement, and he knocked a clear plastic pitcher from his bedside table onto the bed.

"Open the blinds," I cried. "I want this room to be full of sunlight!" The nurse hurried to the window to pull the cord.

As she did so, I noticed a sun catcher in the shape of the rainbow attached to the window, left no doubt by a previous occupant of this room. I caught my breath in wonder. Then, as the light filled the room, it hit the pitcher lying on its side on the bed, and everyone stopped what they were doing in silent awe.

The room was filled with flashes of color, dozens and dozens of rainbows on the walls, the floors, the ceiling, on the blanket wrapped around Andy as he lay in my arms—the room was alive with rainbows.

No one could speak. I looked down at my son, and he had stopped breathing. Andy was gone, but even in the shock of that first wave of grief, I felt comforted. Andy had made the rainbow that he promised me—the one I would never forget.

~Linda Bremner
Chicken Soup for the Grieving Soul

28

The Angels on the Cruise

By emphasizing that which is good in people and in the world,
and by bringing the positive to the fore,
the evil is superseded by the good, until it eventually disappears.
~Rabbi Menachem Shneerson

My husband, Mike, and I lost our soon-to-be eleven-year-old son in a gun accident on December 7, 1993, shortly before his birthday. The journey down the road of grief is very exhausting, and there are many days you don't think you can keep going. We had to keep going; we still had our thirteen-year-old daughter, Jayme, depending on us—besides, Sean would not have wanted us to give up. Many times, remembering his jokes and laughter, and feeling his love, got us through some very rough moments.

Even through the pain, we have had many blessings come to us on our journey through grief. One of these blessings occurred during Thanksgiving of 1994. Thanksgiving had always been a special time for our family. We liked being together, just the four of us. We would take turns cooking our favorite dishes, have a relaxing dinner, decorate the Christmas tree, light the tree when the Plaza lights were turned on, then sit around and eat appetizers while we enjoyed the tree. So that Thanksgiving the three of us needed to have a "different" Thanksgiving holiday. Mike had always wanted to go on a cruise and we thought that might get us through our "first" Thanksgiving. When someone you love dies, you remember things in your life as two parts: before they died and after they died. It's like you're starting a whole new life whether you like it or not.

People think you can get away from your grief by taking a trip, but for those of us going through this journey of grief, you know the pain always goes along. So you have to do the best you can. I did a lot of praying about going on this cruise, hoping it would take a little bit of the edge off the pain.

We got lucky on the cruise: The weather was great and on the second day, on a tender boat going to Key West, we met three really nice people from Orchard Lake, Michigan. It's funny how, when you don't bring a friend along for your daughter, you're always looking around to see if anybody has a daughter, preferably the same age, to hang out with. As luck would have it, Denise Falzon found us first. We all seemed comfortable with each other and agreed to meet later that evening back on ship.

Chris and Denise's daughter, Nikki, was six months older than Jayme, and they had everything in common—from being on student council to being in musicals—except losing a brother. The girls had fun together. The big day arrived and we were out at sea all day. We spent the day on deck with Chris, Denise and Nikki laying out, relaxing and talking. Denise had asked if I had any other kids and I told her no, just Jayme. I guess I didn't expect to see them again or I would have told them. We met for a show later in the evening and I remember looking at the Falzons with envy, thinking "If they only knew of the pain we are carrying" and wondering what it would feel like to just be "normal" again.

We enjoyed the time we spent with the Falzons, and at the end of the cruise we exchanged addresses and said we would write to each other.

A couple of days after Christmas, I received their Christmas card in the mail. As I began to read the card, I started to shake. Denise thanked us for helping them get through another holiday. Their nineteen-year-old son, Brian, had died October 1, 1993, collapsing at his college campus from sudden arrhythmia. So now, Nikki and Jayme were just alike; they both had had a brother who had died suddenly.

With over two thousand people on board that ship, we had met another family who also had lost a son and around the same time—almost as if our sons had matched us up.

I knew the Falzons were spending Christmas out of town, but I hurriedly wrote them a letter about Sean and sent a picture to them. I wanted the letter to be waiting for them when they got back from their trip. They were shocked and called as soon as they read our letter. We just talked and talked—and we're still talking six years later. Denise and I are a mini-support team for each other around the anniversaries of our sons' deaths.

This year Sean would have been graduating from high school, so we are planning a trip to visit Chris and Denise during graduation weekend.

I think being thankful for our blessings, no matter how small, and reaching out to help someone else, especially when we are feeling down, has been a tremendous help to Denise and me and our families. Opening our hearts to the love around us helps us to still feel the love of our sons. Love has no boundaries.

~Shari Dowdall
Chicken Soup for the Girlfriend's Soul

29

Joseph's Living Legacy

The best way to cheer yourself up is to cheer everybody else up.
~Mark Twain

With loving tenderness, I unpacked my son Joseph's Little League trophy, his stack of X-Men comics and the framed pictures of elephants that had decorated his bedroom walls back in our old apartment. Just two weeks before, Joseph had so looked forward to moving into his own room in the new house. Now, making his bed, I couldn't hold back the tears. My little boy will never sleep here, I grieved. I'll never glimpse his smile again or feel his loving hug.

Wondering how I could possibly manage to go on, I began unpacking the dozens of plush animals Joseph loved to collect — bears and monkeys, chipmunks and giraffes.

Sitting on his bed, I hugged the Chris Columbus bear he used to nuzzle when he was little and I read *Love You Forever* or another of his favorite stories. Joseph loved books, and to him they were especially precious because he had a learning disability that made it all but impossible for him to read them himself.

But Joseph was a determined little boy who refused to let his disability stop him from learning. He listened to his schoolbooks and tests on tape, and every night we sat together at the kitchen table so I could read his math problems to him and help him with his spelling. Joseph worked so hard; he always made honor roll at school. He also earned a green belt in karate and was pitcher for his Little League baseball team.

In many ways Joseph was just a regular little boy who loved playing video games with his brother, David, or going to the movies with his sister, Shalom. But Joseph also knew what it was like to feel different and need a helping hand.

I can't remember how many times I spotted Joseph carrying groceries for one of our elderly neighbors or refusing money after shoveling their cars out from the snow. He loved putting on puppet shows for the little girl down the street with Down syndrome, and once, when doctors thought his friend Micah might need a kidney transplant, my son came to me and said, "I sure wish I could give him one of mine."

Joseph, my little mensch, always made me proud, even on the last day of his life.

I was folding clothes in the den that Saturday afternoon when out of nowhere my husband, Lou, shouted for me to call 911. He and Joseph had been discussing a movie they planned to see when suddenly Joseph collapsed onto his bed complaining of a terrific headache. His breathing grew ragged, and then it stopped. Lou, who is a physician, performed artificial respiration until the paramedics arrived. Then he called ahead to the ER while I rode in the ambulance with Joseph and prayed he wouldn't die.

Joseph, always the picture of health, had suffered a massive brain aneurysm. "Is he going to die?" I asked my husband. Holding me tightly he answered, "Yes."

It seemed impossible. Only an hour ago, my son was home watching TV—and now he was on life support with no hope of ever regaining consciousness. I wanted to cry out in shock and grief.

But there wasn't time. There was something important I had to do—and I had to do it right away.

"We have to donate his organs," I told Lou, recalling the time Joseph wanted to give a kidney to Micah. "It's what he would have wanted us to do."

A transplant coordinator made all the arrangements, and a few hours later our family gathered at Joseph's bedside to offer a prayer and say our last goodbyes.

Then we went home, and throughout that night while surgeons recovered my son's organs I lay curled on his bed, clutching his favorite blanket and telling him how much I would always love him.

I don't know how I survived those next two weeks—the funeral and moving into the house we'd already contracted to buy. I cried every time I went near Joseph's new bedroom—the one he would have loved, if only he'd lived. There was a gaping hole in my heart.

Then one day when I felt I could bear my grief no longer, a letter came from the transplant coordinator. "I am writing to share the outcome of your generosity," I read with tears spilling down my cheeks.

Two Kentucky women, one of them the mother of a boy Joseph's age, were now off dialysis because they had each received one of my son's kidneys. Meanwhile, in Missouri, cells from Joseph's liver were helping to keep a critically ill transplant candidate alive while doctors waited for a matching donor organ to become available. In California, two young children would soon be able to run and play with the healthy new heart valves my son had bequeathed them. And two teenagers, one from Kentucky and the other from New York, had regained their eyesight thanks to Joseph's corneas.

Seven people's lives had been changed dramatically because of my son. I carried the letter with me for days, reading and rereading it and marveling especially at the teens who'd received Joseph's corneas. Joseph's learning disability had prevented him from reading. But because of his very special gift, there were now two more children in the world who could. Somehow, this helped me understand that my son had not lost his life in vain.

I wanted each and every one of Joseph's recipients to know who he was. So one night I wrote them each a letter and told them all about the little boy who had given them the ultimate gift. I asked the transplant agency to forward the letters to all seven recipients. With each, I sent along one of his beloved stuffed animals and a copy of a school essay that he'd once written describing how to take care of them.

Knowing the good my son had brought into the world made it easier to walk past his room without bursting into tears. It helped the rest of the family, too, and eventually we became able to share happy memories of Joseph around the dinner table and at other family gatherings.

Lou and I also honored Joseph's memory by speaking to community groups and high school students about the importance of organ donation. After a TV interview, the mother who had received one of Joseph's kidneys contacted us.

"I don't know how to thank you," she sobbed the day we first met.

"Seeing a part of my son living on is thanks enough for me," I said. Because of her new kidney, the woman had been able to attend her own son's eighth-grade graduation. Joseph never reached the eighth grade, but instead of begrudging the woman her happiness, I kvelled in it — because it was my son who had made this miracle possible.

My son is gone, but in a very real way he still lives on, doing what he always did best — offering a helping hand to others in need. Some say Joseph's life was brief. I say it was full.

I once heard that if you save a life, you save the world. Well, my son saved five lives and gave the gift of sight to two others. What mother could possibly ask any more of her child? What mother could possibly be any prouder?

~Kathie Kroot as told to Heather Black
Chicken Soup for the Grieving Soul

Chapter 5

Moms & Sons

Single-Minded Devotion

I remember my mother's prayers
and they have always followed me.
They have clung to me all my life.
~Abraham Lincoln

30

Kitchen Comfort

Very often a change of self is needed more than a change of scene.
~Arthur Christopher Benson

My life is a juggling act. I'm a single mother of two sons; I've got a busy work schedule and limited resources. But there is one thing I don't worry about: when I come home at night, dinner is already started. A typical weeknight at my house looks like this:

My younger child is snapping the ends off the green beans.

My elder is mixing his secret salad dressing.

The babysitter is working on the shopping list for tomorrow's dinner — the kids want to make lasagna.

I throw on an apron, send the babysitter home and join my kids in the dinner preparations.

Sounds too far-fetched for your home? It doesn't have to be. If my family can do it, any family can.

Our meals weren't always such happy group efforts. Seven years ago, my life was shattered by divorce, leaving me with a six-month-old infant and a very angry seven-year-old. I had no family nearby and very little money. The burden of rebuilding my career as a food writer and publicist while simultaneously single-parenting my children seemed insurmountable.

While I did my best to work during my younger's nap times, by day's end I was physically exhausted and emotionally depleted. Typically, I shooed the boys out of the kitchen so I could perform yet another chore: making dinner. When I got the meal on the table, I left them to eat alone so I could have five minutes' peace. Retreating to my bedroom, I collapsed onto my bed and cried. I felt horrible about my family life and helpless to change it.

A year passed, but not much improved. At the end of my rope, one evening I thrust some basil at my youngest, who was then eighteen months old, so he'd leave me alone. Lo and behold, he spent ten minutes happily tearing the basil into little pieces. I was shocked at how he stayed on the task without uttering a peep.

Suddenly, I saw an opportunity. He wanted to help me, and I sure needed help. Why not let him cook with me?

So he and his older brother began doing lots of tasks in the kitchen: peeling vegetables, grating cheese, pushing the blender and food processor buttons, plucking the leaves from herbs, tearing up salad greens, kneading dough, stirring risotto, even helping me make homemade pasta!

It was incredible what they could be persuaded to do—all because I invited them into the process and believed in their ability to really help. Yes, it got messy at times. And at first, I would feel rushed, sabotaging the moment by grabbing something away because they were taking so long. Then I realized I no longer had any reason to be in a hurry. As long as the kids were with me in the kitchen, they were not whining about dinner. They were busy and content. I stopped worrying about the mess or how long it took to cook the meal. And though it was hard to stick to it, I decided to enjoy the process of cooking with my kids and not worry about the meal itself being perfect.

We started to laugh a lot at dinnertime. And my elder son began to rely on that time of day to share his worries and fears. We would talk about tutors and help for him in school, and over time, his problems lessened. He was getting the quality time he needed.

With this mind-set, you won't make the mistake of getting tense and impatient, grabbing food or tools away from the kids because they're too slow. The kids won't end up running off in tears. You'll just be talking, going along cooking, and soon, you'll realize that new lines of communication and strong bonds are forming.

Family cooking has another tangible reward. After preparing the meal together, you'll actually want to sit at the table and enjoy it together. It may well become your favorite part of the day.

~Lynn Fredericks
Chicken Soup for the Single Parent's Soul

Watching Over You

I was a single parent, divorced eleven years and raising my thirteen-year-old son, Michael, alone. Michael had recently taken up skiing at the nearby ski hill. Late one afternoon, I took him and his friend Joe to ski. Given all the trouble teens get into these days, I was always very careful about where they went and who would be there. The community ski facility was quite nice, with an area for food and drinks in the upper loft.

Most parents would drop their kids off and would come back hours later, but before I could feel comfortable about leaving, I had to be sure they were safe and having a good time. I told the boys that I would stay in the loft and watch them ski for a while (even though in the evening with the lights on the hill, you could rarely tell who anyone was as they came skiing down). Hour after hour, I stood there watching each little figure go up in the lift, then ski downward. A couple of times, the boys came in for some food and hot chocolate. They laughed, sharing their triumphs and defeats on the hill, got warmed up and off they went again.

After nearly four hours had gone by, I found myself standing at the window, feeling a bit lonely and sorry for myself—I was tired and weepy. I allowed my thoughts to wander about how my ex-husband was probably out having a great time, with no responsibilities to tie him down. How great it would be to just be able to go clothes shopping or have some fun, something just for me for a change.

Suddenly, a voice broke through my self-pitying mood.

A young man, whom I had never met, said, "Hi, excuse me, but

I noticed you've been standing there for hours. You're watching your kids ski, right?"

Rather taken aback, I responded, "Yes, that's right."

He replied, "Well, I just wanted to tell you, if there were more parents in the world like you, it would be a better place." And then he pushed the door open and left, as suddenly as he had come.

My mood lifted, and a smile spread across my face. I recalled the passage from the Bible: "Don't forget to entertain strangers, for by so doing some have entertained angels unawares" (Heb. 13:1).

The young man's words brought me a very strange but comfortable feeling. I felt God had sent him, this angel, to remind me of what was really important in life. I knew in my heart that there was nothing else I'd rather be doing at that moment, and nowhere else I'd rather be.

~Linda Ferris
Chicken Soup for the Single Parent's Soul

The Fisherman

Fishing is a lot like dating....
Somebody's trying to do the catching
while the other is trying to get away.
~Anonymous

"Mommy, what're you doing?" Jake asked me, rocking a small tackle box by his side.

"Well, I thought I'd curl up with a book and read." I looked at my young son. "Why?"

"Can we go fishing?"

Fishing? I'm a single mom! Worms, fish guts, empty, staring eyes—that is not in my job description.

"I want to catch a fish, a big fish," he said, opening his arms wide.

"But Jake, I don't know how to fish," I answered.

"Me, neither," he said, plopping on the couch next to me. The small pole and string dangled by his leg.

"Sorry, but Grandpa forgot to teach me how to catch a fish," I apologized.

"Life's not fair," he whispered.

"Come on, you're only eight," I said. The guilt factor multiplied in my stomach. "Want to play catch?"

"Nah, Grandpa forgot to teach you that, too."

"Huh?"

"You throw like a girl." He opened the tackle box, pulled out a red bobber and tossed it up and down.

"What do you mean I throw like a girl?" I asked.

"You always throw three feet away from my glove," he said dejectedly, slumping on the couch.

"And that's why you're the best shortstop at Little League. A ball can't get by you." I pointed to the trio of trophies on the mantel.

"But I've never caught a fish." He slid off the sofa, knelt on the carpet and held a colorful fly to the light.

"Grandpa said he'd take you fishing." Guilt twisted a tighter knot in my gut.

"Grandpa lives a hundred miles away." He unscrewed a jar of salmon eggs and played with the round balls.

"Hmm." A well-placed, tactical maneuver. Boy, being a "dad" is hard.

"Isn't today Saturday?" A plan was obviously formulating in his mind.

"Why?" I flipped another page of my book, not a word read. Hmm? What is he up to?

"Isn't there a singles' dance tonight?"

"I hate those dances, Jake." I feigned interest in my crinkled paperback.

"But there are guys there." He established his cause.

"That's right. Lots of guys looking for, well, not me." I am not going to get reeled in.

"Aw, Mom, all the guys love you." Flattery. The bait set.

"You're sweet, but no, I'm still not going."

"All you need is one who likes to fish." He dangled a treble hook and paused.

"What?" I stared at the metal claw.

"Please, Mommy." The sinker. "Go dancing and find me a fisherman."

"I don't have a sitter."

"I'll call Susie down the street." He jumped up from where he sat on the floor and ran to the kitchen phone.

"Jake!"

"Hurry up and get real pretty." Little orders flew from the kitchen. "And don't forget to stink a lot. Old guys like that."

"Wait," I glanced at the clock. It was half past eight. The dance started at nine. "But, I...."

"Susie's on her way over." He pulled me from the comfort of the sofa. "You don't have much time."

"I don't want to go." My heels dragged against the carpet, his little hand in mine. I tripped and fell over the pint-size fishing rod. My ankle tangled in the line.

"Come on. All the good ones will get away."

Let them go. My fishing license is expired. No more pond scum.

I limped to the bedroom, slipped into a black halter dress and fluffed my strawberry tresses. A touch of makeup, an extra spray of musk, and I was off to snag the catch of the day.

A validation stamp on the back of my hand, fifteen dollars at the door, and I entered the dance. I purchased a drink ticket and stood in line at the bar.

"Hi, I'm Tim from Kensington." A Cheshire cat grin spread between the lower lobes of each ear.

"Hello." I inched ahead to the bar.

"Where do you live?" The script rolled off his tongue.

"East of the tunnel."

"Oh, you're geographically unacceptable." With that he turned and scampered away. I gave thanks.

The bartender gestured for the next customer. I ordered my drink and eased my way from the makeshift bar into the large room. Darkened lights created an ambience of what-we-can't-see-will-do-us-no-harm atmosphere. I nursed the cool mixture in my glass and surveyed the crowd. Great music.

As the evening wore on, I tallied the selection of men that had approached me to dance: one accountant, one engineer and one salesman. None of them appealing, none of them appropriate fishing buddies for Jake. The pond dry, the clock marked the eleventh hour. Time for decisive action. I angled to another corner and adjusted my gear. The lure tempted.

"Don't you run at Lake Chabot?" A question of substance floated my way.

"That's me." Intriguing conversation.

"I go there all the time. Do you want to dance?" He motioned toward the arena of swiveling and gyrating hips.

"You go to the lake?" This has possibilities. "Do you like to fish?" A nibble.

"I love to fish." He smiled. "The other day I caught a six-pound rainbow trout." His story is animated. The man knows his sport.

We twisted and turned into the early hours and exchanged phone numbers penciled on little napkin scraps. Later, I paid Susie and watched her walk home.

"You're back." Jake was stretched out on the sofa.

"Hey, sleepyhead."

"Did you have fun?" A yawn caught his words, and they tumbled out in slow motion.

"So-so." I replayed the evening in my head.

"Well?" He sat up slightly, bracing his weight on his elbow.

"Well what?" I reeked of stale tobacco.

"Did you find me a fisherman?" His eyelids were barely open.

"Yeah." I fingered Kevin's number in my hand.

"Thanks, Mommy." He curled back into sleep and hugged the waiting pole.

"You're welcome."

Mom, the fisher of men. What Grandpa forgot to teach, Grandma did not.

~Cynthia Borris
Chicken Soup for the Single Parent's Soul

From Prison to Ph.D.

Turn your wounds into wisdom.
~Oprah Winfrey

The odds were not in favor of my sister, Grace Halloran, when it came to much of anything.

She spent most of her teen years in and out of juvenile institutions for minor offenses, but at eighteen, she hit the big time when she stole a car and traveled across state lines. Arrested, she was sent to federal prison for breaking yet another law—this time, a felony. After three years behind bars, she was released. The guards didn't bother to say goodbye; they were sure she'd be back soon.

Only a few years later, she was given a sentence far worse than the last one: blindness. Grace was summarily told she had two incurable, progressive disorders: retinitis pigmentosa, complicated by macular degeneration. The doctor added coldly, "I hope this will have a maturing effect on you. There are no cures, and nothing can be done to help you. You are legally blind now, and will soon be totally blind."

Grace was also happily pregnant—but terrified she would never see her child's face. How could she raise a child? She believed she had the love, determination and patience to succeed as a mother, although "success" had not been in her vocabulary before. When Ruchell, her son, was born, she managed well despite fading vision, and her son flourished.

Grace kept consulting specialists about her eye problems. She was given even more devastating news when one famous eye specialist said her son would also be blind by the time he was a teenager. She vowed to find something, anything, to prevent her boy from facing her fate. She appreciated the irony that she refused to accept the prognosis for her son that she had so readily accepted for herself.

Conventional medicine offered no hope at all, so Grace embarked on a personal quest. She enrolled in classes at a local college. The office for disabled students arranged to have her reading assignments put on cassette tapes so she could listen and learn. She began studying anatomy, physiology and other health sciences. Fellow students called her "Sherlock," because of her detective skills in ferreting out information, and because of the extra-large magnifying glass she had to use. She followed any and all leads about therapies for eye disorders, including a report from China on the success of acupuncture in improving retinitis pigmentosa. The article gave her a glimmer of hope, and over the next seven years, Grace investigated many alternative therapies—including nutrition, herbal medicine, color healing, yoga, acupressure and acupuncture—adapting many of these modalities for herself and her growing son.

She began to realize that what she was learning related to the health of her whole body, and Grace became a certified Touch for Health instructor, a technique for keeping the body in balance. She also explored sports medicine, which introduced her to the world of bioelectrical stimulation. Everyone who knew her was astonished at her persistence to educate herself, restore her vision and keep focused on her highest priority, raising a son who would have perfect eyesight.

Grace earned her Ph.D. in Holistic Health. She was awarded the degree for her successful work in improving serious eye disorders. Despite the dire medical predictions, Grace's eyesight had slowly improved so much that she was able to qualify for a driver's license.

Word spread of Grace's success with "impossible" cases, and in January 1983, a national magazine featured her story. The response was so great she put together a formal program to present her ideas. Independent assessors were hired to evaluate the data from one hundred participants who used her program, and after two years, the results were overwhelmingly positive. Because European communities are more open to alternative theories than the American medical community, she was invited to teach her program overseas.

Grace was on her way to Sweden the day radioactivity entered Swedish airspace after the Russian atomic power plant exploded at Chernobyl. That fateful flight would become the trigger to a devastating downward health spiral that almost took her life. By 1991, she could no longer work, and her vision was again failing. For two years, she was either in the hospital dealing with radiation exposure, or home struggling to write her autobiography, *Amazing Grace—Autobiography of a Survivor*, and praying she'd live to see it published.

A month after completing the manuscript, Grace lost all her sight and entered a school for the blind to learn independent living skills. She was grateful, though, that after all their work, her son had 20/20 vision and was accepted into the Air Force.

Attitudes toward alternative healing have changed drastically since Grace began her studies. Some American eye specialists have now begun to acknowledge her work and dedication. A leading ophthalmologist, Dr. Edward Kondrot, dedicated his book, *Microcurrent Stimulation : Miracle Eye Cure?*, to Grace, recognizing her as a pioneer in the field. In November 1999, Old Dominion University of Virginia invited her to be a keynote speaker at the First Annual Natural Vision Improvement Conference. Professionals and lay people from all over the world attended, heard her speech and gave her a standing ovation.

She is more determined than ever to regain her sight, and keeps practicing the principles she teaches others in her training seminars.

My sister is slowly regaining her own sight for the second time. She truly is "Amazing Grace."

~Kathleen Halloran
Chicken Soup to Inspire the Body & Soul

34

Love and Cheeseburgers

You can't wrap love in a box, but you can wrap a person in a hug.
~Author Unknown

Things have been hard for a friend of mine. She and her six-year-old son have just moved into their own apartment, a break they needed to get out of a difficult situation. The responsibilities of having their own home puts pressure on her while she tries to support her son, and once in a while, it gets the best of her.

The little guy is a typical six-year-old: mischievous, energetic and curious. His questions deluge her daily as he discovers the world around him. Most of the time, she takes it all in stride, amazed at how easy it is to please him. The promise of a simple cheeseburger from his favorite restaurant is enough for him to be on his best behavior for an entire weekend. His mom is grateful she can give him what he wants, at least for now.

One evening at the end of a very long day at work, the demands of the day were heavy on her mind. After picking up her son at after-school care, the two of them went home for dinner. While going through the motions of preparing his food and looking over his first-grade school papers, the tasks of being a single mom overwhelmed her. Once she had him bathed and tucked into bed, she sat down in the living room and cried. Everything hit her suddenly and without warning. The recent loss of her beloved grandmother, combined with the responsibilities of single-parenting, were just too much. Wiping tears from her eyes, she looked up to see her son peeking into the living room from the hallway.

"Mommy, are you okay?"

"Yes, honey," she replied. "I'm just a little sad."

He walked over to her and wrapped his small arms around her neck. Though she tried to hold them back, her tears fell even more freely, and her son reassured her that everything would be all right. Hurrying back to his bedroom, he returned quickly, handing his mom a small piece of paper folded into a crumpled square.

She opened it and read its message: "I love you, Mom."

She would have reached out at that moment and held him for eternity, but he had gone into the kitchen and was busy making her his special dish. It's the only thing he can cook, and it took him quite a while to prepare it.

Finally, he came into the living room with a plate of buttered toast. It was all he had to give, that and the note.

While he sat there proudly, she ate every bite, even though the butter was in a huge clump in the middle.

"That's what love is all about," she later told me. "He gave me all he had, wrote the words he best knew how to spell, prepared the only food he knew how to prepare. I'm not nearly as alone as I was feeling that evening. I have a wonderful son who loves me."

Sometimes, when you least expect it, a blessing from God shines through your darkest moment. For my friend, that blessing is with her all the time, in tennis shoes and tiny blue jeans.

I asked her what in the world a parent could do when a child has given his all.

She smiled and replied, "The next day, I took him out for a cheeseburger."

~Kathy Bohannon
Chicken Soup for the Single Parent's Soul

Moms & Sons

I Choose You as My Son

Biology is the least of what makes someone a mother.
~Oprah Winfrey

35

Outpouring of Love

A baby is born with a need to be loved—and never outgrows it.
~Frank A. Clark

It was 8 P.M. and cold. The rain, undecided whether to turn to snow, came down in sheets. It didn't matter to us. Three cars filled with family found their way to the Denver airport to meet the plane that was bringing the most precious of all cargoes—a ten-month-old baby boy.

My daughter Katy and her husband, Don, were adopting this boy, who was coming more than five thousand miles from his home in the little country of Latvia. The infant had lived every day of his young life on his back in a crib in an orphanage along with 199 other children. He had never even been outside.

The entire family stood at the end of the ramp leading from the plane to the airport, expectant, awed and barely breathing—waiting for a first glance of this child. As passengers began coming off the plane, a small crowd gathered around us. No one in the waiting group spoke. Every eye was damp. The emotion was almost visible. One of the flight attendants handed us a congratulatory bottle of wine. Even passersby, feeling the electricity, stopped, asked and then stayed to watch.

When finally (they were actually the last ones off the plane) the woman carrying our baby turned the corner and started up the ramp to us, Katy could not contain herself another instant. She started running toward them crying openly, her arms outstretched, aching to hold her baby boy for the first time. Cradling him, she started back up the ramp. Don, with their other adopted child, a two-year-old girl, started running to meet them, he too crying. And when the four of them stepped inside the airport where all of us were standing; it was as if they had stepped into a warm and soft cocoon filled and over-flowing with emotion and love. Everyone was hugging them, and then each other. Overwhelmed by the power of the scene, no longer was anyone a stranger, but then, love is like that.

I stood slightly to one side of the hubbub, so I could really "see" it. This poor little boy, so far from home, was hearing no familiar words. Even his name had been changed. He saw no familiar faces. He had been traveling for over twenty-four hours straight and seemed completely dazed. He was being passed from person to person, each one needing to touch him to believe he was real.

I looked closely at him. He had skin the color of chalk, his every rib was showing, and his nose was running. I reached over and found his forehead was warm to the touch. Clearly, he was ill.

I also noticed he couldn't hold his head up by himself or even sit alone, signs that his development was way behind. Plus, he did not respond to noise. Could he be deaf?

At that moment I knew we probably had saved his life. I also realized with a rush of feeling that I would guard him, nurture him and love him with every fiber of my being. Katy was a wonderful mother, and I would be right behind her all the way.

As we finally left the airport for home, I crawled into the back-seat of the car and sat between the two car seats full of miracles. Now there were two lives dependent on this family for all things. All the way home I had one hand on him and the other hand on her. I think I was praying.

The next morning, we took the baby, who had been named Zachary, to the doctor. She found that Zachary had serious infections in both ears, which had apparently never been treated. She told us that our baby would hear once the infections cleared. The doctor went on to talk about solid foods (Zachary had never had any) and his need for exercise. Sending us home with medicines to help him, she assured us he would "catch up," with care.

And he did, as we watched in amazement! In one short week this child held his head erect, sat alone, then flipped over and crawled on hands and knees. A few weeks later, he reached the stairs, climbed up two of them, then grabbed the rail, and pulling himself to a standing position, stood there looking at his new mom in triumph!

As the doctor predicted, Zachary's hearing returned and rosy apple cheeks replaced his chalky color. But the most important change of all was that our Zachary began to laugh and cry.

This little boy had never cried. When crying hadn't worked to draw the attention he so desperately needed, he quit early on. As for laughter, I doubt there was too much to laugh about.

Now when Zachary laughs, it is no infant giggle, but rather a hearty guffaw right from his toes. When he laughs like that, anyone with him has to laugh too.

Once again, I have seen the tremendous power of love. No one can thrive without it. And with it, all things are possible.

~Jean Brody
Chicken Soup for Every Mom's Soul

Startled by a Dream

Pay attention to your dreams—
God's angels often speak directly to our hearts
when we are asleep.
~ Eileen Elias Freeman, The Angels' Little Instruction Book

I woke from a restful sleep and lay in bed thinking about the day ahead. Soon I drifted off again and dreamed: A teenage boy who looked about fourteen years old sat at a large cherry wood desk, concentrating on a book. Though I had never met him, I felt a sense of intimacy and familiarity with him. Then the Lord spoke: "This is your son."

Startled by this message, I moved in to get a closer look at this studious young boy with brown hair and glasses. The Lord spoke again. "I have a plan, a special purpose for him."

Then a feeling like cold water hit my face and I woke.

I shook my husband. "Stan, we're going to have a baby, a son!"

"Huh?" he said and rolled over, unimpressed. But as I thought about the dream, seeds of hope grew in my heart.

At forty-two, despite major surgery and other medical interventions, I had never been able to conceive. My husband had two grown children, but not having a child of my own grieved me.

My husband and I directed a ranch at Vista, California, for street men from Los Angeles trying to get their lives back together. Part of the summer program included a camp for kids. Under close supervision, teenage counselors shared kitchen duty with the street men.

One day, Jack, a thirty-year-old former Los Angeles street gang leader and drug addict, told us about a sixteen-year-old junior counselor named Robert who shared kitchen responsibilities with him. Robert's foster mother, exasperated by her inability to control him, abandoned him at the ranch. Since she suspected he stole and lied, she turned him over to the police and they hauled him off to a boys' detention home.

Jack pleaded with us. "Robert's mother abandoned him at age eleven. He has been shuffled from home to home since then. He needs a stable place. Please take this boy in, otherwise he will end up like me. I want him to have a better chance than I did."

Our hearts went out to Jack and Robert, but homes for troubled teenagers are almost nonexistent. The staff at the ranch prayed and searched for a month but nothing happened. Jack persisted. "How can you not take care of him when you call yourselves Christians?"

My husband became convinced that God wanted us to take Robert into our home. I didn't have parenting experience. I wanted to start out with a baby, not a teenager. Additionally, I battled chronic fatigue syndrome. I didn't think I had the strength to handle the challenge of a teenager, let alone an abused and troubled one.

Finally, after discussing my fears with my husband, I prayed. Lord, if this is Your will, then I will yield to it. I know that every path You lead us on is fragrant with Your loving kindness and truth, even if it is a hard path. I don't want to miss the blessing You have in mind.

One week after this prayer of surrender, we took Robert in. We faced many challenges working through his problems with him, but ultimately we adopted him. A few months after the adoption, I remembered my dream and wondered if this was the son it had promised.

Robert grew up, married and became the proud father of two little girls. Two years after he left home we thought about adopting another child. We had learned a great deal during the difficult challenge of raising Robert, and he was worth it. After what we had been through with him, we thought we could handle anyone!

We asked the Lord to show us if He wanted us to have more children. Few people adopt older children, yet these older kids yearn for the love of a family as much as the younger ones. We contacted a Christian international adoption agency since we learned that some foreign countries have fewer time and age restrictions. Since my husband is fifteen years older than I, we decided to explore this option, and they accepted us. Three weeks later, they sent us a picture and information about Alex, a fourteen-year-old boy from Brazil.

Alex had a tough background. His father had abandoned him at birth and his mother had abused him and later abandoned him. Despite these negative influences, he had many good characteristics, such as being caring, considerate, a good student and cooperative.

We decided to adopt him—and then the mountain of paperwork began. When we discovered the costs of an international adoption, we blanched. We did not have those kinds of resources.

Discouraged, we talked with a friend who had adopted two older children. She adamantly told us, "Don't let the lack of money stop you. God has ways of providing. Go forward. Begin the process with what you have."

So we began the adoption process, trusting God to provide. Through a series of miracles, and help from others, God made a way for us.

After six months of paperwork, we received approval and flew to Brazil to claim our son. We arrived at the airport and hastened to the courthouse. I wondered how long it would be before we met Alex. A thousand questions went through my head. Is this really God's will for all of us? Are we sure this is the right boy for us—and are we right for him? Will we bond? Will he like us? Will we like him? How will we manage to communicate with the language barrier?

Finally, after lengthy preliminary visits with the social worker and psychologist, they ushered Alex in. He anxiously hugged us and sat down. We talked through an interpreter for forty-five minutes and then we all rose to leave. My husband and the social worker walked out of the room ahead of me. As Alex got up to leave, he put on his glasses for the first time. I gasped. Stunned, I ran out of the room to catch up with my husband. I blurted, "It's him! Alex is the boy in the dream I had years ago!"

During our stay in Brazil, as the three of us spent time with one another, our hearts knit together, and we became a family. About a month later, back in the states, a friend who spoke Portuguese asked Alex, "Weren't you worried that you were nearly sixteen, the cutoff age for international adoptions, and hadn't been adopted yet?"

Alex said, "No. I told Jesus the kind of parents I wanted, and He gave them to me."

~Sharon Gibson
Chicken Soup for the Christian Woman's Soul

37

My Son

Adoption is when a child grew in its mommy's heart instead of her tummy.
~Author Unknown

The war was far from Saigon when I agreed to escort six babies from Vietnam to their adoptive homes in the U.S. Still, the decision to leave my husband and two little girls had not been easy. When the war escalated, I had begged God for a sign that I could back out of my commitment, but he only filled me with a courage and confidence I could explain to no one. Somehow I knew this was all a part of his plan. By the time I landed in Saigon, bombs were falling outside the city limits, Vietnam was falling to the communists, and President Ford had okayed Operation Babylift. Scores of the estimated 50,000 Amerasian babies and toddlers were herded into our headquarters of Friends of Children of Vietnam in preparation for the airlift.

On my third day there, over breakfast of bread and bottled Coke, Cherie, the director, said, "LeAnn, you've probably figured this out...."

I hadn't.

"You and Mark applied for adoption of a son through us, and we told you to expect him in two years." She spoke above the din of dozens of bawling babies. "Obviously, everything has changed. You'll be assigned one of the babies gathered here—or," she paused to touch my hand, "or you can go into the nursery and choose a son."

I was stunned, speechless.

I felt myself flush with excitement—then with fear.

"Really?" I finally croaked. Surely, I had heard her wrong.

Cherie's tired eyes danced. "Really."

"So I can just go in there and pick out a son?"

Cherie nodded again.

Dazed, I turned to my friend and traveling companion, Carol. "Come with me." She jumped up immediately, and we approached the door to the nursery together.

I paused and took a deep breath. "This is like a fantasy. A dream come true."

I opened the door, and we entered a room filled with babies. Babies on blankets and mats. Babies in boxes and baskets and bassinets and cribs.

"Carol, how will I ever choose? There are 110 babies here now."

One baby in a white T-shirt and diaper looked at me with bright eyes. I sat cross-legged on the floor with him on my lap. He seemed to be about nine months old and responded to my words with cute facial expressions and animation. He giggled and clapped his hands.

"We should name you Personality," I said. Then I noticed he was wearing a name bracelet on his ankle. He had already been assigned to a family in Denver. Well, I thought, feeling disappointment rising in my throat, that family is mighty lucky.

Another child caught my eye as he pulled himself to his feet beside a wooden crib. We watched with amusement as he tugged the toes of the baby sleeping inside. Then he dropped to his hands and knees and began crawling to me. I met him halfway across the room and picked him up. He wore only a diaper, and his soft, round tummy bulged over its rim. He looked at me and smiled brightly, revealing chubby cheeks and deep dimples. As I hugged him, he nestled his head into my shoulder.

"Maybe you'll be our son," I whispered. He pulled back, staring into my eyes, still smiling. For the next hour, I carried him around the room, looking at each infant, touching them, talking to them. All the while, the baby in my arms babbled, smiled and continued to cuddle. I couldn't bring myself to put him down as we went upstairs where the floor was carpeted with even more babies. The hallway was like a megaphone, blasting the sounds of chattering workers and crying babies.

"Let me hold him," Carol coaxed, "while you look at the others." The couch against the wall held a half-dozen fussy infants side by side. I picked up each of them. Most seemed stiff and unresponsive. How sad that cuddling could be unfamiliar to them. I weaved my way to the blanket of babies at the end of the room and sat caressing each of them. As I cradled one in my arms, I could feel the bones of his spine press against my skin. Another's eyes looked glazed and motionless. Sorrow gripped me.

I felt the little boy Carol was carrying for me pat my arm. As I turned to look, he reached out his chubby arms for me. Taking him from her, I snuggled him close, and he snuggled back. Someone had loved him very much.

Downstairs, we meandered from mat to crib, looking at all the infants again. I wished I could adopt them all. But I knew there were long waiting lists at the Denver headquarters of hundreds of families who had completed the tedious, time-consuming application process. Each of these precious orphans would have immediate homes carefully selected for them.

"How do I choose?" I asked myself as much as Carol.

The baby boy in my arms answered by patting my face. I had never missed my husband more. "I wish Mark was here."

I turned my full attention to the child I held, waving my hands in front of his face to check his eyes. He blinked and flashed his dimples.

I snapped my fingers by his ears in a foolish attempt to test his hearing. He turned his head, giggled and grabbed at my hands.

Then I sat on the floor, slowly rocking him back and forth in my arms. I whispered a prayer for the decision I was about to make, a decision that would affect many lives forever. The baby nestled into the hollow of my neck, reassuring me that the choice I was about to make was the right one. I could feel his shallow breath and tender skin as he embraced me.

I recalled all the data we had collected for adoption; all the letters of references from friends, bankers, employers; all the interviews with the social workers.

It had all been worth it for this moment.

We rocked in silence and cuddled. Then, with immense joy, I walked back through the nursery door to the office.

"Meet our son, Mitchell Thieman!" I announced, hardly believing my own words. Everyone gathered around and embraced us. I looked at Mitchell's puzzled face and held him closer. Cherie brought a nametag, and I eagerly scrawled on it, "Reserve for Mark Thieman," and placed it on his ankle.

Joyful tears streamed down my cheeks. For a moment, all my fears were gone. I no longer wondered why I had been driven to make this journey. "This is why God sent me to Vietnam," I whispered.

I had been sent to choose a son.

Or had he chosen me?

~LeAnn Thieman
Chicken Soup for the Mother and Son Soul

38

A Cure for Restlessness

Love cures people—both the ones who give it and the ones who receive it.
~Dr. Karl Menninger

Last year, when I went back to China, I paid a visit to Xiaotao, my college friend. He wasn't home, but his wife, Malan, greeted me warmly and led me into their home. As I answered her questions about my life in the United States, I glanced at the expansive living room with elegant furnishings. I knew that what I had heard over the years was true. As China continued to prosper in the last decade, so did my friends.

Half an hour later, when Xiaotao still had not returned, I asked, "Do you think he had to work late?"

"Ah, no," Malan answered pleasantly, pouring tea into my cup. "He's at the orphanage this afternoon."

"Orphanage?"

"Yes," she nodded with a smile. "He began volunteering there three years ago."

During my visit, I heard many things about my friends: Zhang attained wealth; Li obtained a divorce; Wang was laid off... but volunteering in an orphanage sounded alien. I wanted to ask her why, but I didn't. The look on my face must have betrayed my amazement because Malan began telling me the story.

In 1987, she and Xiaotao married. She worked as a copy editor at a magazine, while he taught at our alma mater. Malan gave birth to their son a year later, and their life was good.

But when the government began to allow private enterprise in

1992, Xiaotao became restless. He wanted to make money—lots of it. Borrowing funds from his parents, he quit his job and opened his first restaurant. He was very good at what he did. No one knew how he had learned his business savvy—both his parents were teachers.

After the triumph of the first restaurant, he opened another, then a clothing store, an ice cream parlor and a string of other successful enterprises. In five years, he became a very wealthy man.

Malan momentarily paused. Her smiling face quickly turned somber as she continued. "But trouble began soon after that. Xiaotao's businesses were thriving, and he had more free time on his hands and more money in his pockets than he knew what to do with. He began to frequent bars and discos and spend less and less time with me and our son."

Pausing to control her emotion, she continued. "Then one night he didn't come home. The next morning, he walked in reeking of perfume and liquor. That's when I asked for a divorce. He was so angry that he stormed out of the house, got back into his car and drove away. As he was driving to a nearby village, he hit an old woman.

"That was another turning point in our lives," she said. "The old woman suffered a fractured arm, and Xiaotao visited her every day at the hospital. He was fond of her. They exchanged their life stories, and before long, we called her Aunt Liu.

"On the day she was released from the hospital, Aunt Liu suggested a cure for his restlessness. She told him to spend some time at the orphanage where she worked. He laughed loudly, patted her on the shoulder and assured her he would donate plenty of money. Aunt Liu shook her head and told him that spending time at the orphanage would be more helpful to him than to the orphanage."

Then, looking at me with a proud smile, she said, "After his first visit, he embraced it with his heart and soul. He helped to make cribs and additional rooms for new arrivals. He held the babies when they cried and played with the older children, spending most of his free time there."

An hour later, Xiaotao came home. "Sorry I'm late," he said, shaking my hands with a vise-like grip. "I was about to leave when an abandoned baby girl was brought in."

"What did you do with her?" I asked, my heart in my throat.

"I held her and rocked her until she stopped crying."

Swallowing hard, I tried not to cry. We visited a while longer before I had to take my leave.

The week before my departure, I got a call from Malan asking me to attend Xiaotao's mother's funeral. When I arrived in the old neighborhood, the procession for the funeral was already a mile long and the cry was heard a mile wide. Colorful paper money flew about in the breeze like butterflies. Some things in China will never change, I thought.

As I entered the courtyard and bowed in front of his mother's coffin, Xiaotao came over to shake my hand. "Thanks for coming," he said. He looked somber and pensive.

"My condolences," I said softly.

He nodded. "My mother lived a long life."

"I want you to know something," I said. "Of all the things new in China, what impresses me the most is how the orphanage helped you to regain your life and how you are helping these children."

His lips quivered. "The night before my mother died, she told me about a secret she had kept," he said, staring into the distance. "One night, thirty-seven years ago, she found me lying in a basket on the doorstep... of an orphans' home."

~Linda Jin Zou
Chicken Soup for the Volunteer's Soul

I Am a Mother

Every child begins the world again....
~Henry David Thoreau

was in Portsmouth, New Hampshire, getting my hair cut when my husband called. He didn't even talk to me, but the message he gave to the receptionist was simple, "Stop home on your way to the dentist." It was a beautiful day in July. I had ended work a few days before and had lined up appointments for all those things one puts off when one is working full-time.

Just the week before, we had finished our home study with the adoption agency, and we were told we probably had at least a couple of months before we would be matched up with a baby. My husband, Joe, and I had gone through eight years of medical intervention for infertility, and for much of that time I believed I could not be a mother. After much soul-searching, Joe and I realized that our goal was to become parents and that adoption was just as wonderful a way of building a family as giving birth. Our adoption counselor told me I would be a mother, but was it really true?

As I was driving down the highway after the haircut, I thought about my husband's request to stop home. Did he have some time from work to have lunch at home with me? Then I became curious: Joe has no idea where I get my hair cut, so he must have gone to great lengths to track down the phone number. Now, why would he go through all that trouble to find me and just leave a message to stop home? Could it be we got "the call?" Was I a mother already? My heart began to race with excitement, and then I checked myself as I had a dozen times before when we were trying to get pregnant — no, it couldn't be that.

As I pulled into the driveway, the large quilted heart flag that I had made years before as a Valentine's present for Joe was hanging over the driveway. Where had he dug that up, and why was it hanging? As he walked out of the house with a champagne bottle in his hand, I knew.

"Joan, you're the mother of a baby boy!" he told me. Our adoption counselor had called him at work to give him the wonderful news. He filled me in on the details and told me we could pick up our new son the next afternoon.

What should we do first? We weren't expecting a baby for at least a few months; like a couple that is pregnant, we thought we would have time to plan and get ready. We called our parents first. "Mom, Dad, we have a baby boy!" I told my parents. "Oh, Joan, we're so happy that you're a mother," they said. I didn't feel any different than I had the day before. When will I know I am a mother? I wondered.

The next twenty-four hours went by quickly, yet I remember every moment in great detail. First, we had to talk with the adoption agency to receive more information and directions. They gave us the phone number of the foster mother who was taking care of our son until we picked him up the next day. We dialed the phone and waited what seemed like eternity for an answer. Mary answered. "Hello," I said, "this is Joan and Joe. Do you have our baby?" "Oh, yes," she said, "he's sitting right here on my lap. Do you hear him?" We listened, and heard his voice for the first time, making his baby sounds.

The next fifteen hours were a rush to complete paperwork, get to the bank for payment to the adoption agency, and get to the mall before it closed to pick up a few basics. Although we knew an adoption would happen in the near future, up until that day I could not allow myself to buy or borrow any baby things. For years, each time I would see the grocery aisle that carries diapers and baby food, I would pass by quickly. I believed that aisle was off-limits to me; I was not a mother. It's not a very rational feeling, but one that many infertile women experience, even when they are told a baby is coming for them through adoption.

At the department store, we ran into an old acquaintance. "Hello, what's new?" she asked.

"Oh, nothing," I said out of habit.

"Oh, everything!" Joe said with excitement.

We rushed on, leaving the poor woman quite puzzled. I picked out receiving blankets, diapers, bottles, formula and socks (are baby feet really that tiny?). While I was stocking up on the practical things, Joe ran off and found our son's first stuffed animal—Winnie the Pooh.

Around 1:00 in the morning, while we were trying to figure out how to sterilize bottles, we began to pick a name for the baby. Previously, it was too hard to look at books with baby names; what if our baby never came? Once we picked the name, we tried to get some sleep. Impossible. We had heard his voice, we had given him a name, but was he real? What did he look like? Was he truly going to be ours?

Later that morning, we went to the adoption agency for last-minute paperwork and to meet the birth mother of our son. She had made a careful adoption plan for him and had chosen us to be his parents. It was a very good and touching meeting. She was his birth mother, the one who had given him life, but I was his mother too, the one who would love and care for him every day.

We followed the directions to the foster-care home, and as we pulled up to the house my heart was racing. I don't remember how I got to the front door. Mary opened the door, and as we walked in, she placed in my arms the most beautiful baby I had ever seen. He looked up at me, and said without words, "You are my mother." I will never forget that moment, for that was when all my questions ended.

Looking into his eyes, I knew for certain that I had become a mother.

~Joan Sedita
Chicken Soup for Every Mom's Soul

40

To Have and to Hold

I would thank you from the bottom of my heart,
but for you my heart has no bottom.
~Author Unknown

*I*n the summer of 1959, I flew from Washington, D.C., to Los Angeles accompanied by my father. Nineteen years old, pregnant and frightened, I was flying to this distant city to live with total strangers, so that my unborn child could be born far away from prying eyes and gossiping mouths and then be put up for private adoption.

On September 3rd, I gave birth to a little boy and though I saw him once, lying in the nursery, I was not allowed to hold him. The doctor and nurses felt it would be too painful for me, and I suppose they were right. Shortly after the birth, I flew back to Washington, signed the adoption papers and, as my doctor had suggested, continued on with my life.

Although the pain of the parting diminished with time, I never forgot for a moment that I had a son. Every September 3rd for the next thirty-three years I silently mourned, grieving for the child I had given away. Mother's Day was always the worst. It seemed that every woman I knew was a mom. I'm a mother, too, I wanted to say but couldn't.

And so the years passed and turned into decades, and the memory of my only child lingered just beneath my conscious mind, ready to explode at a moment's notice.

Then on March 26, 1993, I received this message on my answering machine: "Elizabeth," a woman's voice said, "I have some news which I hope will be of interest to you and bring you great joy and happiness."

Her voice broke, and it was quite evident she was crying. "If you are the same Elizabeth Thring who did me a favor thirty-three years ago, please call me in Newport Beach, California. I would very much like to have a chat with you."

I called back immediately and was connected to an answering machine. Three days later, when I finally got through, the woman said her name was Susie. She thanked me profusely for calling and asked if I knew who she was.

"I believe so," I replied, "but I'm not 100 percent sure."

"Oh, Elizabeth," she said, "I adopted your beautiful baby boy thirty-three years ago, and I am just calling to tell you what a wonderful son you have. Bill is married to a terrific girl, and you have two absolutely beautiful little granddaughters."

I couldn't believe what I was hearing. I had fantasized about this very moment in some form or another for years, and now it was a reality. I told her that I couldn't think of another woman I knew with such generosity of spirit. Susie said that one day while watching her two little granddaughters playing, she thought to herself, "What woman wouldn't want to know about such beautiful children?" and so she began to search for me.

She told me that although Bill knew generally that she was looking for me, he had no knowledge of this most recent attempt to locate me, since there was always the possibility that I might not want to see him.

Soon after, I sent Bill a letter. In it I wrote:

Oh, what joy — what pure, absolute, sheer joy, to discover after all these years that you are here, on the same earth, under the same blue heaven and stars and moon at night as I — and that you, my darling boy, want to know me as much as I yearn to know, hold and love you. Billy, it is important for me that you know I never, ever forgot you or ceased loving you. I thank you from the bottom of my heart for wanting to know me and not giving up on me.

Your loving mother,

Elizabeth.

In the middle of April I flew to Los Angeles. On the way, I wrote thirty-three birthday cards to my son with a short description of what I had done for each year of his life. Bill needs, I thought, to learn about me, too.

DeAnn, Bill's wife, videotaped me coming down the ramp at the airport. With her were my granddaughters, and standing just behind her was a very tall, blond, impeccably dressed man.

When he saw me, Bill stepped from behind his wife and walked toward me with arms open wide. Into this circle of love I stepped, feeling just like every other mother in the world holding her baby for the first time.

~Elizabeth Thring
Chicken Soup for the Mother's Soul 2

Moms & Sons

Raising Wonderful Men

Don't wait to make your son a great man
—make him a great boy.
~Author Unknown

41

Baked
with Loving Hands

There's no other love like the love for a brother.
There's no other love like the love from a brother.
~Astrid Alauda

O ur son, Tobey, has always had a generous spirit, as well as a very independent nature. Like many small boys, he liked to show his affection for someone by doing a kind or helpful thing.

"I'm going to make Vanessa's cake," he announced proudly at age nine when his sister's birthday was just a few days away. Somewhat surprised, I was eager to encourage this decision, as well as his interest in cooking. He was tremendously fond of his big sister and wanted to do something very grown-up in honor of her special day.

At the same time, I was a little worried about how he would accomplish this while also accommodating the demands of his twelve-year-old sister's very specific taste. She had big plans for how her birthday would be celebrated with her sixth-grade classmates that year, and was quite specific about exactly what kind of cake she hoped to have for the big day.

Tobey's food-preparation experience was limited to peanut butter sandwiches and microwave popcorn. However, he insisted that this first baking effort, his gift to Vanessa, was something he wanted to do entirely by himself, "With no help from you, Mom." (I would, of course, be allowed to drive him to the store and help him find the necessary baking supplies.)

My confidence in this project was a bit shaky, not only because of the limits of Tobey's experience and the size of his sister's expectations, but because my own cakes are not usually the prettiest things to behold. Fortunately for Tobey—and for me—the cake his sister most desired was available as a boxed cake mix. It included brightly colored sprinkles that baked right into the cake and the instructions certainly didn't sound too difficult.

Tobey and I made a trip to the store to buy the mix along with the other things we needed for the birthday party. On the eve of Vanessa's birthday, he raced through his homework and then excitedly began assembling an assortment of bowls and utensils for his project. As if to reassure me, he sat down first and read and reread the instructions on that package until I'm sure he had them memorized. Then he opened the box and got started.

In a game of parental stealth, I tried to monitor the activities of this young chef without appearing to hover over him. I found a dozen reasons to rummage in the kitchen for things as he went about his task.

Brows knit together, lips pursed in concentration, he carried out the list of instructions carefully. He broke eggs into a bowl for the first time and measured out the other ingredients as though he were handling priceless objects. I was impressed by the fact that he made virtually no mess at all. His eyes darted back and forth to check the instructions constantly.

When it came time to use the electric mixer, he granted me permission only to check that all the parts and pieces were connected properly, then thanked and dismissed me as the beaters began to whir away. He mixed the ingredients into a rich, golden batter. He had only to add the sprinkles and then it could all be poured into the baking pan he'd greased laboriously. Soon the smell of baking cake would scent the house.

Encouraged by his progress, I went to answer a phone call and was horrified to return a few minutes later and find him wrist-deep in cake batter, working his hands in the bowl. I wanted to shout, "What in the world are you doing? Are you crazy?" but thankfully, sheer astonishment kept these words tangled up in my throat unable to escape. I'm so glad I choked on my surprise rather than blurt out something I'd have regretted later.

When he saw my contorted expression, he immediately assured me that he'd washed his hands thoroughly—very thoroughly—before taking this highly unusual step.

Then he gestured with his head toward the empty sprinkles packet on the counter beside him and said, "Can you believe it? I thought it seemed kind of goofy myself, but it's exactly what the instructions said: 'Add sprinkles and mix by hand'!"

I had to agree with him, as I explained the role of spoons in this process, that it might have been helpful for the instructions to mention them. I'm sure that cake tasted even better for the laughter that followed as we waited for it to bake.

The cake—which turned out beautifully—was a smash! Vanessa, who was as surprised as she was thrilled by Tobey's loving gesture, gave him a big hug, right in front of all her "Eew—boys are yucky" friends.

A young man now, Tobey has become an accomplished cook who still likes to show his generosity by feeding others good food. But now he knows to approach at least some of life's instructions with just a grain or two of salt, along with all the other ingredients.

~Phyllis Ring
Chicken Soup for Every Mom's Soul

42

Summer Son

While some kids have bar mitzvahs and others have confirmations to commemorate the beginning of their transition into adulthood, my son Peter—twelve years old, tall for his age with size ten feet, short curly hair and round, wire-rimmed glasses—had a sea kayak trip. It was the first time either of us had ever taken a major outdoor adventure together. His goal was to paddle by himself in a solo kayak; mine was to let him.

Peter is my only child. His father and I have been divorced since he was five—we did not part well. He lives a hundred miles away from us and sees Peter when he can. I wish I could have given my son the mother and father combination I always wanted for him, but it didn't work out that way. After my divorce, I felt that I had failed as a person and as a mom. When Peter's kindergarten teacher called me in and suggested I get my son some counseling, I felt that my failure at life had been passed on to him.

As I worked at shoring up the walls that had fallen around us, he tested their strength by trying to push them down. It took time for Peter to regain a sense of security. It took time for him to rebuild trust in me—and for me to rebuild trust in myself. Slowly, I learned to believe that I had made good choices in life as a person and as a parent, and that not all partings are abandonments—indeed, some are necessary and should be celebrated.

Still, learning to let go is hard, especially when you're raising a boy who's about to become a young man. Just when I thought I was getting the hang of being Peter's mom, I realized there was one more step I had to make.

Three days into our adventure, we slowly awakened inside our bright yellow tent on the small island of Tannøy in a fjord of the Norwegian Sea. However, it wasn't the morning light that had triggered the end of my sleep; the sun is up all night during the summer in this land above the Arctic Circle in northern Norway, and I had grown accustomed to its insistent shine. Rather, it was the smell of boy — campfire smoke in his hair, spicy mosquito repellent on his skin, dried sweaty socks on top of the clothes he had shed the night before.

Our breath had condensed while we slept, forming droplets smaller than tears that clung to the inside of the tent. They released and dropped like rain as I struggled to pull on my shirt and pants.

Peter suddenly sat up. The sun was finally above the mountains that had shadowed us to the east. It was unbearably warm. We needed more air. Both of us reached for the tent zipper at the same time.

"I'll do it, Mom."

The zipper stuck, and my reflex was to offer a suggestion, reach out to help, take command of the whole zipper situation until it was fixed. I caught myself and pulled back. I opened my mouth, then shut it. A moment later, Peter successfully dislodged the zipper, and we both crawled out into the fresh morning air.

We were accompanied by the trip leaders, Tim and Lena, and seven other participants. Everyone got along and shared a mutual appreciation for the dramatic pristine land and seascape. As we paddled, we often paused to take in the towering mountains of the coastal range, their chartreuse-green grassy backs sloping down to the narrow rocky beaches along the shoreline. The unusually windless conditions had made for a smooth passage over the blue-green sea.

From the start, Tim had taken Peter in his double kayak, but on this, the third day of our trip, Tim announced, "Pete, today you solo. Get yourself ready. Take the yellow kayak."

Peter moved quickly, donning the rubbery blue kayak skirt

and cinching up the life jacket. I came forward and watched silently. Before he stepped into the kayak, he looked over and asked, "Can you hold these for me?"

His sweaty hands dropped a collection of white shells, worn black rocks and a long brown feather from a sea eagle into mine. I cradled these treasures of his in my hands.

This first attempt at paddling by himself would be an hour trip around the island we had camped on. He was joined by Tim and two other men from the group. After they returned, we would all paddle over to the next night's stop at the Tranøy lighthouse.

Tim pushed Peter's kayak off its sandy perch. With careful even strokes, Peter backed, turned, pointed the kayak toward the sea, then waited for the others. He slyly peered out from under a wide-brimmed canvas hat.

Everything looked big on him — the sleeves on his jacket were bunched at the cuffs, the thick orange life jacket hugged him front and back. And the way he sat made him look short. I wanted to say, "Be careful. Keep up with the others," but after everything that we had been through over the last few years, I had to show that I could believe in and trust him.

I smiled.

He smiled back.

Soon a flurry of white-tipped paddles rose and fell like a flock of seagulls. The men and the boy moved together out of the protective bay. I waved and waved. Peter didn't look back. I was afraid he would disappear from me without a goodbye.

The kayaks reached the open water and turned to the right.

I kept waving. Nothing.

Then the hat on the duckling-colored boat turned toward shore. Suddenly, Peter lifted his paddle overhead and pumped it up and down victoriously. Two strokes later, he slipped out of sight.

At my feet the sea gently rolled in and out. I was alone on a beach near the top of the world, holding the sharp shells, smooth stones and a feather left behind by a bird that had taken flight — finally able to smile back on the pain and the courage of a little boy and his mother who had lived on a different shore, in another time... long ago.

~Jennifer Olsson
Chicken Soup for the Nature Lover's Soul

Miss You, Love You

Someone to tell it to is one of the fundamental needs of human beings.
~Miles Franklin

Staring at the arrival screen, my eyes searched anxiously for the airline flight number. The flight was expected on schedule. There was still plenty of time since I had allowed myself sufficient leeway to cover any unexpected situation. Now all I had left to do was amuse myself and pass the next long hour. I grabbed a coffee at a nearby kiosk, found a bench facing the arrival lounge doors and made myself comfortable for the wait. As I sipped the steaming liquid and tried to relax, my mind wandered back over the last couple of months.

Had it really been only eight weeks? It seemed like an eternity since I had tearfully kissed my son goodbye and watched him disappear as the departure doors swallowed him up whole. From the time my children had been quite young, we had traveled together regularly. I was a strong advocate of travel as an important educational tool. Logic told me that he was a young adult with a good head on his shoulders and he would be fine, but at that particular moment he seemed like a small child, and my fears could not be assuaged by common sense.

Ryan had set his heart on exploring Europe after high school. We had visited many countries together, and he was familiar with what to expect, but this time he wanted to do it alone.

While I had put on a brave front and encouraged him to realize his dream, inside I was a wreck. I felt myself becoming overprotective and uncharacteristically paranoid. I worried nonstop. Was he eating enough? Would he find a place to sleep? Would he be safe? Would he call?

Ryan had never been one to talk on the phone, but I had given him a long distance calling card hoping that he would keep me up to date. I didn't have to wait long to find out. Shortly after landing in Scotland, he called to assure me that everything was fine. His voice was filled with the excitement and enthusiasm of youth.

The days and weeks slipped by and my son's calls came with increasing frequency. Soon, he was calling every second or third day. When I was out he talked at length to the answering machine as though it were an old friend.

I knew what he saw, what he ate, where he was staying and whom he had met. We laughed together, discussed art and culture, and thoroughly enjoyed each other's company long distance. Every call ended with, "I miss you" and "I love you." By the end of two months, my phone bill was well over two thousand dollars. It was worth every penny.

As Ryan made his way through Holland, Belgium, France and Italy, I could sense that something was troubling him. He insisted that he was fine in spite of the constant rain, which seemed to follow him from country to country. But there was a curious tone in his voice that made me wonder.

Needless to say, I was happy and not entirely surprised when out of the blue he told me that he had decided to come home. And now here I was again at the same airport waiting impatiently.

Sitting on the hard, molded airport seat, I contemplated the crowd of people. They were a mélange of ages and nationalities, each waiting just as I was, each with his or her own personal reason for being there: to welcome home a relative, greet friends or meet a business associate. The arrival screen was our common link as we passed the time, together yet alone.

I'm not certain who noticed it first. His flight began flashing on the screen, and we knew that the flight had touched down. An infectious buzz spread through our rapidly expanding group. My stomach began to churn with anticipation. The milling flock congregated along the rope barriers, blocking my view.

Tense minutes dragged by until finally, in singles and pairs, passengers started to filter through the blank, windowless exit doors. They were met by a sea of hopeful faces. Excited waving and squeals of happiness broke out here and there as friends and families were reunited. I moved closer for a better vantage point.

The door slid open yet again to release a new corps of passengers. My heart jolted. Recognition. There he was. Back home, safe and sound.

Ryan tried to look nonchalant as his eyes scanned the throng for a familiar face. He reached the end of the barriers just as I pushed my way through the wall of bodies, into the opening and flung my arms around him. I couldn't remember when I had felt so happy. Tears of joy streamed uncontrollably down my cheeks. As we embraced, the world stood still. All the airport noise stopped. Silence.

Ryan was the first to speak.

"Mom," he said, looking straight into my eyes, "I have learned so much about myself and what's important. I know that no matter where you go in the world and what you see, you need someone to share it with in order to make it special."

A warm smile spread across my tear-sodden face. And then I felt new, fresh tears — the tears of pride. I may have said goodbye to a child, but a mature young man had come home, and he was my son.

~Penny Fedorczenko
Chicken Soup for the Traveler's Soul

44

Tea Party

You can give without loving, but you can never love without giving.
~Author Unknown

*I*believe every little girl deserves a tea party at some point in her life. Most women have memories of backyard tea parties complete with a little table and chairs, plastic pink tea sets and, of course, the tea. Their moms supplied the good stuff like hot cocoa or soda for tea, or they just used pretend tea. Of course, dolls were invited.

Growing up in the projects of St. Paul, Minnesota, a tea party just never happened for me. I lost my mom one month before I turned nine years old. Her death and my dad's chronic gambling left no room for normal kid stuff. I was too busy raising myself to have a tea party. The county provided food stamps, but tea was not a high-ranking staple.

Sitting on other people's doorsteps became a daily routine. I can still feel the roughness of those concrete stairs, but an eight-hour sit was worth it, knowing that on the other side of the door was a family who might ask me in for a meal and let me play house with them. I lived in a world of make-believe tea parties, family vacations and meals around a real table.

When I married my husband, Rick, nine years later, many of those things were fulfilled... except a tea party. Ten years into my marriage and living in a beautiful home on Lake Superior, I bought my first miniature porcelain tea set at a local gift shop. Over the years I collected many of them, in part to recapture those girlish things, even if it meant only pressing my nose up against my hutch and dreaming about tea parties that might have been.

One perfect spring day, our eighteen-year-old son Marc walked in the dining room as I stood staring at the tea sets.

"Mom, why do you collect those anyway?" he asked.

"I love thinking about what it would have been like to have a tea party as a little girl."

"Why is that so important now?"

"I never had a tea party as a young girl. I miss that connection between a mother and a daughter at a tea, the heart-to-heart talks, the pretending and the silly laughter." I sighed.

At six-feet-two and 225 pounds, Marcus was captain of his football and wrestling teams. As I told my story, I knew he would quickly bore as I reminisced. I peered back into the hutch.

He quickly responded with, "Oh, that's cool... gotta go now," as he got up to leave the house. I understood. After all, this "mom story" had nothing to do with touchdowns or pinning an opponent.

Fifteen minutes later, I noticed Marc's car was still in the driveway. I heard his voice call from the three-season porch, "Mom, can you come in here for a minute?"

As I walked into the sunlight, I couldn't believe my eyes. Tears immediately filled them. There at the little round glass café table were two chairs and a tea set for two. He pointed to the seat across from him and with a big smile said, "This chair is for you, Mom."

As Marc filled my cup, I noticed foam oozing out of the spout.

"Sorry, Mom, but root beer was the closest match I could find," he said apologetically.

It wouldn't have mattered to me if the pot were filled with air; I never wanted this moment to end.

The kid-like pretense started a silly laughter in both of us, followed by heart-to-heart conversation between mother and son. Watching him go through the motion of sipping tea with his big fingers was such a spontaneous gesture of unselfish love that it will be etched in my heart and mind forever. An unexplainable bond formed that perfect spring day, and when we finished drinking our root-beer tea, Marc reminded me, "See, Mom, it's never too late."

Today—fourteen years later—as I gaze into my hutch at the little china tea set that my son so quietly took out that day, I recall the memory of the best tea party ever. It's the only one I'll ever need because it was fulfilled in the most unexpected way... on my own doorstep, with my only son.

~Gloria Plaisted
Chicken Soup for the Mother and Son Soul

45

Mother-and-Son Moment

I can remember the look that he had on his face. So young, cute, innocent and a creation from me with God's help, of course — a true miracle indeed. A blessing that is worth more than anything. I'm talking about my son. I'm talking about raising this little guy as a single mother into a responsible black man.

One day my son caught me by surprise when he came to me and asked me a question. It was a Saturday morning, and I was busy typing away on my computer as I always do. I could hear the Saturday morning cartoons on in his room, which was right across from my bedroom. And here this little guy comes. Face still needs to be washed, eyes big and alive, with his black and gray Batman pajamas on, one pant leg higher than the other.

He says with his arms folded, "Mommy, why am I black?"

I could still hear myself clicking away at my keyboard, when what this little four-year-old boy had just asked me caught my complete attention. My eyebrows raised and I stopped what I was doing. I looked at him. And we were both looking at each other.

I sat straight up in my chair and said, "Baby, why do you ask me that?"

"Well, Mommy, my friend at day care said white is better than black. He said his daddy told him so. So I wanna know why God made me black?"

At this moment I could feel the anger slowly overcoming me.

However, I stopped it in its tracks. I looked at my son, and I just shook my head as I took hold of his little hands.

"Baby, white is not better than black, and black is not better than white. We all are the same, just with different colors. Like your box of crayons, there are a lot of different colors but they are all in the same box. God wanted to make different colors of people. So he did. He didn't want to make everybody the same color because that would be boring. Don't listen to everything everybody says. Some people may not like others because they are a different color, but that's mean and that's not right. God loves us all. Nobody is better than anybody else. Even our hands, we all have different colors. This is a good thing, not a bad thing."

I stopped there, just to see what his reaction was.

He looked at me with his eyes still big, and he said, "Okay, Mommy, nobody's better than anybody else. God likes black people and God likes me. Okay, Mommy." He started to leave, then he came back. "So is that why Elmo is red, and the Cookie Monster is blue and Kermit the Frog is green?"

I smiled at him, "Yes, that is why." What could I say to that sort of reasoning?

Hours later that same day, I went into my son's room to see what he was doing. He was very quiet, which was not usual at all. What I found left me speechless, to say the least. My emotions were mixed between whether I should get mad or whether I should compliment him on getting the point.

My son had drawn different colored hands all over his wall—red, blue, green, brown, orange.... I looked at the wall, keeping my emotions balanced, because I knew it had to be cleaned sooner or later. My son had never drawn on his wall before. Okay, on his dresser drawer, but not his wall.

As I stood there looking at these little small hands all over his bedroom, he tapped me on my side. From behind his back my son pulled out two pieces of paper. One was black construction paper with a lot of little white hands on it, and another sheet of paper was white with a lot of little black hands on it.

My son said, "Look, Mommy! Look what I drew. Look at my two papers. I wanna take them to my daycare tomorrow and show my teacher and friend."

"That's good, baby, you do that. I like your two papers," I answered, leaving the wall out of it, still in shock and not yet sure how to handle it.

"I like them, too. I have to teach my friend and his daddy the truth."

I watched him as he went over to his little backpack and proudly stuffed the two papers inside.

I shook my head laughing to myself as I walked back into my bedroom thinking, kids are so smart. My baby is so smart. Why not let those hands sit on his wall just a few days longer.

I thought about what happened for the rest of the day. Another job well done as a single black mother, I thought.

~Tinisha Nicole Johnson
Chicken Soup for the African American Soul

Song-and-Dance Man

We pardon as long as we love.
~Francois de La Rochefoucauld

After nineteen years of marriage, I made the most difficult decision of my life. The divorce turned my thirteen-year-old son Mike's world upside down. He lived with his dad, and the days strung out between my visitations every other weekend. During that time we struggled, each in a private whirlpool of emotion, often unable to communicate adequately with one another. A typical teen, his need to be with peers left us little time together. I feared not living under the same roof would permanently damage the positive relationship we'd once had.

I prayed often that somehow we'd uncover the common ground the past years of mindful parenting had forged—an irrevocable bond between us. I could see, hear and feel his anger. How could he not be? I didn't know what to do. I had to let go. I had to let God handle it. I asked God to help my son cope with the upheaval the divorce caused in his young life. I fervently prayed that somehow, someday, my son and I would have a healthy relationship.

Eventually technical rock climbing became a mutual pursuit, with Mike and me literally trusting our lives to each other on the ropes. From there we seemed to rebuild our relationship, but I still wondered if he held latent resentment toward me. I worried that he'd soon find other people and activities to fill his time and drift further away from me.

By his late teens, we seemed to overcome the obstacles of

separation and busy lives. I relished each time he'd stop by to give me a ride on his newest motorcycle or show off improvements he'd made to his truck. When he began dating, I enjoyed meeting his girlfriends, always offering to have them over for a dinner date. Sure, I wanted to save Mike the expense of a restaurant, but mainly I wanted the pleasure of his company. Not exactly selfless of me, but it worked! I got to see him a bit more often, and he didn't seem to mind.

Then he met "the right one," and they began to plan their life together. Thrilled for them, I couldn't help but wonder what he may have confided to his fiancée, what he might still harbor inside.

Their wedding arrived, highlighted by a ceremony and reception that impressed everyone. It was a joyous celebration of their love — elegant, meaningful and sincere. They paid attention down to the smallest detail; organized and thrifty, this pair thought of delightful touches, large and small, that lent festivity and significance to their event, creating numerous reasons for guests to "ooh and ahh."

He and his bride chose a well-recommended DJ who, by reputation, knew how to get everyone up and having fun. They had decided to skip the customary "special dances" at the beginning of the reception and simply get down to the music right away. The DJ energetically welcomed all present, and I figured he'd soon be cajoling one and all out onto the floor with his rollicking antics. Imagine my surprise when I heard the announcement, "The mother of the groom is immediately requested on the dance floor." I hesitated, but when I saw the DJ gesturing directly to me, I hustled over. The lights dimmed, and my freshly wed son stepped up to me. I could see my new daughter-in-law smiling and nodding at me from behind Mike.

"How's your two-step, Mom?" Grasping my hand, he chuckled, knowing how I tread on toes with my two left feet. The music began. In one tender motion he began to lead me around the dance floor. Since he stands a full head and shoulders above me, I had to tilt back my head to see his face. I stifled my giggle when I saw the earnest look in his eyes... I didn't know what to expect. "This is called 'She Was' by Mark Chesnutt," he said, and then began singing to me.

I wasn't familiar with the song or the artist, but Mike knew the words and the melody well. I found listening and dancing at the same time quite a challenge. I tripped and lost the beat. Mike laughed softly and got me back on track, but he never stopped singing, "...she started her new life ten dollars in debt... never thought twice...."

As I caught the bits and pieces of lyrics, I began gradually to comprehend what was happening. He continued to squire me around the room, singing, "...she tried to be everything to us... those precious moments turned into years in what seemed like the blink of an eye." The room hushed. My vision blurred with tears. It became evident to all the guests who were aware of our history that my son was using the song to say something profound to his mother. Mike squeezed my hand to gain my full attention and looked directly into my eyes. I could see he meant the words he was singing with all his heart, "...a woman like her would be hard to give up...."

At that moment I got it. He hadn't drifted away from me at all! The healthy relationship I'd feared gone was at this very moment being publicly declared. I was thunderstruck. By the time Mike sang the last line, "...If there ever was a picture of love, she was," my shoulders heaved, tears coursed down my face, and my feet would not even move. Gently he glided me off the dance floor, bent down and kissed me on the cheek. I tried but could not speak. Our eyes met. Mutual understanding, forgiveness and respect passed unspoken between us.

~Maryjo Faith Morgan
Chicken Soup for the Mother and Son Soul

Happy Anniversary

Reflect upon your present blessings....
~Charles Dickens

Often, after she finished her solitary supper, she would just sit at the kitchen table, in no hurry to enter the rest of the house which seemed even emptier at night. She would remember how everyone used to rush off after they had eaten—the boys up to their rooms and Peter to his favorite TV news programs.

Always so much to do, and it seemed at times the boys would never grow up so she could have at least a little time to herself. Time for herself. Oh my, she had lots of time now, big blocks of time which filled so little space in her life. Especially now with Peter gone.

They had planned to travel a little after the boys all left, only Peter had been part of a different plan. She would give anything to have those frenzied days back again, but of course it was impossible. There was her volunteer work and the house work and the occasional baking for bake sales, but she missed the noise and she would have been happy to hear the angry voices in the midst of a fight. "Ma, he took my shirt without asking" and "Ma, he won't let me study." Ma, Ma, Ma. Sometimes she had wanted to throttle them, and now she wanted only to hug them and hold them close. She looked at babies on the street and felt sad, remembering when her arms were also full.

She was being especially silly tonight, and she had told Charlotte, one of her neighbors who had dropped by earlier, that today would have been her fortieth anniversary and they had talked of a special celebration this year. Foolish woman. After Charlotte left, she had baked the chocolate blackout cake that had been a favorite of Peter's, and there it sat in the refrigerator, awaiting its trip to the table.

Last year the boys had all called, and they had laughed and talked about the big forty and how they would all celebrate, only there was nothing to celebrate now. In fact, no one had called, but you really couldn't observe a wedding anniversary with half a couple, could you? At least that's what she had said to Charlotte, who kind of clicked her teeth at her and looked sad.

Feeling sorry for herself, was she? Come on, gal, she scolded herself, let's get our act together and have a big slice of cake and maybe some treats for Max, who must have read her mind because he began to bark. Poor old Max. He had been Peter's dog, waiting for him by the door each night till he came home. Some nights he still waited at the door, which never opened, jumping up and barking at the slightest noise.

Like tonight. What was he barking at? He thought he owned the street, maybe even the world, but certainly anything on this block was his terrain. Tonight something was setting him off. So she walked over to the window to see what it was. There was only a car. "For heaven's sake, Max," she admonished, "we're not the only people on the street." Maybe Mrs. Boris, another neighbor, was having company. She had a big family and they came often to visit their parents.

But Max kept right on, and she thought she heard a noise at the door. Never fearful of the dark or the unknown, she went to the door, flung it open and said, "See, Max—there's no one—oh my Lord!" They were standing there, the three of them, and they yelled, "Surprise, surprise" and suddenly there were hugs and kisses every-where—her boys had come home.

"I didn't think you'd remember and besides, with Dad...." Her voice trailed off in a blur of tears.

"Ma," that was Josh's voice, "you and Dad were always here for us, always in our hearts and our memories, and every anniversary will be our special day." The others nodded, and now the tears were rolling down her face. "Hey, Ma, where's the cake?" That was Chuck's voice. "We want to party." Suddenly she smiled and ran back to the kitchen, thanking the divine force that had directed her to bake her cake today and had given her three wonderful sons.

~Evelyn Marder Levin
Chicken Soup for the Golden Soul

A Lesson from My Son

If you want others to be happy, practice compassion.
If you want to be happy, practice compassion.
~Dalai Lama

I was one of those lucky children for whom learning came easily. So, when I became a parent, I naturally assumed that if I read to both of my children faithfully and offered them fun, educational playtimes, they would follow in my footsteps. They, too, would learn, retain materials and receive all As as I had done.

Amanda, my first child, was right on target. She learned quickly and earned good grades. However, even though I practiced the same methods with my second child, Eric, I sensed that life would be a challenge, not only for his teachers, but for Eric and myself personally.

I did my part for this sweet, loving youngster who was never a discipline problem for anyone. I made sure his homework was completed each night, kept in touch with his teachers, and enrolled him in every assistance program the school had to offer. But, no matter how hard he struggled, report cards with Cs were met with frustration and tears. I could see his discouragement and feared he would lose all interest in learning. Soon I doubted myself.

Where had I failed my son? I wondered. Why couldn't I motivate him to help him succeed? I felt if he didn't excel in school, he would be unable to create a life of his own or support himself—and perhaps a family someday.

Eric was a sixteen-year-old blond when my eyes were opened. We were sitting in the living room when the phone rang; a message that my father had suffered a massive heart attack and died at age seventy-nine.

"Papa," as Eric had called him, had been such a part of my little boy's life during his first five years. Since my husband worked nights and slept days, it was Papa who took him for haircuts, ice cream and played baseball with him during those earlier times. Papa was his number-one pal.

When my father left and moved back to the town where he grew up, Eric was lost without him. But time healed those wounds. Gradually, he came to understand his grandfather's need for old friends and roots of the past. For Eric, phone calls and visits from the grandfather he loved became a way of life. And his Papa never forgot him.

When we entered the funeral parlor, I stood in the doorway and looked at my father, so still, so unlike the man I knew. My children were on either side of me, and I felt Eric take my hand as we walked up to his grandfather. We shared our moments together then took our places on the side of the room as hundreds of friends filed by. Each person shared sympathies and memories of my father's life. Others just touched my hand and walked away.

Suddenly, I realized Eric wasn't beside me. I turned to look around the room and noticed him near the entranceway helping the elderly in need of assistance with the stairs or the door. Strangers all, some with walkers, others with canes, many simply leaning on his arm as he led them to his grandfather to pay their last respects.

Later that evening, the funeral director mentioned to me that one more pallbearer was needed. Eric immediately said, "Please Sir, may I help?"

The director suggested he might prefer to stay with his sister and myself. Eric shook his head. "My papa carried me when I was little," he said. "Now it's my turn to carry him." When I heard those words I started to cry. I felt as though I could never stop.

From that moment on, I knew I would never berate my son for imperfect grades. Never again would I expect him to be someone I had created in my own mind, because that individual I envisioned was nowhere near the fine person my son had become. His compassion, caring and love were the gifts God had blessed him with. No book could have taught him these things. No degree framed behind glass would ever convey to the world the qualities Eric possessed.

He is now twenty years old and continues to spread his kindness, his sense of humor and compassion for his fellow man wherever he goes. Today I ask myself, "What difference do science and math grades make? When a young man does the best he can, he deserves an "A" from the heart.

~Kathleen Beaulieu
A 5th Portion of Chicken Soup for the Soul

Moms & Sons

Special Moments

Remembrances last longer than present realities.
~Jean Paul Richter

Mama Can't Read

I've never known any trouble that an hour's reading didn't assuage.
~Charles de Secondat, Baron de la Brède et de Montesquieu

Last night, sitting with a group of friends who share my love for words, someone wondered what my mother would think if she read a silly thing I had written.

"My mother doesn't read or write," I told them. I saw their shocked expressions.

I've never been ashamed of my mother's illiteracy. Never. They could assume it was some kind of culturally deprived circumstance or a measure of my family's lack of intelligence. I knew better. I tried to explain.

"She's not ignorant or lacking," I said. Then I caught myself. Why should I explain? Yes, I wish she could have had the chance to read, but that's the way it's always been. In spite of the hardship not reading has been for her, what was missing ended up bringing us closer. Some of my most cherished memories are of sitting in the kitchen and reading the newspaper to my mother. How could they possibly understand this special link, my personal bond to my mother?

"How awful it must be to not be able to read," one woman commented.

I glanced around the roundtable of educated faces and saw disbelief and pity in their eyes. I didn't want to glorify my mother's lack of education or be insensitive to it, but I resented having to defend my mother's illiteracy. Then I thought about my own love of books. As a child, I escaped my hopelessly poor surroundings through the magic of reading. From the depths of our struggling existence, reading was my ticket out.

But what about Mama?

I wondered if Mama's life could have been different. If I should have at least asked how she felt about it or offered to teach her. I was filled with guilt and sadness, and I longed to be with her, feel her arms around me.

I remember waking up early and reading portions of the newspaper to Mama in the kitchen. She'd always have a cup of steaming atole for me. I felt closer whenever I read to her: Her interest or excitement was mine. Her eyes lit up in various shades, depending on the subject. If it was a killing or scandal, her eyes got wide as silver dollars. She'd raise her hands to her cheeks and cry, "Ay, Dios mío!" She'd want to hear every detail twice. If I read news of something especially nice, her eyes would melt into tears of happiness, "Ay, qué suave, m'ijo." She hung on every word, savored every line. I became her eyes, her window to the world.

Mama's favorite part of the newspaper was the obituary section. After the main news, she'd always press me for it. It was a game I played. Save the best for last. "Who died?" she'd ask anxiously. To an outsider, it might seem like a depressing way to view life, but to me, and especially to her, there was something about the obits section that brought great anticipation.

My own anticipation came from watching her reaction. I must admit, I'd get caught up in the drama, too. As I read, my mood would change, and my tone would soften, almost to a whisper. I'd solemnly read the list of deaths, pausing briefly for effect. If there was one even slightly familiar, I was to go over and over it until we understood exactly where the connection was. My mother's heart would race, she'd shake her hands, wipe her brow and talk about how we knew this person. If it was someone very close, or worse, family, then she'd grab for her apron to wipe away the tears of sadness and shock.

Eventually, I grew up and moved away. I wrote letters to Mama whenever possible. Sometimes I'd write a short story about our family and send it to one of my sisters with instructions to read it to her.

I knew she'd cry because my stories were gentle slices of our family, reminders of our lives. I pictured exactly how she would hear them, the words winding their way into her heart.

"Look, Mama, this is about us, our stories," I'd write. Her face would light up, tears in her eyes.

"Read it again, m'ija," she'd beg my sister. "I want to hear it again."

Last week, I drove home to visit her in the early morning. She no longer stands over the table patting masa for tortillas, as she'd like to do, to please me. Her hands are wracked with arthritis, barely able to hand me the cup of atole as I sit down and unfold the newspaper. Her figure, once proud and upright, is now slumped, and she uses a walker to move slowly across the kitchen. It hurts to see her this way. I wish I could buy something to rejuvenate her tired body, to keep her with me.

Our days are slipping away.

I stop, look lovingly at her and ask, "Mama, did you ever feel bad because you couldn't read?"

She stares at me, then scolds, "Don't be silly. I have you to read to me." Then, with that familiar twinkle in her eyes that magically erases all doubt, she asks, "A ver, m'ijo, tell me who died."

~Charles A. Mariano
Chicken Soup for the Latino Soul

Dissed

Positive lessons are not always taught in positive ways.
~Anonymous

Chad was intimidated by the burly professor yelling into his face, "Your work is sloppy! Your study habits are horrible! Your grades are slipping! I hate sloppy work! I hate poor study habits! And I hate that shirt you are wearing!"

The class was dead silent as the professor chastised Chad for several minutes. Then a collective gasp filled the room when the professor turned and began to yell at the entire class.

"You guys have made it through high school because your mommies babied you. Now you have to grow up! Your mommies are not here!"

Chad spoke in a quivering voice. "You'd better be glad my mom's not here. She bought me this shirt!"

~Mary J. Davis
Chicken Soup for the College Soul

Together, We Can Do Anything

Sticking together as a family has always been important to my sisters, my mom and me—especially after my dad left us. I guess he didn't feel the same way about us as we did about him, and he went off to start a whole new family.

I didn't always want to talk to my mom about my feelings, because she had her own problems taking care of our ranch without my dad around. I was old enough to help out and we all pitched in, but it was still hard on her. I talked to my older sister, Alana, while we worked—and I talked to the Sisters B.

That's what we called our six cows. All of their names started with a B. They were definitely part of the family. I got my first calf when she was three days old. We bottle-fed her and named her Belle. She grew into a beautiful cow who gave birth to two other cows, Brandy and Betsey, and was grandmother to Bootsie. I gave Bootsie to my little sister, Adena. Then I got one other cow that I gave to my older sister, Alana. We named her Blue, and Blue had a calf named Bailey.

All six of the Sisters B hung out and stayed close to each other all of the time. It was clear to us that they loved each other. And we loved them, too. We showed them at local 4H shows and took really good care of them.

When my dad left, he moved down the street from us. We would see him every day, driving down the street in his truck or working in his yard. He never visited us and had a new family to keep him busy. Finally, it was just too painful for all of us, especially my mom. We decided to sell our home and move.

We had to sell all the animals on our ranch, and we wanted to sell the Sisters B together. They were family, in more ways than one. We wanted them to go to someone who would love them like we did, and be willing to keep them together. We put an ad in the paper.

We thought it was an answer to our hopes when a man called and told us he wanted to buy our cows for breeding. He told my mom that he could only pay eighteen hundred dollars for all of them, but that he had other cows, lots of pasture and a large barn.

That afternoon, my mom, my sisters and I went to his place. It looked really nice, and we were happy that we had found the right home for the Sisters B. He looked right at my sister, Adena, and told her that she could visit Bootsie anytime and that he would take special care of her. My mom told him once again that we would only sell the cows to him if he would not sell the cows separately or kill them for meat, and he promised us that he would not.

The next day it was my job to help put the Sisters B in the trailer for delivery to their new owner. They trusted us, and wanted to please us so much that they went right into the trailer without even a fuss. My sisters both had tears on their faces and I could feel tears stinging my eyes, too. But I convinced myself that the Sisters B would be better off in their new home—and besides, they couldn't go with us when we moved.

A week later, while we were having our moving sale, one of our neighbors came up to my mom and told her that she had almost bought my "big red cow" before the cow went to auction. My mom said she had to be mistaken and asked who was selling the cow. When our neighbor told us who it was, I felt sick. We had trusted him, and just a week later he was selling Belle away from her baby and from the rest of her family. He had lied to us.

My mom piled us in the car and we drove to his house. When he answered the door, my mom told him what the neighbor had said and he shut the door right in our faces. My sisters were really crying now, and my mom was begging him to tell us where the Sisters B were, and to sell them back to us. Mom was crying too, but he wouldn't open the door.

I have never seen my mother so determined in my life. She told us she was going to find out where the cows were. She started calling a lot of auctions and finally found one that had a record of our cows, and told us that the cows would be auctioned off the next morning at 8:00.

That night, I couldn't sleep. I kept thinking, How could someone do something like this? Finally, the sun started to come up and we were on our way. We arrived at the auction at 7:00 in the morning.

When we got there, we found the cows in a pen. They looked pretty bad. They had cuts all over them and looked thin, but we were just thankful that they were still alive. Belle saw us first, and came right up to where we were standing. They were just as glad to see us as we were to see them. Just then a man came by who was there to buy stock, and he said it would cost us about three thousand dollars to buy our cows. I couldn't believe it! That's why we'd been deceived: the man who bought the cows from us had just wanted to make a profit.

I suggested to my mom and sisters that we get busy praying. We didn't know what else to do; we sure didn't have three thousand dollars to buy back our cows, and we didn't even know how to bid at an auction. We prayed really hard for God to show us the way.

Then Alana had an idea. She had brought some pictures of the Sisters B with her from our showing at the county fair. Every time someone arrived at the auction, she would hurry over to them, show our photos and share our story. The man who had bought the Sisters B from us was watching Alana, and when he realized that people were talking about him, and what he had done, he got all red in the face and left in a hurry. Most of the men that Alana talked to said that they wouldn't bid on our cows when they came out for auction, and that's when we got excited. Maybe we did have a chance, after all!

We waited until almost 11:00 before we saw the first of our cows. It was Brandy. Because we didn't understand the bidding process well,

Alana didn't hold her number up fast enough and the men bidding on Brandy didn't see Alana. The price went up too high and we lost her. But then we understood how it worked.

Every time one of our cows would come into the ring, Alana would raise her number, and no one would bid on the cow. At one point the auctioneer stopped the whole auction and yelled that this had better stop, but everyone ignored him. Alana kept holding up her number, and the men resisted bidding on our cows. By 5:00, we had bought back all of the cows, except for Brandy, for twenty-two hundred dollars. Belle, her mother, kept mooing for her baby, and we were all sad to lose her. Mom used the eighteen hundred dollars we had from selling the cows, and we had to use our moving-sale money to make up the difference, but we had done it. We had them back!

Some friends of ours gave the Sisters B a new home. At first, we didn't get any money for them, but money wasn't as important to us as what could have happened to our cows. Recently, our friends sent us fifteen hundred dollars for the cows. After all we had sacrificed, it was a really nice surprise.

Family needs to love and protect family, and they were our family. Now when we go to visit them, they are always together — just like my mom, my sisters and me.

What happened to us was hard, but we survived and we learned a lot. Although there are dishonest people in the world, there are also many kind people who are willing to help you, even if they don't know you. But the best part is that we did it together. Together, we can do anything.

~Jarod Larson
Chicken Soup for the Preteen Soul

52

It's Baseball Season

Love is the most important thing in the world, but baseball is pretty good too.
~Greg, age 8

The team members' attention spans stretch barely the length of a cartoon. Their eyes are invisible beneath oversized batting helmets. They wear T-shirts with messages like "Critter Ridders Pest Control: 30 Years of Service in Roaches."

All across the country, it's T-ball season.

I became a T-ball mom when my seven-year-old son signed up to be a Giant (an obvious misnomer for a team where no one can bench press a Nerf ball). I should have been prepared. We limped through flag football last fall.

I still remember that day when the youngest kid on the football field kept interrupting the game squealing, "Coach, are we winning yet?"

It's a significant question.

In T-ball, no one even keeps score. That's good. It makes me think of Megan, a little girl I met before I moved to Idaho. Megan could neither hit nor throw a ball, but she wanted to play T-ball. I saw a few of her games.

Megan's parents and coaches practiced with her, encouraged her and never once considered calling her a klutz. But when the last game of the season rolled around, Megan still hadn't connected with the ball.

When she finally did, she hit an easy pop fly and her team lost. But the people in the bleachers stood up and cheered for Megan. Because, by that time, everyone knew she was a winner.

I moved away before Megan grew up, but I'm sure she grew

up successful. Not because she had any more talent than the boy whose dad yelled at him whenever he didn't get a hit. In fact, she probably had much less. But Megan had something else. She had people around her who cared, not about her batting average, but about her.

Not long ago, I sat listening to a speaker who insisted that we are living in the midst of a generation of kids who see themselves as potential failures.

Among the causative factors, she said, parental influence is the greatest. I'm determined to be the right kind of T-ball mom. My husband may do a better job with practice sessions, but I'm pretty good at screaming, "Way to go, slugger!" Even when (and all of this has happened this season):

The second baseman is turning cartwheels when he's supposed to be fielding the ball.

A child is lying flat on the ground refusing to budge after he's been thrown out—and the other kids are trampling over him.

A batter is rounding the bases because the right fielder doesn't want to give up the ball.

The coach is yelling, "Take your base, Son," but the kid is standing there pointing toward center field. His mother yells from the stands, "That means he has to go to the bathroom."

In spite of it all, these children are making their first stabs at growing up. They're taking their first steps toward life in the major leagues. They may be chewing bubble gum instead of tobacco and they may not have learned how to scratch themselves yet, but they take their base hits seriously.

I'm glad they haven't yet "arrived." I'd hate to give up being a T-ball mom, because I think I really like the game.

After all, anything that ends with Reese's Pieces and Kool-Aid Kool Bursts can't be all bad.

~Denise Turner
Chicken Soup for the Baseball Lover's Soul

53

The Best Days of Our Lives

Every experience, every thought, every word, every person in your life
is a part of a larger picture of your growth.
~Macrina Wiederkehr

Newly divorced, with a seven-year-old son to support, I attempted recently to reenter the teaching profession I had left when Steven was born. As the job hunt stretched into weeks, however, I experienced a growing sense of panic. But one of the things I have learned in becoming suddenly single has been to reach out to good and gentle friends. One of them shocked me when he said I worried so much about the future that I had no time to enjoy the present.

"Go ahead and look for your job," he said. "But live in the now. Perhaps this time is a gift, one that may never be given again. Use it to discover who you are and what it is that is really important to you."

I began to see, just a little bit, what I had been doing to myself, what I have been doing all my life. Living in the future. Never really being present in my own here and now. What a thief I had been — stealing from myself. And I had absolutely no idea of how to change.

I searched my heart and memory for origins of the "work now, live later" ethic. And for the beginnings of the deeply held belief that if I was not actively productive in a way that was immediately visible — either in a paycheck, or a shiny floor or a possession — then

I was somehow unworthy. Perhaps, I finally decided, the important thing is the awareness and the opportunity to become free, just a little bit.

That afternoon, I thought about Steven, and wondered how long it had been since I had taken time to be truly, fully, with him.

When Steven returned from school, I offered to play some of his games with him. He had tried to get me to play many times, but I always had something "more important" to do. He got out the games, and I noticed immediately that every one of them was somehow linked with achievement. How many points scored, words made and in the least amount of time. And don't forget to keep score. So we are teaching it to them, too, I thought.

I suggested to Steven that we might play without the scorecards. After his initial shock, and even reluctance, he agreed. Eventually, we even progressed to the point where we were able to make up our own words—though they were not in the dictionary—and to laugh at our own inventiveness. The experience left me hungry for more.

At Steven's bedtime, I said to him: "Honey, we haven't had much time together lately. You and I ought to just go off on an adventure. I just might show up at your school one morning, and steal you away for the day."

Steven's face registered surprise, then impish delight. "Oh, make it a Thursday, Mommy. We have book reports on Thursday, and I hate book reports."

"Teachers love book reports, Steven. It gives them a chance to sit down. I will make it a Thursday."

Two weeks later, I got to the school as California's December morning coolness was beginning to dissolve into warmth. When I entered the classroom, Steven eyed me calmly, but his teacher looked incredulous when informed, without explanation, that my son would be leaving for the day. I merely smiled and hoped the delicious sense of mischief in my heart was not evident in my eyes.

Looking sober and serious, Steven and I made our way safely into the parking lot, where we laughed until tears came streaming. Quickly, we made our getaway. I had packed everything that we might need—lunches, snacks, books, soft drinks, bathing suits, beach balls, warm jackets.

We turned off the Pacific Coast Highway, coming to a halt in front of gently rolling waves that sent white foam bursting on brilliant sunlit sand. Except for about fifty large seagulls and two men, a woman and a little girl, the beach was entirely ours. Steven changed into his swimming trunks and was in the water before I could even spread the towels and snuggle down with a book.

The little girl, attracted by Steven's beach ball, joined us in digging deep holes and tunnels in the sand. The child's father introduced himself and his party. They were Sioux Indians, he said. This was their first day in California and the very first time they had seen the ocean. They taught us the Sioux words for perfect day and beautiful children. Steven taught them the word Kool-Aid.

Then our visitors left. As I lay back on the sand and saw that little boy who is so special to me, really saw him, rushing out to meet the foaming waves, and heard his laughter and basked in his and in my own deep pleasure, my only regret was that I had not brought my movie camera. What I didn't know in that moment is that I will be able to run that scene over and over for as long as I live.

Later, we made footprints in the sand and wrote our names again and again, and laughed as the waves washed away all traces of our being there. We climbed rocks. We found a friendly dog and some fossils. We met a boy and a girl having a picnic lunch and asked them if they were playing hooky, too. They laughed; we all laughed.

The day seemed to flow from one good thing into another. When at last the breeze became cool, and the sun fell a little and our stomachs told us that it might be time to have another meal, Steven ran to me with his new treasures—seaweed, shells, bits of pretty rock—and said, "Mommy, do we have to go home?" There seemed to be a question beyond the words.

"No, Steven, let's drive down the beach to that restaurant with the big old booths in the windows, right smack on top of the waves."

As we were seated, with the surf pounding only a few feet below, we noticed a man running and jumping over the giant rocks that were covered with moss and looked to be slippery. He had only a few sandpipers, the wind and the sunset for companions.

From the next booth, we heard a man exclaim, "Look at that nut out there hopping on the rocks. And it's almost dark!"

Steven looked at me and smiled. After a while, he said softly, "I bet there are things some people just don't know about."

My son fell asleep in the back seat of our car on the way home. I could hear his soft snoring. When I carried him into his bedroom, he awakened and said, "Oh, Mommy, this has been the very best day of my life."

"Mine, too, Steven dear," I replied. "Mine, too."

~Colleen Hartry
Chicken Soup for the Working Mom's Soul

I Flushed It

The best way to get a puppy is to beg for a baby brother
—and they'll settle for a puppy every time.
~Winston Pendelton

It was a hot day in Florida. The school year had just ended and it was time for summer vacation. We had just gotten a little black dog who we named One-Eyed. We chose that name because he could only see out of one eye.

Everybody wanted to do something for the dog: feed him, teach him tricks and take long walks with him. Everybody was so happy to have this active, playful, shaggy, sable-coated new addition to our family. Everybody, that is, except my mom and me.

All my mom saw when she looked at the dog was someone else to clean up after. Shedding, messy, muddy, he pounced all over the house. All Mom seemed to care about was getting the house cleaned. My mom began to put Clorox in the tub. There was no messing with Mom when she started cleaning, so I decided to move out of the way. Actually, getting out of the way is a move I'd been practicing for a long time.

Being the youngest in my family has had its advantages, of course. I won't deny that. More than a few times I was spoiled or everyone was convinced that I was the cutest. It wasn't all bad to get this attention.

But being the youngest also came with its fair share of troubles. I was often told what I couldn't do and why. I realize that I practiced getting out of the way because most of the time I was being pushed out of the way. "You're too young!" "You're too little!" "You'll mess this up!" they'd often say.

I also knew that my family loved me. They always tried to protect me, help me and take care of me, but I couldn't wait to show them I could do things by myself.

Every time I asked my brother or my sister if I could pet One-Eyed, they would shout, "No!" or tell me that I had germs. Once, they even convinced me that I had so many germs, if I touched One-Eyed he would die! I really believed them and was scared that something terrible would happen to the dog. Once I even confessed to my mom that I touched the dog when no one noticed. At first, my mom seemed very confused about what I was telling her, but then she realized that they were playing a joke on me to keep me away from the dog. My mom scolded my brother and sister, "You better stop teasing your little brother!" Little brother! That's exactly what I was. That really got my blood boiling. I was so mad, I wanted to break something!

I wasn't going to let them make me move out of their way this time! I took one look at the dog and decided, "I'll show them what a little kid can do!" I took the dog into the bathroom. "I'm going to give you a bath!" I said. One-Eyed looked at me strangely; he obviously didn't understand what I was saying. I looked at the sink. Too small, I thought. I looked at the tub. "It stinks like Clorox." Then I saw it. The perfect place for a dog bath — the toilet!

I took my sister's shampoo and poured it into the toilet. Then I put the dog in. I was scrubbing all the dirt off the dog with our towels. The finishing touch was to pull down the lever, which I did. But the sound of the toilet made the dog panic like crazy! He tried to escape, but the shampoo was too slippery. While the water was going down, One-Eyed's legs were going down with it. I was scared, and I didn't want One-Eyed to get hurt. I didn't want to get into trouble or for anyone to find out. I went running down to the garage.

My mom was standing there and laughing, as if she was expecting me. I didn't know what to say. I tried to catch my breath. Then I told her what just happened. I thought she would punish me. I didn't expect my mom would be... laughing!

As it turns out, I later discovered that my mom knew what was happening all along. She always seemed to be a pretty good spy, I guess.

Oh, and if you're wondering, One-Eyed was fine: but he did stay away from me for a while. Even though we never actually had a conversation about my being the youngest, I think Mom understood what I was trying to do. I was trying to make my own place in our family... trying, maybe sometimes in a weird way, to declare my independence. Flushing the dog down the toilet might not sound like a Declaration of Independence, but for a six-year-old, well, it was my best shot!

~Pier Novelli
Chicken Soup for the Preteen Soul

55

So How Do You Boost an Ego?

Those who bring sunshine to the lives of others
cannot keep it from themselves.
~James Matthew Barrie

*M*r. Rickman, our psych teacher, doesn't give the kind of assignments other teachers do, such as read a thousand pages; answer the questions at the end of the chapter; work problems 47 through 856. He's more creative than that.

Mr. Rickman led up to last Thursday's assignment by saying that behavior is a means of communicating. "'Actions speak louder than words' isn't just an empty phrase," he told us. "What people do tells you something about what they are feeling."

He paused a minute for that to sink in before he gave the assignment. "Now see if you can build up somebody, boost his or her ego enough that you notice a change in the way the person acts. We'll report the results in class next week."

When I got home from school that afternoon, my mom was really feeling sorry for herself. I could tell the minute I came in. Her hair was straggling around her face, her voice was whiny and she kept sighing while she got dinner. She didn't even speak to me when I came in. Since she didn't speak, I didn't either.

Dinner was pretty dreary. Dad wasn't any more talkative than Mom and I were. I decided to try out my assignment. "Hey, Mom, you know that play the university drama club is putting on? Why don't you and Dad go tonight? I've heard it's really good."

"Can't make it tonight," Dad said. "Important meeting."

"Naturally," Mom said. Then I knew what was bugging her.

"Well then, how about going with me?" I asked. Right away, I wished I could take back the invitation. Imagine a high school kid being seen out in the evening with his mother!

Anyway, the invitation was hanging there in the air, and Mom said in an excited voice, "Really, Kirk?"

I swallowed a couple of times. "Sure. Why not?"

"But guys don't take their mothers out." Her voice was getting more pleasant all the time, and she pushed the straggles of hair up on top of her head.

"There's no law that says they can't," I told her. "You just go get ready. We're going out."

Mom started toward the sink with some dishes. Her steps were perky now instead of draggy.

"Kirk and I will take care of the dishes," Dad offered, and Mom even smiled at him.

"That was a nice thing for you to do," my dad said, after Mom left the kitchen. "You're a thoughtful son."

Thanks to psychology class, I thought gloomily.

Mom came back to the kitchen looking about five years younger than she had an hour earlier. "You're sure you don't have a date?" she asked, as if she still couldn't believe what was happening.

"I do now," I said. "C'mon, let's go."

That evening didn't turn out so badly after all. Most of my friends had more exciting things to do than watch a play. The ones who were there weren't at all startled to see me with my mom. By the end of the evening, she was genuinely happy, and I was feeling pretty good myself. Not only had I aced a psych assignment, I had also learned a lot about boosting an ego.

~Kirk Hill
Chicken Soup for the Teenage Soul II

56

A Scarf, Earrings, Necklace, Bottle of Perfume

The reason it hurts so much to separate is because our souls are connected.
~Nicholas Sparks, The Notebook

Growing up in the Bronx during the 1950s, I was a mama's boy—and an extreme case at that. When I started Public School 105 as a five-year-old, I couldn't last a full day because I missed my mother. I found that the quickest way to be with her was to complain that I had a stomachache. The school nurse would then call my mom, and she'd come and pick me up and take me home. But before we even reached our apartment, my stomach problem was miraculously cured.

My mother soon realized that my formal education would never be completed at the rate I was going. She decided to give me one of her pearl earrings to keep in my pocket. She said that the next time I had stomach cramps, I could reach into my pocket, touch her earring, which had magical healing powers, and I would feel better.

The next day at school, right on schedule, my stomach started acting up. I reached into my pocket, touched my mother's earring, and to my astonishment, I felt better.

I continued this healing process every day for a few weeks. Then one day, my stomachache didn't go away as quickly as it had on the other days. That afternoon I asked my mother if it was possible that the magical powers were wearing off the earring. "Sometimes that happens," she said. But she had a solution. She explained that any personal possession of hers would work. She went to her dresser and pulled out one of those white gloves that women wore back in the 1950s. The glove worked just fine for me for a couple of weeks. Then it, too, lost its power, so I selected one of my mom's scarves and used that to cure my problem. This process went on for months, eight months, in fact.

One spring morning in April, the principal announced on the public-address system that all classes needed to report to the gym. We filed in pairs down the stairs to the gym, where we were told that all the classes should form large circles by holding our neighbor's hand and then dropping it. Mrs. Hallorhan explained that we had a serious problem at P.S. 105. One of the students had taken another student's property. She explained that she was going to point to each of us and we would then turn our pockets inside out.

Now my stomach started to really hurt. I wasn't stealing anyone else's property; I was only five years old. Yet, I knew how it would look when I emptied my pockets and all of my mother's items came tumbling out. You see, I hadn't exchanged the glove for the earring, or the scarf for the glove, and so on. I'd kept all of them in my pocket.

Slowly Mrs. Hallorhan went around the circle, my anguish increasing as she got closer and closer. When she did reach me, I started to cry. I reluctantly turned my pockets inside out. The teachers must have thought that they had caught the Bronx cat burglar, because out came the first earring, a couple of other earrings, the white glove, the scarf, a pearl necklace, a couple of stick pins, a small bottle of perfume, various charms, and four rings.

Embarrassed and ashamed, I ran to the boys' bathroom and locked myself in a stall. I wouldn't come out until my mother came and got me.

Almost forty years later, my mother passed away. That night, the rabbi who would conduct the memorial service called my sister and asked her to tell him about our mother. Roberta spent over an hour telling him about the wonderful, humorous, loving and thoughtful person our mother was. She said that most of all, our mother loved to make people smile. Among my sister's stories was the one about the day her brother holed up in the school bathroom.

The service was respectfully sedate. Near the conclusion, the rabbi asked everyone to stand for a final prayer. He then said he wanted to tell just one more story about my mother and her son. The rabbi was a fine storyteller, and his timing was perfect. As he described the earrings, the white glove, the scarf... dropping out of my pocket, the laughter grew louder and louder.

I was laughing; I was crying. It was all true. I was a mama's boy. Even in her absence, my mother worked her special powers and was able to bring a smile to all of those at her funeral one more time.

~Andy Strasberg
Chicken Soup to Inspire a Woman's Soul

57

The Last First Day

When you are a mother, you are never really alone in your thoughts. A mother always has to think twice, once for herself and once for her child.
~Sophia Loren

This was my last first day of school. My baby Rob, the youngest of my three sons, was starting kindergarten. I had already gone through this twice before with his older brothers, but this time it was different. I knew this was my last time. Being the third boy in our family, he was more than ready for his first day of school. I, on the other hand, was not. I was a wreck.

What if he was scared? What if he missed me? What if he needed me? I decided to try and do the grown-up thing and not tell him how I felt. I assured him that he was a big boy now and that everything would be just fine. He, on the other hand, knew that everything would be fine — but he wasn't absolutely sure I would be.

The night before school started, Rob and I went into his bedroom, just the two of us. I wanted to have a few minutes alone with him. I sat down with him, hugged him and asked if he had any questions about what he could expect tomorrow when he went to his big new school. We had visited the school, been to his classroom and met his teacher.

"I'm really excited, Mommy, but I'm a little worried about what I should do if I miss you," he confided sheepishly.

I had just the answer for him.

I opened my hand and showed him a brand-new, shiny penny. "This is a lucky magic penny you can take to school with you. If you're scared or lonely or if you miss me, just put your hand in your pocket and hold on to this lucky penny. Every time you hold it and think of me, I will know and be thinking about you, too."

It was absolutely true. I'd be thinking about him every minute.

School started bright and early the next day. Tucked in the pocket of Rob's new jeans was that lucky penny. As he entered his schoolroom, he looked back at me, put his hand in his pocket and smiled. My baby looked so sure of himself. I smiled back at him and hoped that he didn't see the tears in my eyes.

The hours moved slowly, but finally it was time to pick him up. Out of the room he bound, still smiling.

"I had a great day!" he cheered. "There were a few times I was worried, but I held on to my lucky penny, and I knew you were thinking about me and that made me feel all better."

Rob carried that lucky penny to school with him for about a week. Then, one day after I had dropped him off and returned home, I found it on his dresser. I guessed he was secure enough in his new situation that he didn't need it anymore.

I, on the other hand, tucked it in my pocket for a few more days.

~Barbara LoMonaco
Chicken Soup for the Mother and Son Soul

58

Jimmy's New Shoes

You are my sonshine.
~Author Unknown

My son Jimmy has sky-blue eyes, curly hair and a smile that lights up a room. Two days before Jimmy's fifth birthday, my husband (whose nickname is Chooch) and I took Jimmy to buy a new pair of high-top tennis shoes. At the store, after looking up and down the display of shoes, Dad found a pair in the colors of Jimmy's favorite basketball team. Jimmy's eyes widened as he asked, "Let's try these, okay, Mom?"

I found the style in his size, and he sat down on a nearby stool. I had a lump in my throat as I took off his old shoes and then removed the braces he had worn since he was sixteen months old, when the doctors had told us he had cerebral palsy.

Of course, we had bought shoes before, but never shoes like these. Normally we could only pick shoes that would fit over his braces, but Jimmy's therapy had been going so well, his specialist said he could wear a pair of shoes without braces a few days a week.

I bent down, adjusted his socks and slipped the shoes on Jimmy's feet. I laced them up, and the instant I finished tying the second bow, Jimmy slid off the stool and went to the mirror. He stood for a moment gazing at himself, his hands on his hips, like Superman.

Chooch and I were as excited as he was. "Jimmy," I said, "why don't you walk around and see how they feel?"

He took a few steps and turned to see if we were watching.

"Go on, Honey," I told him. "You're doing great."

I was holding Chooch's hand, and we both squeezed tightly as we watched Jimmy walk faster, and then almost run in his new shoes. Jimmy—almost running! My heart was full to bursting.

Still watching my son march around the shoe department with a great big smile on his face, I asked Chooch, "How much are they?"

We both laughed. "Who cares?" he answered. "Jimmy is getting these shoes."

I put the old shoes in the box, and we paid for the new ones.

As we walked to the car, Jimmy thanked us. On the ride home, he sat up front with Dad, clicking his feet and admiring his new shoes the whole way. I sat quietly in the back, thinking of all we had been through, especially Jimmy, to get to this point.

At home, Jimmy hummed happily as we went inside the house. He was eager to call everyone and tell them about his new shoes, but he accepted my suggestion that we call just a few people and then surprise the rest at his birthday party. After our calls, we went through our nightly routine of a warm bath, lotion massage and a few stretches. I put on his night braces and kissed him good night.

"Thank you for my new shoes," he said again. "I love them!" He fell asleep with the shoes right next to him on the bed.

The next morning, as I helped him dress for school, I gently reminded him that he would still have to wear his braces most days. "The therapist says you can wear your new shoes only a few days a week. Remember?"

"I know, Mom. My braces are cool," he assured me. "I can wear them, too."

As we walked to the front door to catch the bus, Jimmy smiled up at me and said, "I bet Miss Cindy will say, 'Oh my gosh! I can't believe it!'"

When the bus came and the driver, Miss Cindy, opened the door, Jimmy walked up the steps holding on to the rail and paused at the top. "Look!" he said, "look at my new shoes! And no braces!"

"Oh my gosh! I can't believe it!" Miss Cindy said. Jimmy turned to me and grinned. Then he went to his seat and blew me a kiss, giving me the thumbs-up sign, the way he always did.

I walked slowly back to the house, wondering about how his teachers and friends would react. I wished I could be there. I paced a lot during the day and wrote in my journal. I prepared some snacks for his school birthday party the next day. Chooch was decorating the house and yard for Jimmy's big family birthday party the next night. I couldn't wait to see the smiles of Jimmy's grandparents, aunts, uncles and cousins, as they watched him parade around in his new high-tops. It was something we'd all hoped for but had been afraid to believe was possible.

It was a beautiful day, so I went outside to wait for the bus fifteen minutes early. I couldn't wait for Jimmy to come home. I feel this way every day he goes to school, but that day, when the bus turned the corner, I wanted to run down the street to meet it. But I didn't. I stayed put until the bus pulled up. There was my son, that big smile still on his face.

He blew everyone kisses goodbye. We walked across the street, Jimmy telling me all about his day. One of his teachers, Miss Susan, had "screamed when she saw me," he said. "I think she cried a little, too." He stopped. "Mother, this was my happiest day ever."

I couldn't speak and tears welled up in my eyes as I bent down to hug him. He wrapped his arms around my neck and said, "I know. Me, too." We both cried and hugged each other, then laughed.

Holding hands, we walked slowly up our driveway, both of us getting used to Jimmy's new shoes.

~Marie A. Kennedy
Chicken Soup for the Mother's Soul 2

Chapter 9

Moms & Sons

Love through the Generations

It takes a village to raise a child.
~African Proverb

59

The Gravy Boat Rescue

Remembrances last longer than present realities.
~Jean Paul Richter

Not long ago my wife and I had a dinner party for some good friends. To add a touch of elegance to the evening I brought out the good stuff—my white Royal Crown Derby china with the fine gold and blue border. When we were seated, one of the guests noticed the beat-up gravy boat I always use. "Is it an heirloom?" she asked tactfully.

I admit the piece is conspicuous; it is very old and it matches nothing else. Worst of all, it is scarred by a V-shaped notch in the lip. But that little gravy boat is much more than an heirloom to me—it is the one thing in this world I will never part with.

Our history together began over fifty years ago when I was seven years old and we lived across the street from the river in New Richmond, Ohio. In anticipation of high water, the ground floor of the house had been built seven feet above grade.

That December, the river started to overflow west of town. When the water began to rise in a serious way, my parents made plans in case the river should invade our house. My mother decided that she would pack our books and her fine china in a small den off the master bedroom. Each piece of the china had a gold rim and then a band of roses. It was not nearly as good as it was old, but the service had been her mother's and was precious to her.

As she packed the china with great care, she told me, "You must treasure the things people you love have cherished. It keeps you in touch with them."

I didn't really understand her concern. I'd never owned anything I cared all that much about. Still, planning for disaster held considerable fascination for me.

The plan was to move upstairs when the river reached the seventh of the steps that led to the front porch. We would keep a rowboat in the downstairs so that we could get from room to room. The one thing we would not do was leave the house. My father, the town's only doctor, felt he had to be where sick people could find him.

The muddy water rose higher and higher until at last the critical mark was reached. We worked for days carrying things upstairs, until late one afternoon the water edged over the threshold and poured into our house. I watched it from the safety of the stairs, amazed at how rapidly it rose.

Every day I sat on the landing and watched the river rise. My mother turned a spare bedroom into a makeshift kitchen and cooked simple meals there. My father came and went in a fishing boat that was powered by a small outboard motor.

Before long, the Red Cross began to pitch tents on high ground north of town. "We are staying in our house," my father said.

One night very late I was awakened by a tearing noise, like timbers creaking. Then I heard the rumbling sound of heavy things falling. I jumped out of bed and ran into the hallway. My parents were standing in the doorway to the den. The floor of the den had fallen through and all the treasures, including my mother's china, that we had attempted to save, were now on the first floor beneath the steadily rising river.

My mother had been courageous, it seemed to me, through the ordeal of the flood. But the loss of the things she loved broke her resolve. That night she sat on the top of the stairs with her head on her crossed arms and cried. My father comforted her as best he could, but she was inconsolable.

My father finally told me to go to bed, and I watched him help my mother to their room. In a few minutes he came to see me, to tell me everything would be all right and that my mother would be fine after a good night's sleep.

I wasn't sure about that at all. There was a sound in her weeping that I had never heard before, and it troubled me. I wanted to help her feel better, but I couldn't think of what I could possibly do.

The next morning she made me breakfast, and I could tell how bad she still felt just by how cheerful she pretended to be.

After breakfast, my mother said I could go downstairs and play in the rowboat. I rowed the boat once around the downstairs, staring into the dark water, but could see nothing. It was right then that I thought of trying to fish for my mother's china.

I carefully put a hook I cut from a wire coat hanger onto a weighted line. Then I let it sink until I felt it hit bottom. I began to slowly drag it back and forth. I spent the next hour or so moving the boat back and forth, dragging my line, hoping against hope to find one of my mother's treasures. But time after time I pulled the line up empty.

As the water rose day after day, I continued to try to recover something, anything, of my mother's lost treasure. Soon, however, the water inside had risen to the stairway landing. On the day the water covered the rain gutters, my father decided we would have to seek shelter in the tents on the hill. A powerboat was to pick us up that afternoon.

I spent the morning hurriedly securing things in my room as best I could. Then I got into my rowboat for the last time. I dragged my line through the water and just as I made the last turn to go back to the stairway, I snagged something.

Holding my breath, I raised my catch to the surface. As the dark water drained from it, I could see it was the gravy boat from my mother's china service. The bright roses and gold leaf seemed dazzling to me.

Then I saw what had helped my line catch: There was a V-shaped chip missing from the lip of the boat. I stowed the treasure inside my jacket and rowed as fast as I could to the stair landing. My mother had called me for the second time, and I knew better than to risk a third.

We left from the porch roof and the boat headed to higher ground. It began to rain, and for the first time I was really afraid. The water might rise forever, might cover the whole valley, the trees, even the hills. The thought made me cold, and I did not look out at the flood again until we landed at the shelter.

By the time we were settled in a Red Cross tent, we were worn out. My father had gone off to help with the sick people, and my mother sat on my cot with her arm around my shoulder. I reached under my pillow and took out the gravy boat.

She looked at it, then at me. Then she took it in her hands and held it a long time. She was very quiet, just sitting, gazing at the gravy boat. She seemed both very close to me and far away at the same time, as though she were remembering. I don't know what she was thinking, but she pulled me into her arms and held me very close.

We lived in the tent for almost two weeks, waiting for the flood to end. When the water eventually receded, we did not move back to our old house, but to a house in a suburb of Cincinnati, far from the river.

By Easter, we were settled in and my mother made a special kind of celebration on that sacred Sunday. My mother asked me to say grace, and then my father carved the lamb. My mother went into the kitchen and returned with the gravy boat. Smiling at me, she placed it on the table beside her. I said to myself right then that nothing would ever happen to that gravy boat as long as I lived.

And nothing ever has. Now whenever I use it, guests almost always ask about it and sometimes I tell the whole story—at least most of it. But there really is no way to tell—beyond the events of the flood—how deeply that small treasure connects me to the people and places of my past. It is not only the object but also the connection I cherish. That little porcelain boat, old and chipped, ties me to my mother—just as she said—keeping me in touch with her life, her joy and her love.

~W. W. Meade
Chicken Soup for Every Mom's Soul

60

The Blessing

I grew up in a poor neighborhood in Philadelphia, and, when I was a child, I didn't care at all for the custom of asking for my mother's blessing. It seemed too old-fashioned and sort of meaningless in those days. The few times I did ask, I did it just to please her.

I felt ashamed because the mothers of Anglo kids never required their children to ask for a blessing when they left the house. A simple "See ya later!" was more than enough. In those days, the Anglo way seemed like a more "manly" goodbye, and I didn't want to be laughed at by my friends or have them think I was less of a "guy" than they were.

When I was a child, I couldn't put my feelings into words, but I knew that somehow the act of asking for bendición made me feel stained or dirty. As the years passed, I buried the memory of that shame. I hid it deep in my soul like a dark and bitter thorn that would prick my conscience every so often.

With the passage of time, life's experiences have given me a different perspective on things. After my mother's death in 1978, I began to miss that beautiful Puerto Rican custom of asking for and receiving your mother's blessing. My mother's death woke me up, as I was devastated to suddenly realize that I would never have that opportunity again.

I returned to Puerto Rico in 1987 to visit my grandmother, Doña Carmelina Eustaquia Rivera de Font. We were talking about things, nothing of any real importance, when suddenly my nose began to itch. I was instantly overcome by a sneeze so strong it seemed to rock the entire neighborhood of Santa Teresita, Santurce, where my grandmother lived.

My grandmother eyed me silently with feigned gravity and pronounced, "Bless you...! And may the germ that made you sneeze, die!"

Her response caught me off guard. I looked at her, and we both burst out laughing. I realized how wonderful it felt to have received that verbal display of affection from the mother of my mother, and I was struck by the tenderness and beauty of relationships that exist between mothers, grandmothers and sons.

When it was time for me to leave, I stopped at the doorway and said, "Abuela... give me your blessing."

"Que Dios te bendiga, m'ijo," my grandmother said.

I breathed in deeply, and the secret thorn buried deep in my soul disappeared. I felt lighter and purified.

My grandmother died in 1994, but the memory of the sweet blessing she gave me that day is still with me.

Today, at times when I least expect it, I yearn to ask for and receive bendición from the elders in my family. A few weeks ago, I had a long and pleasant telephone conversation with my uncle Agapito who lives in Río Piedras, Puerto Rico. We talked about all kinds of things, like family, politics and music. But before we said our goodbyes, I said, "Uncle, give me your blessing..."

~Aurelio Deane Font
Chicken Soup for the Latino Soul

The Light

And the mother of the child said, As the Lord liveth, and as thy soul liveth,
I will not leave thee. And he arose, and followed her.
~2 Kings. 4:30

My family was a close-knit group, and my grandmother was the center of our universe. Although a stern disciplinarian, she ruled her children and her children's children with affection. We never doubted her love, even when she corrected us.

It was during the heat of World War II that her youngest son, my uncle Raymond, turned nineteen. Shortly after his birthday, he found himself in Italy fighting his way toward Berlin. A farm boy, he had never spent a night away from home until he shipped out for basic training. Homesick and scared, he slugged his way through towns, vineyards and woods, thinking of home and his family.

I remember the terrible day the Western Union car pulled up and a man got out. By the time the messenger walked up the sidewalk, all of us children were out on the porch, waiting silently for the news. Grandma moaned softly, not crying, but frightened. Grandpa stood next to her, his face grave. Grandma took the envelope in trembling hands and ripped it open. It was the longest wait of our lives as she began to read the message inside.

A wide grin spread across her face and she clutched Grandpa's hand. "He's alive! Raymond's injured and coming home, but he's alive!" she cried.

There was much crying, dancing, hugging and cheering as we embraced one another.

The day Raymond got home, he looked so pale and tired, I thought we'd wear him out with our welcome. He was hard of hearing and still sore from his wounds, but he was in one piece and back with us. We pulled him inside, where we sat gathered around the table, while Raymond told us about the day he'd been injured.

"We had been fighting a battle for several days and were marching forward, bone tired, cold and frightened, yet happy that we continued to inch closer to the German border," he began. "It was late afternoon, and snow was on the ground. I was marching down a muddy, half-frozen road when an armored tank rolled by. Several of my buddies and I hitched a ride on it. We hopped on the tank, glad to rest for a short spell. We were laughing and talking when, out of the blue, a mortar round exploded around us.

"The next thing I remember is hearing Mama calling me to get up. 'Raymond, get up!' she shouted. 'Get up right now!'

"At first, I thought I was back home and she was calling me for school. Then I opened my eyes and realized I was in Italy. The world had gone totally silent. I knew I was deaf first, then I noticed the blood on my hands, where it had streamed down from my head.

"I was frightened and confused. My buddies and other soldiers lay dead all around me. I was in shock. I was disoriented and didn't know where the enemy lines were or where my troops had moved. By now, it had grown dark, and it was a night without stars. Panic set in because I couldn't hear. I felt helpless.

"Then Mama said, in her sternest voice, 'Raymond, go toward the light! Go toward the light.'

"Her voice sounded as clear as though she were standing over me. So I staggered down the road, confused, my head aching, too dazed to fully comprehend the danger, not even understanding what the light I saw might be. I hobbled around a bend in the road and fell into the arms of a medic.

"As soon as they checked me out, the medics evacuated me to a field hospital. They said that I was lucky to have caught them. They had already searched the area I was in for wounded, shipping them out first and then returning for the dead. Had I not regained consciousness and moved toward them, I'd have bled to death from the leg injuries before they found me."

Raymond stopped talking, and he and Grandma just sat there, looking at each other. No one spoke, and then my grandfather said loud enough for Raymond to hear, "Well, do you want to hear the rest of the story?" Raymond nodded, and Grandpa started telling what had happened here that same night.

"Your mama and I were asleep," he said, "when Mama awoke from a dream and shook me awake. 'Alston,' she said, 'something has happened to our boy. I dreamed he was calling to me for help. I thought he was a little boy again and he was crying, so I called to him to get up and come to the light so I could see what was wrong with him.'

"She got up and dressed, refusing to go back to sleep. All that day and for the next several days, your mama sat on the front porch waiting for the Western Union boy to bring us the telegram she knew was on the way."

The rest of us looked at Grandma in surprise, but Grandma wasn't paying any attention to us. She and Raymond just kept looking at each other, the tears running down their faces.

After the war, Raymond regained most of his hearing, married, and went on to live a long and happy life. Over the years, I heard him tell the story about Grandma and the light often. He always ended it by saying, "I was all the way over in Italy, stone deaf, but I heard her all the same.'Go to the light, Raymond,' she said. 'Go to the light.' I'll never understand how she did it, but it was my mama that saved my life that night. My mama and the light."

~Patricia S. Laye
Chicken Soup for the Veteran's Soul

62

The Power
of Our Family History

Notebook in hand, my nine-year-old son Michael plopped down on the sofa in our living room where I had been paging through a writer's magazine and said, "What did Grandpa Leal's father do for a living?"

I was startled by his question. He had never shown the slightest interest in his ancestors. When I asked him why he wanted to know, he explained that his fourth-grade teacher had given the class an assignment to research their family histories. I felt an excitement stir within me. There was almost nothing I loved more than talking about my family's roots, since I had recently researched and written genealogies about both sides of my family. But I also knew that my son had a typical nine-year-old's attention span, and that he would drift off in boredom if I started a lengthy discourse about his ancestors.

My son is of Irish, Hungarian and Mexican descent — a "melting pot" American. I knew little about his father's Irish-Hungarian side, but enough about his Mexican side to keep him writing for days. This, I realized, was the perfect time to tell Michael the story about his Mexican roots.

He asked again. "What did Grandpa Leal's father do for a living?"

I put my magazine on the coffee table and leaned back into the cushion of the sofa. "That would be my grandfather, your great-grandfather, Agapito. He was a field laborer, and later, he became a groundskeeper at a high school. He loved to work outdoors. His flower garden at home was gorgeous. Whenever I smell jasmine, I think of his garden."

Michael looked up at me, his brown eyes wide and round. "What do you mean by a field laborer?"

"He picked cotton, vegetables, fruit—you know, whatever was in season."

"Like out in the fields?"

"Yes, like out in the fields!" I smiled, amused at his incredulity. "In fact, your grandma's father also was a field worker for a while." I suddenly realized that the lives of his great-grandparents were as alien to Michael as if they had been born on another planet.

"Where were these fields?"

"Your grandfather's dad worked in the valley, near the Texas-Mexico border. There are a lot of citrus orchards down there, also commercial vegetable fields, with acres of beets, carrots and tomatoes. Every kind of vegetable you can imagine."

"What about Grandma's dad?" He stopped writing and looked up expectantly.

"He worked for a little while as a picker, but then he went into business as a labor contractor. He took field workers with him all over Texas and Mississippi to pick cotton."

Michael bunched up his eyebrows. "By hand?"

I nodded.

"Anyway, back to your grandfather's father, my abuelo—that's the Spanish word for grandfather—moved to Texas in 1912 because of the Mexican Revolution. He was seventeen at the time. He got a job helping to clear the land in the town where he lived. After his field work, he got a job at a packing shed, washing, gathering and then packing thousands of pounds of fruits and vegetables into crates for shipping. After he retired from that job, he worked for many years as a high school groundskeeper.

"His wife, my abuela, was a strong woman. She was the same age as Grandpa and was born in a little ranch in south Texas, though her parents were from Mexico. Grandma and Grandpa Leal were married in the early 1920s. They lived in Weslaco, north of the Missouri

Pacific railroad tracks, in a pink, three-room house on the Mexican side of town."

"On the Mexican side of town?" Michael interrupted.

"Yes, in those days, Mexicans lived on one side of the railroad tracks, and the Anglos lived on the other side."

"That's weird."

"Yeah," I said.

"If I lived then, where would I have lived?" He put his notebook on his lap, his eyes intense.

"You mean being part Mexican?" I crossed my arms.

"Yeah."

"I'm not sure, but since your dad is Anglo, probably on the Anglo side of town."

He nodded, then picked up his notebook.

"Anyway, neither of your great-grandparents could read or write, but they were responsible and wise. They were married for more than fifty years. My grandmother died seven years after their fiftieth anniversary, and then Grandpa died just a few months later. Before he died, abuelo often roamed around the house calling for her."

"That's creepy."

I smiled. "He missed her. They were married a long time."

He frowned.

"Anyway, even though my grandparents were not educated, they were honest, God-fearing people who expected their children to better themselves and to be good American citizens."

Michael looked down at what he had written. "I didn't know I had relatives who were field workers and one who was a janitor."

"Does it bother you?"

"No... I mean, I just never thought about it, about what it must have been like to have to work in the fields."

"People still do that kind of work today, and many of them are Mexicans who travel all over the country. It's hard work. During the time your great-grandparents were alive, they had few choices but to work in the fields. But they didn't complain about it. They knew that one day their children, grandchildren and great-grandchildren would have a better way of life."

Michael pursed his lips. "Wow, this is really something. My great-grandparents worked in the fields." He slapped his notebook shut. "I'm done. I'll type it up later." He jumped off the sofa, walked over and plopped down on the recliner, then turned on the television with the remote control.

I felt strangely deflated. Had anything I said meant anything to him? As I reached over to pick up my magazine, Michael turned to me.

"Mom, the janitor at our school is Mexican. I've never talked to him before. I think I'll say hi to him tomorrow."

That day, because of a fourth-grade project, Michael learned about his immigrant forefathers, and I learned about the power of our family history. The story of our ancestors can have a positive effect on how we view others—the men and women working in fields, in restaurants, in hotels, in the multitude of menial labor jobs our society gives to new, uneducated immigrants—no longer faceless individuals, but people who want to achieve the American dream. People like our own ancestors. People like us.

~Cynthia Leal Massey
Chicken Soup for the Latino Soul

63

The Longest Week

A sweet new blossom of humanity,
fresh fallen from God's own home, to flower the earth.
~Gerald Massey

It was a wintry Saturday morning and I was still asleep when the phone rang, but the urgency in Matthew's voice startled me awake. "Esmaralda's water broke," my oldest son told me. "We think she's in labor."

I felt my heart sink. As a longtime childbirth educator and breastfeeding counselor, I knew all too well the potential risks and challenges of a baby born two months early.

We spent the next hours walking the halls of the hospital as Esmaralda's contractions grew ever stronger. Finally, the midwife knelt in front of her, Matthew sat behind her supporting her back, and Esmaralda's mother and I took our places, one on either side, holding her legs. In just a few pushes, the baby emerged — pink and healthy, a beautiful boy.

Beautiful, yes, but oh-so-incredibly tiny. Sebastian Rhys Pitman weighed just four pounds, six ounces.

Esmaralda's face glowed with joy as she held him against her. But within minutes, his breathing began to falter. We could see him struggling to take in each breath, and newborn Sebastian was moved to the nursery and placed in an incubator.

I was a grandma! But although I'd been there to rejoice in his arrival, I had barely seen, let alone touched, my new grandson, and my heart ached with worry.

By midnight we had even more to worry about. His breathing had continued to deteriorate, and eventually the pediatrician decided Sebastian needed to be transferred to a larger hospital where he could be placed on a respirator. An ambulance arrived to take him away, and a team of health-care professionals put tubes down his nose and throat and hooked him up to monitors for the trip. It scared us all to see this tiny, scrawny baby with so much of his little body covered by tubes and wires.

There wasn't room for my son in the ambulance, so I drove him to the hospital, an hour away. Matthew's a foot taller than me, but he leaned his head against my shoulder and wept as we drove through the dark and snowy night.

We were fortunate there was a Ronald McDonald House next to this larger hospital, offering a place to stay for parents whose children had been admitted. It became Matthew and Esmaralda's home as Sebastian struggled to stay alive. They spent most of their time sitting alongside his incubator, talking and singing to him so he would know he was not alone.

The nurses encouraged his parents to participate in Sebastian's care from the beginning. He was too frail to tolerate much handling and needed to be on the respirator to keep him breathing, but when his diapers needed changing or when he needed to come out of the incubator for a few minutes, Esmaralda and Matthew were the ones who changed and held him.

I longed to cuddle him just once, but I knew that it was far more important for his parents to have that connection with him. I remembered how hard it was for me, as a new mother, to hand over my baby to someone else. I didn't want to steal even one minute of the precious time these new parents had to hold their son.

I could be patient. But my arms ached to hold him.

I was used to being the mother—the one who had that very intimate connection with the baby. I didn't know yet how to be a grandmother, and it was hard feeling relegated to the sidelines. Maybe if I held him just once, I'd feel more like a real grandma.

But I could be patient. I saw the happiness in Esmaralda's eyes as

Sebastian responded to her touch and her voice, familiar to him from the months before he was born. I would wait.

After four days, he was growing stronger. He began to breathe on his own, and the respirator tube was removed and replaced with a smaller oxygen tube. The nurses began to feed him the breast milk Esmaralda had pumped, and she was able to hold him longer each day.

I continued to drive there daily to encourage them and to marvel at Sebastian's progress. Sometimes, as Esmaralda cuddled him to her, I would stroke his tiny hand or gently touch a foot that peeked out from the blanket. But my arms ached to hold him.

When he was a week old, the nurses informed us that he was almost ready to return to the hospital in the small town where we lived and he had been born. Yes, he still needed to be kept warm and fed by a tube for a few more weeks before he could come home, but he no longer needed all the special equipment.

As we celebrated this good news with smiles and hugs, the nurse said, "Now that he can be out of the incubator longer, would Grandma like a turn holding him?"

Would I? Would I?! I'd dreamed of little else for the past seven days.

I settled myself in the rocking chair and the nurse handed him to me. He was so light in my arms... such a tiny bundle. But he nuzzled his face against me and snuggled close. I felt a rush of love and emotion surge through me, and the tears flowed down my cheeks. Here he was, my beautiful little grandson, in my arms at last, breathing on his own and healthy and one step closer to coming home. I couldn't speak. All I could do was cry. My arms no longer ached as I held him near and took in the magic of the moment as I held him for the very first time.

~Teresa Pitman
Chicken Soup for the Grandma's Soul

64

It Just Isn't Fair

No language can express the power
and beauty and heroism and majesty of a mother's love.
~Edwin Hubbell Chapin

I'd wanted a child for so long. I'd endured the diabetes testing and the pelvic exams. I'd cried during my ultrasound when I saw my son for the first time, and I'd laughed through the baby shower my sisters had given me. I was thrilled with my pregnancy, but now, as I prepared the bedroom down the hall for my new son, try as I might, I couldn't shake the thought: It just isn't fair.

As I got closer to motherhood, thoughts of my own mother came more and more frequently. My mother had died of cancer when I was thirteen. In my memory, she had been the very best mother in the whole world—patient, kind and loving. She had enjoyed her children, caring for us and meeting our every need the way only a mother can.

Her death at the age of forty-one had been no beautiful, poignant *Love Story* death; she'd fought hard for her life and the struggle had consumed the last year of her time with us. After she died, I missed her with a bottomless ache in my soul that never went away. When I graduated from high school I pushed away thoughts of my mother. I tried to ignore how unfair it felt that she wasn't there to see me get my diploma. At my wedding, I deliberately closed the emotional door to memories of Mom. But now, as I waited for our son, I found I couldn't stop thinking about my mother.

Growing up, I'd found substitutes as best I could. My father kept his family together, trying hard to make up for Mom's death. My five sisters and I made a tight-knit, loving unit, and we all mothered one another.

Then God gave me a second mother in my wonderful mother-in-law, Ethel. In the early years of my marriage Ethel never intruded but also never failed to give good advice when she felt it justified. Ethel died three years before I got pregnant, and although her death was more peaceful and less painful than my mother's, I still missed her terribly. As my baby grew inside me, I felt keenly the fact that I had no mother to help me.

I'm ashamed to admit I felt jealous of other pregnant women who had mothers. I saw them together shopping for maternity clothes while I went, alone, to buy my own. They were there cooing over cribs and cradles when my husband and I shopped for the perfect bed for our baby. Even in our Lamaze class there was a mother-daughter team, huffing and puffing right alongside the counting husbands and the eagerly attending ladies.

I had this little fantasy that I'd let my mind play: my mother and I, enjoying lunch together at a restaurant while she told me wise stories about the wiles and ways of babies. I could picture myself, listening intently and laughing at tales of her own mothering. But of course, it was just a fantasy. It just wasn't fair.

I knew I could never forget my mothers; their faces are etched in my memory. But I wanted my son to somehow "know" his grand-mothers, so a few months before our baby arrived, Tom and I decided to hang a picture of each of our mothers on the wall. In my mother-in-law's picture, taken when she was a lively, vibrant young woman, Ethel looks a lot like her son — complete with the slightest sugges-tion of faint lines under her eyes, a hereditary trick of the skin that my husband shares. It's a distinctive feature, and I noticed it in Ethel the first time I met her.

My own mother's picture looks down at me with the large, beau-tiful and smiling brown eyes I remember so vividly from my child-hood. I'd found comfort in those eyes when I hurt myself. I'd loved the way she smiled and how her eyes lit up with laughter when she felt delighted. And despite the stress and strain of raising six children, with a husband in Vietnam, there had always been deep peace in her eyes.

For me, labor lasted thirty-three hours and ended in an emergency C-section. The doctor whispered the word "brain damage" into the phone while she summoned the high-risk pediatrician, and I knew from the way the nurse frowned at the monitor and from her honest answers to our questions that my baby was in trouble.

It was a far cry from the delivery I'd planned, the one where my husband and I would participate joyously in the miracle of birth. I was sure that I'd cry the first time I heard the baby cry out, and I knew my husband would, too. But I wasn't awake to see my baby born. Right before the general anesthesia put me to sleep, my last conscious thoughts were prayers for his safety.

When I woke up from the delivery, my husband and my sister were with me. My first thought, even before I could open my eyes, was for the baby. I'll never forget my sister's voice saying, "He's beautiful — and he's huge!" In spite of the doctor's fears, Ben was healthy, hearty and weighed nearly ten pounds. Finally they brought my son to me. I was groggy and in pain from the staples in my incision, but I couldn't wait to meet him.

I took the heavy bundle they handed me — they didn't tell me he'd be so heavy! Someone put a pillow on my belly so I could hold him more easily, and I did what I'm sure every new parent does — I held his hand and counted his fingers, amazed at the tiny, perfect little fingernails. He made a face when I did that, his eyes still closed in sleep. I watched him breathe, watched the way his barrel chest went in and out, in and out. I savored the bowed, pudgy little legs and the perfect roundness of his head. I held him while he slept, breathing in that unforgettable fragrance of new baby. An hour later, he stirred and woke. I watched as his eyes opened, held my breath as he looked at me for the first time.

Considering that his grandmothers were absent, I'm proud to say that up until then I'd done pretty well. I'd felt too full of joy and thanksgiving at Ben's safe arrival to feel the "just isn't fair" feeling. And, when my son opened his eyes, "it just isn't fair" ended for good.

You see, my son has my mother's eyes—big, deep brown, and full of sparkle and life. And there's a funny little skin fold under his eyes—just like his father, just like Ethel.

When I see my two mothers smile at me from my son's face, I no longer have any thoughts about "fairness." I just know that I have been blessed with a beautiful son whose smile gives me back both of my mothers every day of his life.

~Nancy L. Rusk
Chicken Soup for the Mother's Soul 2

Moms & Sons

Through the Eyes of a Child

There is a garden in every childhood,
an enchanted place where colors are brighter, the air softer,
and the morning more fragrant than ever again.
~Elizabeth Lawrence

Two Little Boys Named Chris

Character is what you know you are, not what others think you have.
~Marva Collins

When my firstborn child, Christian (Chris), was a little over three years old, he was diagnosed with cancer. After two to three years of treatment and several surgeries, it became apparent that his learning abilities had degenerated. With the help of Cancer Institute personnel, we were able to get Chris into a special-education class in a local school.

His teacher soon realized there was a problem in identifying two little boys in the class named Chris. Every time she called the name Chris, both boys answered. So she decided to ask each one what his mother called him at home. The other little boy answered, "Chris," and my son answered, "Sweetheart."

~Delores Lacy
A 6th Bowl of Chicken Soup for the Soul

The Sandbox Revelation

You can learn many things from children.
~Franklin P. Jones

I spent all morning cleaning the house because my mother was coming over for dinner that night. When I was through, I decided to take my four-year-old out so that no new messes would accumulate before my mother arrived.

We were sitting at the park having a snack when I noticed that he was watching a father and son playing in the sandbox together. I asked him what he was looking at. Gazing up at me, he said, "Why don't I have a daddy?" I was so shocked by the question that I couldn't think of a thing to say. Noticing my confused expression, he stood up and gave me a big hug. With his arms still around me, he looked me in the eye and said, "It's okay, Mommy. We don't need anyone else making a mess in our house, anyway."

~Christine E. Penny
Chicken Soup for the Single Parent's Soul

The Two Eyes

To be upset over what you don't have is to waste what you do have.
~Ken S. Keyes, Jr., Handbook to Higher Consciousness

My son, one of triplets, was playing with his brothers in their room a few days before the Jewish Holiday of Scholars, Lag B'Omer. The triplets were almost eight years old at the time. They had made bows and arrows out of twigs for Lag B'Omer, and I decided to let them play with them a few minutes before getting them into bed.

One of the boys was showing his brothers how to shoot the bow in a safe manner, with the bow pointing downward. As he was about to demonstrate this, one of the other boys banged into him, lifting his arm up and causing him to shoot the arrow. The arrow flew across the room at the very moment that the third boy, Elishama, happened to turn around to face his brothers. The arrow struck him in the eye.

Filled with horror at this freak accident, we rushed Elishama to the hospital. He was immediately sent into emergency surgery to try to save his eye. But when the surgery was over and the surgeon came to tell us the news, it was not good. Elishama's vision in his left eye was destroyed.

The next day, as Elishama was recovering from surgery, he asked me from his hospital bed, "What am I going to do now?"

I had been thinking carefully about what I could tell him, how I could comfort him.

I took his hand and said to him very gently, "God created everyone with two eyes—one to see the world with a good eye and one to see the world with a bad eye. Right now God has given you the privilege to be able to see the world with only a good eye."

Elishama considered this for a moment. Then he said, "Boy, I'm sure glad the arrow didn't hit my other eye!"

~Leah Golomb
Chicken Soup for the Jewish Soul

68

The Pencil Box

was deep in thought at my office, preparing a lecture to be given that evening at a college across town, when the phone rang. A woman I had never met said she was the mother of a seven-year-old boy and that she was dying. She said her therapist had advised her that discussing her pending death with her little boy would be too traumatic for him, but somehow that didn't feel right to her.

Knowing that I worked with grieving children, she asked my advice. I told her that our heart is often smarter than our brain, and that I thought she knew what would be best for her son. I also invited her to attend the lecture that night since I was speaking about how children cope with death. She said she would be there.

I wondered later if I would recognize her at the lecture, but my question was answered when I saw a frail woman being half-carried into the room by two adults. I talked about the fact that children usually sense the truth long before they are told, and they often wait until they feel adults are ready to talk about it before sharing their concerns and questions. I said that children usually can handle truth better than denial, even though the denial is intended to protect them from pain. I said that respecting children meant including them in the family sadness, not shutting them out.

At the break, she hobbled to me and said through her tears, "I knew it in my heart. I just knew I should tell him." She said that she would that night.

The next morning I received another phone call from her. I managed to hear the story through her choked voice. She said she awakened him when they got home the night before and quietly said, "Derek, I have something to tell you."

He quickly interrupted her, saying, "Oh, Mommy, is it now that you are going to tell me that you are dying?"

She held him close, and they both sobbed while she said, "Yes."

After a few minutes the little boy wanted down. He said he had something for her that he had been saving. In the back of one of his drawers was a dirty pencil box. Inside the box was a letter written in simple scrawl. It said, "Goodbye, Mom. I will always love you."

How long he had been waiting to hear the truth, I don't know. I do know that two days later Mom died. In her casket was placed a dirty pencil box and a letter.

~Doris Sanford
Chicken Soup for the Grieving Soul

69

Dusting in Heaven

$\mathcal{M}$y eight-year-old son, Jonathan, is an exceptionally inquisitive and cheerful child who must have an answer for every question that enters his mind. I truly admire this awe-inspiring quality in him. However, I'm stumped when I do not have an answer for him.

While tucking him into bed one night, I faced the hardest question he'd posed to me up until then.

"Mommy," he said, "where is my granny now, and what is she doing there?"

I was entirely lost for words. There was a long pause as I searched my heart and soul for an appropriate answer.

My mother-in-law had been diagnosed with lymphoma and suffered through two long years of chemotherapy and radiation. Our family, being very close, prayed together as we watched this horrible disease claim her life twenty-six months later. My son was very close to his grandmother, and her death was a great mystery to him. I always knew this time would come, but how to prepare for such a question was a mystery to me.

Granny must have been listening to the conversation between her only grandson and me because my answer to him came out as if someone was talking for me.

"Jonathan," I began, "Granny has gone to live in heaven." Recalling the special care and tidiness she took with her home, I added, "She is dusting the clouds and keeping them shiny white."

After a brief thought, Jonathan smiled as if he could imagine

Granny working hard in heaven, and he kissed me good night. Relieved that I had satisfied his curiosity, I let out a breath of relief. I, too, missed her, and was happy I had moved through the interrogation without tears. Jonathan fell asleep, happily as always.

The next morning, he ran through the house and jumped into bed with me. "Mom!" he said, "please come and look out your window!"

I half opened my eyes and gazed at the rays of sunshine filtering into my bedroom. "Yes, Jonathan, it is going to be a beautiful day."

Jonathan had a glow about him as he looked at me with his wide-open eyes. His face beamed like a shaft of light as he looked out the window where the sun came shining in. He said, "Granny is doing a great job up there in heaven. Just look at those clean, white, fluffy clouds!"

~Denise Peebles
Chicken Soup for the Grandma's Soul

70

The Plum Pretty Sister

Brothers and sisters are as close as hands and feet.
~Vietnamese Proverb

Justin was a climber. By one and a half, he had discovered the purple plum tree in the backyard, and its friendly branches became his favorite hangout.

At first he would climb just a few feet and make himself comfortable in the curve where the trunk met the branches. Soon he was building himself a small fort and dragging his toy tractors and trucks up to their new garage.

One day when he was two, Justin was playing in the tree as usual. I turned my back to prune the rosebush, and he disappeared.

"Justin, where are you?" I hollered.

His tiny voice called back, "Up here, Mommy, picking all the plums for you!"

I looked up in horror and disbelief. There was Justin on the roof of the house, filling his plastic bucket with the ripe juicy plums from his favorite tree.

When Justin was three, I became pregnant. My husband and I explained to him that we were going to have another baby as a playmate for him.

He was very excited, kissed my tummy and said, "Hello, baby, I'm your big brother, Justin."

From the beginning he was sure he was going to have a little sister, and every day he'd beg to know if she was ready to play yet.

When I explained that the baby wasn't arriving until the end of June, he seemed confused.

One day he asked, "When is June, Mommy?"

I realized I needed a better explanation; how could a three-year-old know what "June" meant? Just then, as Justin climbed into the low branches of the plum tree, he gave me the answer I was looking for... his special tree.

"Justin, the baby is going to be born when the plums are ripe. You can keep me posted when that will be, okay?" I wasn't completely sure if I was on target, but the gardener in me was confident I'd be close enough.

Oh, he was excited! Now Justin had a way to know when his new baby sister would come to play. From that moment on, he checked the old plum tree several times a day and reported his findings to me. Of course, he was quite concerned in November when all the leaves fell off the tree. By January, with the cold and the rains, he was truly worried whether his baby would be cold and wet like his tree. He whispered to my tummy that the tree was strong and that she (the baby) had to be strong too, and make it through the winter.

By February a few purple leaves began to shoot forth, and his excitement couldn't be contained.

"My tree is growing, Mommy! Pretty soon she'll have baby plums, and then I'll have my baby sister."

March brought the plum's beautiful tiny white flowers, and Justin was overjoyed.

"She's b'ooming, Mommy!" he chattered, struggling with the word "blooming." He rushed to kiss my tummy and got kicked in the mouth.

"The baby's moving, Mommy, she's b'ooming, too. I think she wants to come out and see the flowers."

So it went for the next couple of months, as Justin checked every detail of his precious plum tree and reported to me about the flowers turning to tiny beads that would become plums.

The rebirth of his tree gave me ample opportunity to explain the development of the fetus that was growing inside me. Sometimes I think he believed I had actually planted a "baby seed" inside my tummy, because when I drank water he'd say things like, "You're watering our little flower, Mommy!" I'd laugh and once again explain in simple terms the story of the birds and the bees, the plants and the trees.

June finally arrived, and so did the purple plums. At first they were fairly small, but Justin climbed his tree anyway to pick some plums off the branches where the sun shone warmest. He brought them to me to let me know the baby wasn't ripe yet.

I felt ripe! I was ready to pop! When were the plums going to start falling from that darn tree?

Justin would rub my tummy and talk to his baby sister, telling her she had to wait a little longer because the fruit was not ready to be picked yet. His forays into the plum tree lasted longer each day, as if he was coaxing the tree to ripen quickly. He talked to the tree and thanked it for letting him know about this important event in his life. Then one day, it happened. Justin came running into the house, his eyes as big as saucers, with a plastic bucket full to the brim of juicy purple plums.

"Hurry, Mommy, hurry!" he shouted. "She's coming, she's coming! The plums are ripe, the plums are ripe!"

I laughed uncontrollably as Justin stared at my stomach, as if he expected to see his baby sister erupt any moment. That morning I did feel a bit queasy, and it wasn't because I had a dental appointment.

Before we left the house, Justin went out to hug his plum tree and whisper that today was the day his "plum pretty sister" would arrive. He was certain.

As I sat in the dental chair, the labor pains began, just as Justin had predicted. Our "plum" baby was coming! I called my parents, and my husband rushed me to the hospital. At 6:03 P.M. on June 22, the day that will forever live in family fame as "Plum Pretty Sister Day," our daughter was born. We didn't name her Purple Plum as Justin suggested, but chose another favorite flower, Heather.

At Heather's homecoming, Justin kissed his new playmate and

presented her with his plastic bucket, full to the brim with sweet, ripe, purple plums.

"These are for you," he said proudly.

Justin and Heather are now teenagers, and the plum tree has become our bonding symbol. Although we moved from the home that housed Justin's favorite plum tree, the first tree to be planted in our new yard was a purple plum, so that Justin and Heather could know when to expect her special day. Throughout their growing-up years, the children spent countless hours nestled in the branches, counting down the days through the birth of leaves, flowers, buds and fruit. Our birthday parties are always festooned with plum branches and baskets brimming with freshly picked purple plums. Because as Mother Nature—and Justin—would have it, for the last fifteen years, the purple plum has ripened exactly on June 22.

~Cynthia Brian
Chicken Soup for the Gardener's Soul

Grandma and the Chicken Pox

The first duty of love is to listen.
~Paul Tillich

My twin boys were only seven years old when their paternal grandmother announced she was getting remarried. We were all thrilled for her, since she had seemed so lonely since Grandpa passed away a few years before. We broke the news to our boys, who were sitting in the back of the car. "Grandma is getting married again," we said.

Jon had a look of thoughtfulness on his face for a while. He finally asked, "Is she going to have more children?"

Before we had a chance to respond, his twin brother Mike shot back this answer: "No! She can't. She already had them. It's like chicken pox. Once you get them, you can't get them again."

~Susan Amerikaner
Chicken Soup for the Grandparent's Soul

I Want It in Ink

My son was nine years old and beginning to recognize he had a life to manage. Asking me to schedule a commitment to him for the following week, I picked up a pencil to write it in my calendar.

He said, "I want it in ink."

The light bulb went on. He knew that when I wrote things in my calendar in pencil, they were subject to being rescheduled. He didn't want to be "rescheduled."

This was a reminder that children notice the littlest things, and if we are listening to them, we can learn a lot. Needless to say, from then on, I wrote all commitments to my children in ink.

~Dorothy M. Neddermeyer
Chicken Soup for the Single Parent's Soul

Moms & Sons

Courage and Persistence

*When faced with a challenge,
look for a way, not a way out.*
~David L. Weatherford

73

Hand-Me-Down Love

*I*t was a typical spring day in my local high school science class. Each student was to show proficiency in anatomy by dissecting a frog. We were called up in alphabetical order. My day was today, and I was ready for the task.

I wore my favorite power shirt—the one I knew I looked good in, the one everyone told me I looked good in. I had studied and was ready for the assignment. When my name was called I walked confidently to the front of the room, smiled to the class and grabbed the scalpel to begin the task.

A voice from the back of the room said, "Nice shirt."

I beamed from ear to ear, when suddenly another voice from the back of the room said, "That shirt belonged to my Dad. Greg's mother is our maid and she took that shirt out of a bag headed for the Salvation Army."

My heart sank. I was speechless. It was probably one minute, but it felt like ten minutes of total emptiness and embarrassment in front of my peers. Vice President of Student Government, born with a gift of gab, I stood for the first time in my life speechless with nothing to say. As I looked to the left, another African American whose mother was also a maid, looked down; to my right, the only other African American in the class laughed out loud. I wanted to crawl into a hole.

My biology teacher asked me to begin the dissection. I stood speechless; he repeated the question. After total silence, he said, "Mr. Franklin, you may be seated. Your grade, a D."

I don't know which was more embarrassing, receiving the low mark or being found out. At home, I stuck the shirt in the back of the closet. My mom found the shirt and brought it to the front. This time I put it in the middle of the closet. Again, she moved it to the front.

A few weeks passed and my mom asked why I had not worn the shirt. I responded, "I just don't like it anymore."

She pressed with more questions. I didn't want to hurt her, but I had been raised to tell the truth. I explained what had happened in front of the whole class.

Mom sat in total silence while tears fell from her eyes. Then she stood and called her employer, "I will no longer work for your family," she told him, and asked for an apology for the incident at school. My mom was quiet for the rest of the day. At dinner, where she was typically the life of the family, Mom was totally quiet. After the kids were down for the night, I stood outside my mom and dad's door to hear what was going on.

In tears, Mom shared her humiliation with my dad—how she had quit her job and how embarrassed she felt for me. She said she couldn't clean anymore; she knew her life's purpose was something greater.

"What do you want to do?" Dad asked.

"Teach children," she answered with sudden clarity.

"You have no education." Dad pointed out.

With conviction she said, "Well, that's what I want to do, and I am going to find a way to make it happen."

The next morning she met with the personnel manager at the Board of Education, who thanked her for her interest but told her without an education she could not teach school. That evening, Mom, a mother of seven children and a high school graduate far removed from school, shared with us her new plans to attend the university.

Mom started her studies by taking nine hours. She spread her books on the dining room table, studying right along with the rest of us.

After her first semester, she immediately went back to the personnel manager and asked for a teaching assignment. Again she was told, "Not without an education."

Mom went back to school the second semester, took six more hours and again went back to the personnel manager.

He said, "You are serious, aren't you? I think I have a position for you as a teacher's assistant. This opportunity is dealing with children who are mentally challenged, slow learners with, in many cases, little to no chance of learning. This is the highest area of teacher turnover due to sheer frustration."

Mom leaped at the opportunity.

She got us kids ready for school in the morning, went to work and came home and fixed dinner. I knew it was tough, but it is what she wanted to do and she did it with so much love. For almost five years my Mom was a teacher's assistant at the Starkey Special Education Center. Then, after three teacher changes during that five-year period, the personnel manager and the principal showed up in her classroom one day.

The principal said, "We have watched you and admired your diligence over the last five years. We have watched how you interact with the children and how they interact with you. We've talked to the other teachers, and we are all in agreement that you should be the teacher of this class."

My mom spent twenty-plus years with the Wichita Public School System. Through her career, she was voted Teacher of the Year for both her work with the Special Olympics and the special education center. All of this came about because of the thoughtless comment made in the classroom that day.

It has been said children learn not from what you say, but what you do. Mom showed me how to look challenging situations in the face and never give up.

As for me, my biology teacher approached me as I gathered my books to leave the classroom that day. He said, "I know this was a tough day for you, but I will give you a second chance on the assignment tomorrow."

I showed up, dissected the frog, and he changed my grade from a D to a B. I challenged him for an A, but he said, "You should have gotten it right the first time. It would be unfair to others."

As I grabbed my books and walked toward the door, he said, "Do you think you are the only one who has had to wear used clothes? Do you think you are the only one who has grown up poor?"

I responded with an assured, "Yes!"

My teacher put his arm around me and shared his story of growing up during the depression, and how on his graduation day he was laughed at because he did not have enough money for a cap and gown. He showed up with the same pants and shirt he wore to school every day.

He said, "I know how you felt; my heart went out to you. But you know something, kid? I have faith in you. I think you are going to be something special. I can feel it in my heart."

I was speechless again. Both of us were fighting back the tears, but I felt the love from him—a white man reaching out to a young black student who had been bussed across town.

I went on to become President of the Student Body, and my teacher was my mentor. Before I opened assembly, I would always look for him and he would give me a thumbs-up—a secret only he and I shared.

It was at that point I realized that we are all the same—different colors, different backgrounds, but many of our experiences are the same. We all want to be happy; we all want great things in life. My teacher and my mother showed me that it's not what you wear, your education or your money, but what's in your heart that counts.

~Greg Franklin
Chicken Soup for the African American Soul

74

Music That Might Never Be Heard

Music is the medicine of the breaking heart.
~Alfred William Hunt

Spring had slipped quietly into our neighborhood and across the mountains with wildflowers and the scent of fresh earth reminding me of happy yesterdays. It was Mother's Day and we were celebrating with our three grown children and their families, picnicking and playing volleyball in our backyard. We were having a wonderful time, yet I ached for the one lost sheep.

Our youngest son, Brian, was gone. He had changed from a loving, tender, family-oriented person into an irritable stranger before he'd left school and the tennis team, and disappeared into the streets six months ago.

I longed for the days when he would bounce into the house yelling, "Mom, want to go over to the school and watch me practice my serve?" On Sunday afternoons, he would set up "Olympic" hurdles for his nieces and nephews and cheer them on to victory, making sure they all got a ribbon. Sometimes, he made beds for us all on the deck, inspiring summer sleepovers and star-watching.

We missed him.

Though Brian's sensitivity and compassion had endeared him to adults and small children, he didn't make friends of his own age easily and faced relentless torment all through school.

At seventeen, he battled depression. Unable to cope, he ran away and lived on the streets where he was accepted, but after a short time, he returned home with the promise to obey house rules and get his life together. One winter afternoon, his sobs broke through the house. "Mom, come here," he said. "I'm scared. The world is so ugly."

I ran to my six-foot-three son and cradled him in my arms. Sweat mingled with tears on his cheeks. I wiped his forehead. I could smooth his hair but not his pathway. "Brian," I said. "You're going to come through this hard time. The world needs a boy like you. We'll get professional help, and we'll all work together on this."

But within days he had disappeared again.

I knew when Brian was born I would have to give him up some-day—but not like this. At three, he had played outside rain or shine, laughed up at the clouds, shoveled sunlight, built roads and tunnels for his trucks. One morning, he ran in breathless. "Mom," he shouted, waving his arms, then whispering his secret, "Mom, my heart is so happy it's tickling me."

During his junior high years, he made friends with folks on his paper route. He would come home laden with plants to begin a gar-den. One widow gave him her whole stamp collection. Another of his customers was running for reelection as state representative. He left a note in her paper. "Mrs. North, I watched the election on TV last night. I'm glad you won." He later served as page at the State Capitol with her recommendation.

A former teacher was on his route, and he helped with her sick dog. He sat with them many evenings and listened to tales about Chiquita, who could fit into Mrs. Hall's pocket. The day Chiquita died, he took lilacs to his grieving friend and left his dinner untouched.

I had rocked him through nightmares and fevers, panned "gold" with him at the river, led him up mountainsides and run with him in 5Ks. I wouldn't give up on him now.

I opened the door to his room, stung by the lingering trace of his familiar aftershave as the silence screamed at me. I smoothed the quilt on his bed and kneeled down, burying my head in the softness, clutching for his presence, praying as mothers all over the world pray when a child is in need.

I grieved for the music in him that might never be heard, remembering his childhood notes—scrawled messages on paper—sailing under the bathroom door when I was bathing, his teenage knock on the wall to say goodnight after all the lights were out.

All those memories helped me through sleepless nights and dark days. After several weeks, Brian called again. "Mom, do you think I could come back? It's awful here. I think I'm going crazy. Can you meet to talk?"

My feet barely touched the ground as I scrambled for my keys and ran to the car, praying all the way. There, in the dark restaurant, sat my son, hollow eyes peering from his haggard face. He looked like an old man, and at the same time, a lost child. As I approached the booth, he brightened briefly. "Hi, Mom. Thanks for coming."

I sat down facing him, and he said, "I'm so confused. My head feels like it will explode."

I put my hand on his arm. "If you can live by the rules, you can come home. You're stepping in the right direction."

He cupped his chin in one hand and looked out the window. "Last week I walked over to the park where I used to play tennis matches. If I hadn't messed up, I could have earned a tennis scholarship to college. I climbed the hill where you always sat to cheer for me. It was lonely and quiet. I sat there in the rain till dark, then walked back to where I'm staying and slept in someone's car."

The pain in my son's eyes tugged at my already weary heart.

He came back home only to disappear within a few days. Again he was lost to us. Worse, we had to live month after month with the terror of not knowing.

Somehow, the time passed. Mother's Day came, my first without him. Bravely I'd picnicked and played, but in the evening, after our children had returned to their own homes, emptiness jabbed at my insides. I had enjoyed spoiling our grandchildren, grateful for our family day, but the house was all too quiet in the soft twilight. When a knock came at the door, I welcomed the distraction.

There stood Brian, his face thin, clothes wrinkled and stale, but his eyes revealing a faint spark behind the pain. "I had to come," he said. "I couldn't let Mother's Day go by without letting you know I'm thinking of you." He straightened his shoulders and smiled, holding out two pink carnations cradled in baby's breath. I read the card: "Mom, I love you, and you're thought of more often than you'll ever know."

His arms wrapped around me like sunshine breaking through black thunder, his voice barely a whisper, "Mom, I wanted to take my life, be through with the pain, but I could never do that to you." I leaned against his shoulder and buried my face in the sweet, stale sweat of his shirt.

This time, Brian stayed. It was difficult at first, but now ten years later, he is doing well. And each year on Mother's Day, I celebrate my son's final homecoming, and deep inside I relive the wonder of this secret anniversary of my heart.

~Doris Hays Northstrom
Chicken Soup for the Mother's Soul 2

75

A Mother's Test

If one dream should fall and break into a thousand pieces,
never be afraid to pick one of those pieces up and begin again.
~Flavia Weedn

My mother and father were married for ten years before she discovered that he was having an affair. He begged her forgiveness and then promised he would never be unfaithful again. Although she was devastated by my father's unfaithful acts, she apprehensively gave him a second chance. She did so because she felt it was in the best interest of her three sons; she felt that we needed our father. When she discovered that he continued the affair, what little chance he had of regaining her trust and restoring the marriage was completely destroyed. Realizing that she could take no more, she kicked him out of the house and filed for divorce.

Though my father agreed to the divorce, and the proceedings went pretty smoothly, it was still the most difficult time of my mother's life. The custody decision was left to us, and we all chose to live with our mom. She didn't have a job. When my parents married, they agreed that she would be a housewife and full-time mother. Although she finished medical school in the Philippines, where my parents had met, she wasn't qualified to practice medicine in the United States since she hadn't taken the ECFMG, the difficult cumulative medical exam that graduates of foreign medical schools have to pass in order to practice medicine in America. She did not have a driver's license, because my father didn't believe that she needed one. Because public transportation in the suburbs was almost nonexistent at the time, doing everyday tasks was very difficult for her. There were times when all four of us would hitchhike to Kmart.

Her entire family was thousands of miles away in the Philippines. I was five, my brothers were seven and ten, and we were not equipped to provide her with the kind of support that she needed. My mom cried an awful lot during those times! I remember listening through the walls of my bedroom at night, hearing her cry and repeatedly asking the Lord to help her get through this. After phone conversations with my father, she would cry uncontrollably. Each time I heard her, I would do what she taught me to do when I really needed something: I prayed to God. I prayed to God to make my mom stop crying.

Mom could've picked us up and moved us to the Philippines, where her parents were financially well-off. However, she wanted to be an American, and she wanted her kids to grow up as Americans. In 1979, I was in kindergarten, and my brothers were in second and fifth grade. They were in school all day, but I was out at noon. Soon after the divorce was complete, she registered for driving lessons. I went with her to every lesson right after I got home from kindergarten. After a few months, she finished the lessons, passed her driving test and got her driver's license.

She was getting alimony from my father to support the family, but it was only about one-tenth of what he was making as an anesthesiologist. She made use of the money, though. She bought a 1980 Toyota Corolla. She drove this little car to a facility that helped prepare her for that very important exam: the ECFMG. After ten years of not reading a medical book or gaining any medical experience, she decided to register for the examination.

While mothering three boys, she prepared to take one of the hardest exams in the world. For a whole year, she read for hours a day. She read book after book after book, and then followed that up by reading study guide after study guide. She went to Stanley Kaplan classes two or three days a week. She prayed, both at church and at home... oh, how she prayed. She was relentless. When it was time to take the test, we drove from Frankfort, Illinois, all the way to Des

Moines, Iowa. A friend of hers, who had graduated from the same university in the Philippines as my mother, came with us. She was going to take the test, too.

We waited for months for the results to come in the mail. Her friend got her results first and she did not pass. When my mother's results came in the mail, my brothers and I crowded around her as she opened the letter. She began crying. Then, fighting through her tears, she gleefully screamed, "I passed, my darlings! I passed! Now we can have everything we want. I am so happy." I remember thinking after she said that, I do have everything I want; Mom's happy again. From that point on, she began laughing and smiling a lot more, and she stopped wasting tears on my father.

My mother never had to preach the most important lessons in life. She showed us by example: how to get up after falling down, how anything is possible as long as you are willing to work hard. She showed us not to give up on love. Although, at times, love may fail you, if you keep trying, you will eventually find the one who is meant for you. After she became the woman she wanted to become, she fell in love with and married a man who is truly deserving of her. They remain happily married to this day.

~Ervin DeCastro
Chicken Soup for the Single Parent's Soul

76

The Price of a Dream

God gives us dreams a size too big so that we can grow in them.
~Author Unknown

I grew up poor—living in the projects with six brothers, three sisters, a varying assortment of foster kids, my father, and a wonderful mother, Scarlette Hunley. We had little money and few worldly goods, but plenty of love and attention. I was happy and energetic. I understood that no matter how poor a person was, they could still afford a dream.

My dream was athletics. By the time I was sixteen, I could crush a baseball, throw a ninety-mile-per-hour fastball and hit anything that moved on the football field. I was also lucky: My high-school coach was Ollie Jarvis, who not only believed in me, but taught me how to believe in myself. He taught me the difference between having a dream and showing conviction. One particular incident with Coach Jarvis changed my life forever.

It was the summer between my junior and senior years, and a friend recommended me for a summer job. This meant a chance for money in my pocket—cash for dates with girls, certainly, money for a new bike and new clothes, and the start of savings for a house for my mother. The prospect of a summer job was enticing, and I wanted to jump at the opportunity.

Then I realized I would have to give up summer baseball to handle the work schedule, and that meant I would have to tell Coach Jarvis I wouldn't be playing. I was dreading this, spurring myself with the advice my mother preached to us: "If you make your bed, you have to lie in it."

When I told Coach Jarvis, he was as mad as I expected him to be. "You have your whole life to work," he said. "Your playing days are limited. You can't afford to waste them."

I stood before him with my head hanging, trying to think of the words that would explain to him why my dream of buying my mom a house and having money in my pocket was worth facing his disappointment in me.

"How much are you going to make at this job, son?" he demanded.

"Three twenty-five an hour," I replied.

"Well," he asked, "is $3.25 an hour the price of a dream?"

That question, the plainness of it, laid bare for me the difference between wanting something right now and having a goal. I dedicated myself to sports that summer, and within the year I was drafted by the Pittsburgh Pirates to play rookie-league ball, and offered a $20,000 contract. I already had a football scholarship to the University of Arizona, which led me to an education, two consensus selections as All-American linebacker and being chosen seventh overall in the first round of the NFL draft. I signed with the Denver Broncos in 1984 for $1.7 million, and bought my mother the house of my dreams.

~Ricky C. Hunley
Chicken Soup for the Sports Fan's Soul

77

Bound by Love

Can I see another's woe, and not be in sorrow, too?
Can I see another's grief, and not seek for kind relief?
~William Blake

When my son was only five months old, he had to have major surgery on his head. My husband, Chris, and I were shocked and devastated. Cole's skull had fused together prematurely; he had no "soft spot." No one knows why this happens to some babies. The only remedy is surgery.

How could this have happened to my baby? What did I do wrong? I had been so careful during my pregnancy, eating well and refusing caffeine. No matter how many doctors explained to me that the condition was not my fault, I felt responsible.

The surgery and the ensuing five days at the hospital were the scariest, darkest, most exhausting days of our lives. Cole lay in his tiny hospital bed, IVs poking from his perfect little body. My faith faltered with his every breath. If not for the kindness and sensitivity of people—family, friends and hospital staff—I do not know how we could have made it through.

Even Cole tried to help. When Cole's head swelled so badly that his eyes fused shut and his eyelashes disappeared, I sang to him, my eyes never leaving his face. I was amazed to see him force a weak smile for me. To this day, I'm convinced he was trying to make me feel better.

After Cole's surgery, his head was swollen and bruised, and he had a dramatic zigzag scar from one ear to the other. I was hesitant to go out in public with my sweet boy. I felt defensive and protective, as if I might snap if anyone asked me what was wrong with my baby.

A few days after coming home from the hospital, Cole and I ventured out to buy some groceries. Still on pain medication, Cole was unhappy and cranky. On the way home, I noticed the gas tank indicator was flashing red for empty, so I stopped for some gas. Cole whined as I tried to get the keys out of the ignition. I needed the keys to open the gas tank, and for some reason I could not manage this simple maneuver. For some minutes, I tried pulling and tugging, until finally I feared I might break the key. Trying to compose myself, I reached for Cole and headed for the pay phone. Chris was not home. My heart raced. Cole began crying, and tears welled up in my own eyes.

I found my AAA card and called for help. This, after all, qualified as an emergency. Minutes later, the AAA truck pulled up, and a burly man stepped down and walked toward our car. His eyes immediately focused on Cole's head, the scar fresh and frightening. "You poor fellow," he said, "what have you been through?"

His kind words directed toward Cole opened a flood of tears in me. I began to sob. The stranger, whose name tag read Ron, simply placed a hand on my shoulder until I calmed down. Then he said to me, "As parents, we go through some very hard things. There's nothing worse than seeing your child in pain. I have two kids of my own, and I know all about it. Even an earache can seem like the end of the world. The thing is—we simply get through it." He reached for his wallet and pulled out numerous pictures of his son and daughter.

Cole and I sat with Ron as he talked about each picture. By the time he finished, Cole was sitting contently on my lap, and I felt a smile, the first in weeks, spontaneously come to my lips.

Although it took Ron less than one minute to get the keys from my ignition, this kind stranger spent over an hour with us, taking the concept of Roadside Assistance to a whole new level.

It's been five years since Cole's head surgery. Sometimes, Cole's red hair parts so that I can see the thick scar that crisscrosses his head; otherwise there are no visual reminders of his surgery.

Yet there are things unseen. The way I feel toward Cole is difficult to describe — it's as though our hearts had been bound together during that surgery.

Recently, at the park, a Guatemalan woman asked me about the scar. She said, "The angels came into him while his head was open." I don't know if I believe that, but the thought makes me feel better.

My younger son, Ry, fell from his bed one night when he was two years old and had to have stitches on his chin. I was with him as the nurses at the emergency room held him down while the doctor stitched. He clutched my hand and screamed, and it reminded me of Cole's surgery.

The room started to spin, and I was having trouble breathing. One of the nurses yelled, "Mom going down! Mom going down!" The next thing I knew, there was a wet towel on the back of my neck, and I was being instructed to put my head between my legs.

Going through these difficult things with my children doesn't end — whether it's watching them get stitches or seeing them be teased by other children. My heart is constantly being ripped in unexpected ways, despite both children, ultimately, doing fine. The hard times usually end up bringing us closer together.

Now four years old, Ry likes his scar. He points to it all the time. The other day, Cole complained that he didn't have a scar to show off like Ry.

"Yes, you do honey, I said, "Remember, you have that big zigzag scar that goes from ear to ear?"

"Oh, yeah," he said. "I guess I forgot."

I'm glad that he's forgotten about the scar, and I hope all the trauma behind it — as long as he remembers the love we forged going through it together.

~Victoria Patterson
Chicken Soup for Every Mom's Soul

78

The Day Mother Cried

Never look where you're going. Always look where you want to go.
~Bob Ernst

Coming home from school that dark winter's day so long ago, I was filled with anticipation. I had a new issue of my favorite sports magazine tucked under my arm and the house to myself. Dad was at work, my sister was away, and Mother wouldn't be home from her new job for an hour. I bounded up the steps, burst into the living room and flipped on a light.

I was shocked into stillness by what I saw. Mother, pulled into a tight ball, with her face in her hands, sat at the far end of the couch. She was crying. I had never seen her cry.

I approached cautiously and touched her shoulder. "Mother?" I asked. "What's happened?"

She took a long breath and managed a weak smile. "It's nothing, really. Nothing important. Just that I'm going to lose this new job. I can't type fast enough."

"But you've only been there three days," I said. "You'll catch on." I repeated a line she had spoken to me a hundred times when I was having trouble learning or doing something important to me.

"No," she said sadly. "There's no time for that. I can't carry my end of the load. I'm making everyone in the office work twice as hard."

"They're just giving you too much work," I said, hoping to find injustice where she saw failure. She was too honest to accept that.

"I always said I could do anything I set my mind to," she said, "and I still think I can in most things. But I can't do this."

I felt helpless and out of place. At age sixteen I still assumed Mother could do anything. Some years before, when we sold our ranch and moved to town, Mother had decided to open a day nursery. She had no training, but that didn't stand in her way. She sent away for correspondence courses in child care, did the lessons and in six months formally qualified herself for the task. It wasn't long before she had a full enrollment and a waiting list. Parents praised her, and the children proved by their reluctance to leave in the afternoon that she had won their affection. I accepted all this as a perfectly normal instance of Mother's ability.

But neither the nursery nor the motel my parents bought later had provided enough income to send my sister and me to college. I was a high-school sophomore when we sold the motel. In two years, I would be ready for college. In three more, my sister would want to go. Time was running out, and Mother was frantic for ways to save money. It was clear that Dad could do no more than he was doing already—farming eighty acres in addition to holding a full-time job.

Looking back, I sometimes wonder how much help I deserved. Like many kids of sixteen, I wanted my parents' time and attention, but it never occurred to me that they might have needs and problems of their own. In fact, I understood nothing of their lives because I looked only at my own.

A few months after we'd sold the motel, Mother arrived home with a used typewriter. It skipped between certain letters and the keyboard was soft. At dinner that night I pronounced the machine a "piece of junk."

"That's all we can afford," Mother said. "It's good enough to learn on." And from that day on, as soon as the table was cleared and the dishes were done, Mother disappeared into her sewing room to practice. The slow tap, tap, tap went on some nights until midnight.

It was nearly Christmas when I heard her tell Dad one night that a good job was available at the radio station. "It would be such interesting work," she said. "But this typing isn't coming along very fast."

"If you want the job, go ask for it," Dad encouraged her.

I was not the least bit surprised, or impressed, when Mother got the job. But she was ecstatic.

Monday, after her first day at work, I could see that the excitement was gone. Mother looked tired and drawn. I responded by ignoring her.

Tuesday, Dad made dinner and cleaned the kitchen. Mother stayed in her sewing room, practicing. "Is Mother all right?" I asked Dad.

"She's having a little trouble with her typing," he said. "She needs to practice. I think she'd appreciate it if we all helped out a bit more."

"I already do," I said, immediately on guard.

"I know you do," Dad said evenly. "And you may have to do more. You might just remember that she is working primarily so you can go to college."

I honestly didn't care. In a pique, I called a friend and went out to get a soda. When I came home the house was dark, except for the band of light showing under Mother's door. It seemed to me that her typing had gotten even slower. I wished she would just forget the whole thing.

My shock and embarrassment at finding Mother in tears on Wednesday was a perfect index of how little I understood the pressures on her. Sitting beside her on the couch, I began very slowly to understand.

"I guess we all have to fail sometime," Mother said quietly. I could sense her pain and the tension of holding back the strong emotions that were interrupted by my arrival. Suddenly, something inside me turned. I reached out and put my arms around her.

She broke then. She put her face against my shoulder and sobbed. I held her close and didn't try to talk. I knew I was doing what I should, what I could and that it was enough. In that moment, feeling Mother's back racked with emotion, I understood for the first time her vulnerability. She was still my mother, but she was something more: a person like me, capable of fear and hurt and failure. I could feel her pain as she must have felt mine on a thousand occasions when I had sought comfort in her arms.

Then it was over. Wiping away the tears, Mother stood and faced me. "Well, Son, I may be a slow typist, but I'm not a parasite and I won't keep a job I can't do. I'm going to ask tomorrow if I can finish out the week. Then I'll resign."

And that's what she did. Her boss apologized to her, saying that he had underestimated his workload as badly as she had overestimated her typing ability. They parted with mutual respect, he offering a week's pay and she refusing it. A week later Mother took a job selling dry goods at half the salary the radio station had offered. "It's a job I can do," she said simply. But the evening practice sessions on the old green typewriter continued. I had a very different feeling now when I passed her door at night and heard her tapping away. I knew there was something more going on in there than a woman learning to type.

When I left for college two years later, Mother had an office job with better pay and more responsibility. I have to believe that in some strange way she learned as much from her moment of defeat as I did, because several years later, when I finished school and proudly accepted a job as a newspaper reporter, she had already been a reporter with our hometown paper for six months.

Mother and I never spoke again about the afternoon when she broke down. But more than once, when I failed on a first attempt and was tempted by pride or frustration to scrap something I truly wanted, I remember her selling dresses while she learned to type. In seeing her weakness, I had not only learned to appreciate her strengths, I had discovered some of my own.

Not long ago, I helped Mother celebrate her sixty-second birthday. I made dinner for my parents and cleaned up the kitchen afterward. Mother came in to visit while I worked, and I was reminded of the day years before when she had come home with that terrible old typewriter. "By the way," I said. "Whatever happened to that monster typewriter?"

"Oh, I still have it," she said. "It's a memento, you know... of the day you realized your mother was human. Things are a lot easier when people know you're human."

I had never guessed that she saw what happened to me that day. I laughed at myself. "Someday," I said, "I wish you would give me that machine."

"I will," she said, "but on one condition."

"What's that?"

"That you never have it fixed. It is nearly impossible to type on that machine, and that's the way it served this family best."

I smiled at the thought. "And another thing," she said. "Never put off hugging someone when you feel like it. You may miss the chance forever."

I put my arms around her and hugged her and felt a deep gratitude for that moment, for all the moments of joy she had given me over the years. "Happy birthday!" I said.

The old green typewriter sits in my office now, unrepaired. It is a memento, but what it recalls for me is not quite what it recalled for Mother. When I'm having trouble with a story and think about giving up, or when I start to feel sorry for myself and think things should be easier for me, I roll a piece of paper into that cranky old machine and type, word by painful word, just the way Mother did. What I remember then is not her failure, but her courage, the courage to go ahead.

It's the best memento anyone ever gave me.

~Gerald Moore
Chicken Soup for the Christian Family Soul

79

Doubting Thomas

"*T*homas Tucker rarely stands in front of a crowd," the reporter wrote. This is true. Thomas gets excited around large crowds. When he is overstimulated, he needs an outlet to help calm himself down, like spinning.

My eight-year-old son is autistic. A very polite and loving boy, Thomas is considered "high functioning," which means that he can interact with others. His speech is significantly below age level, and he goes to speech therapy four times a week, but my husband and I try not to treat Thomas like he is different, and we expect him to do and learn things just like any other child. Because of his autism, he can become very focused on a specific subject, and it isn't always easy to get his attention.

We live in a small community in Kentucky, near Fort Campbell. Thomas is very well known here. It seems we cannot go anywhere in town without someone saying "hi" to him. Usually, I have to remind him to say "hi," back; otherwise, he would just walk right by. He has no idea how popular he is.

My husband had been deployed with the 86th Combat Support Hospital a month earlier for Operation Iraqi Freedom, when the Cadiz Renaissance Society planned a rally to support the troops. They called to see if Thomas would say the Pledge of Allegiance.

I was concerned about whether or not he would be able to maintain his focus in front of a large crowd. But he did know the pledge by heart. And he had been in school for five years. I knew I was probably more frightened than my son, so I told the society that Thomas would be glad to do it.

Decisions like these are usually made in tandem with my husband, but we hadn't heard from him since his deployment, and I had no idea when we would get to speak to each other. Especially since the rally was to support his father and the rest of the troops, I wanted my son to be able to participate. But what I really wanted, I realized, was for Thomas to tell me what he wanted. Was he interested in reciting the Pledge of Allegiance at the rally? And, could he do it?

Thomas doesn't understand war or why Poppa is gone. The only thing he seems to understand is that Poppa is at work, although he isn't sure why we took him to work one day but can't go and pick him up. Showing my feelings around Thomas is difficult because of his limited comprehension, so my sobbing and sadness are reserved for the times when he is at school or in bed. And determining how Thomas feels is near to impossible. So without input from my son or my husband, I agreed that Thomas would recite the Pledge of Allegiance.

We arrived at the rally a little before 2:00 P.M. It was supposed to be held at the high school football field, but the April rains forced us inside the local Baptist church, a building that has large and very beautiful stained glass windows. When we walked in, all Thomas could see were the windows. He began talking about *The Hunchback of Notre Dame* and was so fixated on the windows that he couldn't answer any of the reporter's questions.

I started to worry. Usually, when Thomas is focused on something, it's very hard to redirect him. Thomas has not been able to participate in the school productions because he wants to make up his own show when he gets to the microphone. Would that happen today?

Our seats were in the front pew of the church, right in front of the stage. There were numerous speakers and presentations, and Thomas enjoyed the music. He seemed to be focusing less on the windows and more on the rally, but I was definitely getting nervous about him being onstage.

The local VFW brought in the colors to post. Then the unthinkable happened. The VFW did not know that Thomas was supposed to say the pledge, and it is usually routine for them to recite it while posting the colors. We followed suit and recited the pledge along with them. When it was over, I was crushed: Thomas thought we were done and it was time to go home. We sat through the rest of the rally, but I'm sure my disappointment was visible to others around me. As the rally concluded, they sent the VFW back in to retire the colors. To our surprise, they asked if Thomas could come up and say the pledge as they took the colors out. This was it!

Thomas and I walked up to the stage. He stepped up to the microphone and spoke confidently and clearly as he recited the Pledge of Allegiance. His words were so precise that I had to take another look to make sure it was really him at the microphone. When he was done, he stepped back and remained still and quiet. I was astounded, and I could feel my eyes beginning to water. My heart swelled with such pride, and I wished my husband had been able to witness this.

My son stood still and quiet as an audience of two hundred people applauded.

I will never doubt Thomas again.

~Leah Tucker
Chicken Soup for the Military Wife's Soul

Moms & Sons

Making a Difference

*The best and most beautiful things in the world
cannot be seen, nor touched... but are felt in the heart.*
~Helen Keller

A Child's Playground

A child's playground could be anywhere—a backyard, the sidewalk, a ball field, a nursing home. A nursing home? That's exactly where I spent my afternoons as an eight-year-old. The red brick building, whose back door opened up into our church parking lot, had been the local medical clinic until a modern hospital opened just a mile down the road.

As the new hospital opened, my mother informed me of another business opening in its former residence. It would be called a convalescent center. Those were mighty big words for an eight-year-old.

"A what?"

"A convalescent center. It's like a hospital but only for older people."

I had no reason to question my mother on this subject, especially after learning that she would be working at the conva... well, nursing home, which is what everyone else called it. This would be her first job, at least since my memory was established, and would most likely alter my convenient everyday routine. Coupled with the departure of my sister, who married earlier that year, this was really going to shake up my world.

Luckily the nursing home was a short distance from school, which allowed me to walk there some afternoons. At first I enjoyed my visits as educational, learning about my mother's job and getting to know the patients. My mother walked me down the hall and into the individual rooms, introducing me to the occupants of each bed.

Some I knew already, many I knew by name, and most I knew by association with their families.

Few of the patients were mobile, most not able to venture out of their beds or much further than a nearby chair. Many could not feed themselves or tend to their personal needs without at least some assistance. Others could not even express themselves well enough to make their wants and wishes known.

My mother thrived on assisting the less fortunate. As a first-grader, I often waited outside the cafeteria for her to pick me up and take me home for a special-order lunch. Waiting along with me were members of the poorer families who couldn't afford to buy or even bring lunch. Before long, she was providing them homemade meals and delivering right to their chairs.

Some afternoons, as we waited for our ride home, she would go out of her way to come inside the school auditorium and give them money to spend on candy or ice cream, a luxury not always afforded to her own children. When I objected, she replied with New Testament logic.

"We must always take care of those who can't care for themselves."

Always spreading cheer, Mother was an angel-in-waiting to many of the patients, just what the doctor ordered or should have, and I was the tag-along on her skirt tail. Peeping around from behind her, too shy to speak aloud, I would be introduced even to the ones who couldn't see beyond the foot of their bed or remember my name after I left.

Still, I enjoyed walking the halls behind my mother and seeing the wrinkled faces light up as she entered each room. When tired of being a shadow, I took a seat in the front waiting room, which retained its clinical aroma and reminded me that the people here were either sick or in need of assistance. It was there that I met my friend.

She was old like all the others, though at age eight it's hard to tell the difference between fifty and ninety. To a child there is no degree of old, just old. The skin of her face was wrinkled and her hair was white, two of my prerequisites for old age. What made her different was the way she moved about, as though she were dutifully carrying out a task and stopping only long enough to check on the child sitting alone in the brown Naugahyde chair, rubbing my hands along the silver, metal arms that appeared more like the guardrails on the patients' beds.

Pausing in front of the chair and peering from up above me like the Grinch looking down over Whoville, she grabbed under my arms and hoisted me into the air before settling into the chair herself as I plopped into her lap. Story after story she told until I became antsy and bolted, sprinting down the hall to find my mother.

Occasionally my friend chased after me and I would discard my shoes, sliding down the hall in stocking feet until a heavy wooden door or a concrete wall blocked my path. When the hallway wasn't my track, it was my playing field. I sometimes brought my own playthings, like a rubber baseball or a miniature football, and she tossed these to me as I slid down the hall and made diving catches up against the wall.

Having to retrieve an errant pass or fumble, I frequently ventured into various rooms where I happened upon surprised but delighted patients who were pleased to be visited by an eight-year-old with football in tow. Lonely and longing to belong, many were happy to be visited by anyone.

Some of the patients I knew by name, their great-grandchildren were friends or classmates, but my friend had no relatives with whom I was acquainted. I knew her by sight, by voice, by action. Every day I thrilled to hear her stories, none of which remain with me in my mental scrapbook, and every day I delighted to play outdoor games inside this clinical stadium, displaying recently learned skills which I continued to develop.

One year later I grew from an atypical eight-year-old into a typical nine-year-old. At that age, one year represents a generation of transformations. The time came for my mind to wander and my interests to change. After school, playtime with friends and neighbors took priority and captured the place of my trips to the nursing home. My visits became sporadic and eventually ended completely.

In that year, I'd learned more about life than school had taught me about any subject matter. From the men and women in those rooms, I learned that what we need most is one another. From my mother, I saw that one caring soul can make a difference in the health and happiness of others. From my friend, I learned that age doesn't matter and the differences in people, when measured by age, are far less than we envisioned.

Never forgetting that year of fun and frolic in the nursing home, my mother kept me abreast of the latest proceedings on a regular basis. Occasionally, I would inquire about the status of certain individuals, particularly those who were related to my friends and classmates. Some were doing well, some weren't, and some had passed to a better place.

Remembering my friend and worried that she may have met that same fate, I asked my mother if that patient I used to play with was still alive. If so, I wanted to know how she was doing.

She gazed at me with a quizzical look on her face. "Which patient?"

"You know. The white-haired lady that used to play ball with me and tell me stories."

Quickly her appearance transformed to one of comical disbelief. "Son, she wasn't a patient. That lady was the director. She was my boss."

I was humiliated. Maybe I should have guessed because of her behavior, but I was basing things on how she looked, which to me was "old."

Through the years, my nursing home days found protective shelter far back into my recollection. High school passed and college arrived, while that year in the nursing home was hidden from my thoughts, only to be revived on the evening news.

The year was 1976, and I was back home for a few weeks, taking a break from college studies. One Saturday evening our family was relaxing in the den with the television on, not that anyone was watching closely.

Reading the paper, I only glanced up if something caught my

attention. While sewing, Mother occasionally peeked up at the screen, only to go right back to her household chores.

Suddenly, she pointed at the screen and looked over at me. "Do you recognize her?"

Not really paying attention, I asked, "Who?"

"Her," and she pointed at the white-haired lady being interviewed by the newsman. "Do you remember her?"

"Not really," and that was an honest answer. I had seen her on TV before but as far as knowing her personally, I couldn't say that I did.

"That's the lady you used to play with at the nursing home. Remember now?"

I did. Her face and mannerisms were no different than they were thirteen years earlier. She still seemed young and active though she again looked old. A chill came over me as I realized this was the same woman that used to tell me stories as I sat in her lap, and chased me down the hall, laughing as I slid and crashed into the wall.

Now, here she was on the national news, doing what she had been for the past several months. They called her Miss Lillian. She was helping her son, Jimmy Carter, campaign for president.

~Tony Gilbert
Chicken Soup for the Working Mom's Soul

81

The Flight of the Red-Tail

*T*he hawk hung from the sky as though suspended from an invisible web, its powerful wings outstretched and motionless. It was like watching a magic show until—suddenly—the spell was shattered by a shotgun blast from the car behind us.

Startled, I lost control of my pickup. It careened wildly, sliding sideways across the gravel shoulder until we stopped inches short of a barbed-wire fence. My heart pounded as a car raced past us, the steel muzzle of a gun sticking out the window, but I will never forget the gleeful smile on the face of the boy who'd pulled that trigger.

"Geez, Mom. That scared me!" Scott, fourteen, sat beside me. "I thought he was shooting at us! But look! He shot that hawk!"

While driving back to the ranch from Tucson along Arizona's Interstate 10, we had been marveling at a magnificent pair of red-tailed hawks swooping low over the Sonoran Desert. Cavorting and diving at breathtaking speeds over the yucca and cholla cacti, the beautiful birds mirrored each other in flight.

Suddenly, one hawk changed its course and soared skyward, where it hovered for an instant over the interstate as though challenging its mate to join in the fun. But the blast from the gun put an end to their play, converting the moment into an explosion of feathers dashed against the red and orange sunset.

Horrified, we watched the red-tail spiral earthward, jerking and spinning straight into the path of an oncoming eighteen-wheeler. Air brakes screeched. But it was too late. The truck struck the bird, hurling it onto the median strip.

Scott and I jumped from the pickup and ran to the spot where the stricken bird lay. Because of the hawk's size, we decided it was probably a male. He was on his back, a shattered wing doubled beneath him, the powerful beak open, and round, yellow eyes wide with pain and fear. The talons on his left leg had been ripped off. And where the brilliant fan of tail feathers had once gleamed like a kite of burnished copper against the southwestern sky, only one red feather remained.

"We gotta do something, Mom," said Scott.

"Yes," I murmured. "We've got to take him home."

For once I was glad Scott was in style, with the black leather jacket he loved, because when Scott reached for the terrified hawk, it lashed out with its one remaining weapon: a hooked beak as sharp as an ice pick. To protect himself, Scott threw the jacket over the bird, wrapped him firmly and carried him to the pickup. When I reached for the keys still hanging in the ignition, the sadness of the moment doubled. From somewhere high in the darkening sky, we heard the plaintive, high-pitched cries of the other hawk.

"What will that one do now, Mom?" Scott asked.

"I don't know," I answered softly. "I've always heard they mate for life."

At the ranch we tackled our first problem: restraining the flailing hawk without getting hurt ourselves. Wearing welding gloves, we laid him on some straw inside an orange crate and slid the slats over his back.

Once the bird was immobilized we removed splinters of bone from his shattered wing, and then tried bending the wing where the main joint had been. It would only fold halfway. Through all this pain, the hawk never moved. The only sign of life was an occasional rising of the third lid over the fear-glazed eyes.

Wondering what to do next, I telephoned the Arizona-Sonora Desert Museum. When I described the plight of the red-tail, the curator was sympathetic. "I know you mean well," he said, "but euthanasia is the kindest thing."

"You mean destroy him?" I asked, leaning down and gently stroking the auburn-feathered bird secured in the wooden crate on my kitchen floor.

"He'll never fly again with a wing that badly injured," he explained. "He'll starve to death. Hawks need their claws as well as their beaks to tear up food. I'm really sorry."

As I hung up, I knew he was right.

"But the hawk hasn't even had a chance to fight," Scott argued.

Fight for what? I wondered. To huddle in a cage? Never to fly again?

Suddenly, with the blind faith of youth, Scott made the decision for us. "Maybe, by some miracle, he'll fly again someday," he said. "Isn't it worth a try?"

For three weeks the bird never moved, ate or drank. We forced water into his beak with a hypodermic syringe, but the pathetic creature just lay there staring, unblinking, scarcely breathing. Then came the morning when the eyes of the red-tail were closed.

"Mom, he's... dead!" Scott pressed his fingers beneath the matted feathers. I knew he was searching, praying for a heartbeat, and the memory of a speeding car and a smiling boy with a gun in his hands returned to haunt me.

"Maybe some whiskey," I said. It was a last resort, a technique we had used before to coax an animal to breathe. We pried open the beak and poured a teaspoon of the liquid down the hawk's throat. Instantly his eyes flew open, and his head fell into the water bowl in the cage.

"Look at him, Mom! He's drinking!" Scott said, with tears sparkling in his eyes.

By nightfall, the hawk had eaten several strips of round steak dredged in sand to ease digestion. The next day, his hands still shielded in welding gloves, Scott removed the bird from the crate and carefully wrapped his good claw around a fireplace log where he teetered and swayed until the talons locked in. As Scott let go of the bird, the good wing flexed slowly into flight position, but the other was rigid, protruding from its shoulder like a boomerang. We held our breath until the hawk stood erect.

The creature watched every move we made, but the look of fear was gone. He was going to live. Now, would he learn to trust us?

With Scott's permission, his three-year-old sister, Becky, named our visitor Hawkins. We put him in a chain-link dog-run ten feet high and open at the top. There he'd be safe from bobcats, coyotes, raccoons and lobos. In one corner of the pen, we mounted a manzanita limb four inches from the ground. A prisoner of his injuries, the crippled bird perched there day and night, staring at the sky, watching, listening, waiting.

As fall slipped into winter, Hawkins began molting. Despite a diet of meat, lettuce, cheese and eggs, he lost most of his neck feathers. More fell from his breast, back and wings, revealing scattered squares of soft down. Pretty soon he looked like a baldheaded old man huddled in a patchwork quilt.

"Maybe some vitamins will help," said Scott. "I'd hate to see him lose that one red tail feather. He looks kinda funny as it is."

The vitamins seemed to help. A luster appeared on the wing feathers, and we imagined a glimmer on that tail feather, too.

In time, Hawkins's growing trust blossomed into affection. We delighted in spoiling him with treats like bologna and beef jerky soaked in sugar water. Soon, the hawk—whose beak was powerful enough to snap the leg bone of a jackrabbit or crush the skull of a desert rat—had mastered the touch of a butterfly. Becky fed him with her bare fingers.

Hawkins loved playing games. His favorite was tug-of-war. With an old sock gripped tightly in his beak and one of us pulling on the other end, he always won, refusing to let go, even when Scott lifted him into the air and swung him around like a bolo. Becky's favorite game was ring-around-the-rosy. She and I held hands and circled Hawkins's pen, while his eyes followed until his head turned 180 degrees. He was actually looking at us backward!

We grew to love Hawkins. We talked to him. We stroked his

satiny feathers. We had saved and tamed a wild creature. But now what? Shouldn't we return him to the sky, to the world where he belonged?

Scott must have been wondering the same thing, even as he carried his pet around on his wrist like a proud falconer. One day, he raised Hawkins's perch to twenty inches, just over the bird's head. "If he has to struggle to get up on it, he might get stronger," he said.

Noticing the height difference, Hawkins assessed the change from every angle. He scolded and clacked his beak. Then, he jumped—and missed, landing on the concrete, hissing pitifully. He tried again and again with the same result. Just as we thought he'd give up, he flung himself up at the limb, grabbing first with his beak, then his claw, and pulled. At last he stood upright.

"Did you see that, Mom?" said Scott. "He was trying to use his crippled wing. Did you see?"

"No," I said. But I'd seen something else, the smile on my son's face. I knew he was still hoping for a miracle.

Each week after that, Scott raised the perch a little more, until Hawkins sat proudly at four feet. How pleased he looked—puffing himself up grandly and preening his ragged feathers. But four feet was his limit. He could jump no higher.

Spring brought warm weather and birds: doves, quail, roadrunners and cactus wrens. We thought Hawkins would enjoy all the chirping and trilling. Instead we sensed a sadness in our little hawk. He scarcely ate, ignoring invitations to play, preferring to sit with his head cocked, listening.

One morning, we found him perched with his good wing extended, the crippled one quivering helplessly. All day he remained in this position, a piteous rasping cry coming from his throat. Finally we saw what was troubling him: High in the sky over his pen, another red-tail hovered.

His mate? I wondered. How could it be? We were at least thirty miles from where we'd found Hawkins, far beyond a hawk's normal range. Had his mate somehow followed him here? Or through some secret of nature, far beyond our understanding, did she simply know where he was?

"What will she do when she realizes he can't fly?" Scott asked.

"I imagine she'll get discouraged and leave," I said sadly. "We'll just have to wait and see."

Our wait was brief. The next morning, Hawkins was gone. A few broken feathers and bits of down littered his pen—silent clues to a desperate struggle.

Questions tormented us. How did he get out? The only possibility was that he'd simply pulled himself six feet up the fence, grasping the wire first with his beak, then his one good claw. Next he must have fallen ten feet to the ground.

How would he survive? He couldn't hunt. Clinging to his perch and a strip of meat at the same time with one claw had proven nearly impossible. What about the coyotes and bobcats? Our crippled hawk would be easy prey. We were heartsick.

A week later, however, there was Hawkins perched on the log pile by our kitchen door. His eyes gleamed with a brightness I'd never seen before. And his beak was open! "He's hungry!" I shouted. The bird snatched a package of bologna from Scott's hand and ate greedily.

Finished, Hawkins hopped awkwardly to the ground and prepared to leave. We watched as he lunged, floated and crashed in short hops across the pasture, one wing flapping mightily, the other a useless burden. Journeying in front of him, his mate swooped back and forth, scolding and whistling her encouragement until he reached the temporary safety of a mesquite grove.

Hawkins returned to be fed throughout the spring. Then one day, instead of taking his food, he shrank back, an unfamiliar squawk coming from his throat. We talked to him softly like we used to do, but suddenly he struck out with his beak. The hawk that had trusted us for nearly a year was now afraid. I knew he was ready to return to the wild.

As the years passed, we occasionally saw a lone red-tail gliding across our pastures, and my heart would leap with hope. Had

Hawkins somehow survived? And if he hadn't, was it worth the try to keep him alive as we did?

Nine years later, when Scott was twenty-three, he met an old friend in Phoenix, who had lived near our ranch. "You won't believe this, Scott," he said, "but I think I saw your hawk roosting in a scrub oak down by the wash when I was home for Christmas. He was all beat up, broken wing just like Hawkins."

"You gotta go take a look, Mom."

The next day I drove north until the dirt roads became zigzagging cattle trails and finally no trails at all. When a barricade of thorny mesquite trees and wild rose bushes stopped me, it was time to walk. Finally an opening through the maze led me down to a twisting, sandy river bed; a paradise for lizards, toads, tarantulas, snakes and small rodents of the desert. It was also an ideal feeding ground for a hawk.

Flanked by the spiny overgrowth on the banks above, I walked for hours, but saw no trace of Hawkins. But hope plays such tricks on the eyes, ears and mind, I confess there were moments when the rustling of leaves, the clumps of mistletoe swaying on high branches and the shifting shadows against gnarled tree trunks both kindled my fantasies and snuffed them out in a single second. Finding him was too much to hope for.

It was getting cold when I sensed I was being watched. All of a sudden, I was looking straight into the eyes of a large female red-tail. Roosting in a mesquite less than fifteen feet away, she was perfectly camouflaged by the autumn foliage surrounding her.

Could this magnificent creature have been Hawkins's mate? I wondered. I wanted so much to believe she was, to tell Scott I had seen the bird that had cared for her mate, scavenged for his food and kept him safe. But how could I be sure?

Then I saw him!

On a low branch, beneath the great dark shadow of the larger bird, hunched a tattered little hawk. When I saw the crooked wing, the proud bald head and withered claw, my eyes welled with tears. This was a magic moment—a time to reflect on the power of hope.

A time to pray for the boy with a gun. A time to bless the boy who had faith.

Alone in this wild, unaltered place, I learned the power of believing, for I had witnessed a miracle.

"Hawkins," I murmured, longing to stroke the ragged feathers, but daring only to circle around him. "Is it really you?"

Like a silent echo, my answer came when the yellow eyes followed my footsteps until he was looking at me backward, and the last rays of sunlight danced on one red feather.

Then, finally, I knew—and, best of all, my son would know. It had been worth the try.

~Penny Porter
Chicken Soup for the Unsinkable Soul

82

My Son the Rabbi

My mother never wanted me to be a rabbi. Her dream was that I receive a graduate degree in mathematics, learn accounting and take over my father's flourishing CPA practice. She was shocked and sad when I took her out to lunch and told her, "I am dropping out of graduate school. In the fall, I am beginning my rabbinical studies at the Jewish Theological Seminary."

My mother was deeply Jewish, but her Jewishness had nothing to do with religion. It was ethnicity, memories and a few eclectic religious observances. She had the greatest disdain for Jews who were observant. "They are more interested in the law than in people," she would say. I heard stories about the poor kids from a kosher family who had to bring their own hot dogs to neighbor kids' birthday parties because they could not eat the food.

My mother was disturbed when I began keeping kosher. "Now you won't eat in my house." When she and my dad first married, he wanted her to keep a kosher home. She said, "No, there are too many rules." Now, with her oldest son studying to be a rabbi, she bought a separate set of kosher dishes for me to use. When I told her that I would no longer drive on the Sabbath, and when I began to wear a yarmulke all the time, she became more concerned. "Why can't you be one of those liberal rabbis, who don't worry so much about the picayune laws?" That was not to be my dream.

For the first three years of rabbinical school, my mother waited for me to drop out and go into the family business. She described to me how delicious lobster was and asked me not to be too religious. One day she said, "I can live with you being a rabbi. But please don't make law more important than people."

Then one summer day, I finally convinced my mother that I would be a good rabbi. I shared with her a story of what happened to me on a cross-country drive.

During summer break from the seminary, another rabbinical student and I took off to drive across the country. As we mapped out our route, we discovered that we could reach Rapid City, South Dakota, by Shabbat. In Rapid City, there is one small synagogue that meets on an army base. It serves the few Jewish families in town, as well as those in the military. They were having Friday night services and invited my friend and me to join them.

"My friend and I would love to join you, but we do not drive on Shabbat. Is there any chance we can stay within walking distance?" The members of the Rapid City Jewish community were wonderful, arranging for us to sleep at the army base, and even getting us an invitation for a vegetarian dinner at someone's home. So began a beautiful Shabbat in South Dakota.

Friday night, the lay people led the service. More people than usual attended, intrigued that two seminary students were in town. At the Oneg Shabbat afterwards, my friend and I led a discussion on Judaism.

Suddenly, a little boy of about nine came up to me all excited. He had some things that his grandfather had left him, and he did not know what they were. The boy proudly showed me a velvet bag and took out a pair of tefillin. I explained that they are phylacteries worn by Jewish men on their head and on their arm during the weekday morning prayers. They literally fulfill the commandment, "You shall bind them for a sign upon your hand, and they shall be for reminders between your eyes."

The boy was excited. "Rabbi, show me how to put them on."

"I am not yet a rabbi, only a student," I responded. And I thought about what to do. It was Friday night. The sun had gone down. On Shabbat it is forbidden by Jewish law even to handle a pair of tefillin, let alone put them on. I was tempted to say, "Put them away until a weekday."

On the other hand, how many observant Jews pass through this small South Dakota town each year? Who else could show the boy how to wear his grandfather's tefillin? The opportunity might not present itself again. I told him to roll up his sleeve. And slowly, at this Friday night Oneg Shabbat, I taught the boy how to wear tefillin. Wearing his grandfather's tefillin on his arm and forehead, we said the Sh'ma together. I could see tears in his father's eyes. There was a joy in the boy's steps as he went home that evening.

When Shabbat was over, I called my mother. She said, "Do you mean that you broke the laws of Shabbat to put tefillin on that little boy?"

"Yes," I replied.

"Maybe you will be a good rabbi after all."

From that moment on, my mother supported my decision to enter the rabbinate. "Now I know that for you, people are more important than laws." She cried when I received my rabbinic ordination and proudly spoke of her son the rabbi. And my mother made one more promise: "I will not eat lobster anymore. At least, when I go out with you."

~Rabbi Michael Gold
Chicken Soup for the Jewish Soul

Mother of Three Thousand Sons

Who gives to me teaches me to give.
~Ancient Proverb

Thirty years ago, when I was a journalist in Philadelphia, I founded a small magazine called Umoja (Swahili for unity), which dealt with the issues confronting African Americans.

Because of the many letters the magazine received about the gang problem in our city, I asked my husband, Dave, to do some research. He began walking the streets, asking questions, talking to people and observing the problem firsthand.

My interest in the subject was purely professional—until the day Dave returned from a fact-finding mission and reported that our second son, Robin, was a member of a gang. Even worse, Robin was the gang's favorite, called the "heart of the corner." The heart is the favorite target if gang wars occur. I was shocked and frightened. How could this be happening in my home, in my family? But it was true. My son was a walking bull's-eye.

We had six sons, ranging in age from eleven to eighteen. I looked carefully at sixteen-year-old Robin that evening when he came home. I hadn't noticed it before, but Robin was different. He wore his clothing differently, and his manner was tougher. I confronted him, and he didn't lie. Yes, he was a gang member—and nothing I said or did was going to change that.

It was as if the bottom dropped out of my world. I stopped eating; I couldn't sleep. In an effort to save my son, I talked to social service agencies and the police, but no one seemed to have an answer. No one seemed able to do anything.

But everyone agreed that the breakdown of the family was the main source of the gang problem. I thought our family was strong, but for Robin, obviously something was missing.

Then an idea came to me. If family was the problem, could family also be the solution? Why not invite Robin's gang to live in our home? We could show them how real families work.

"Are you out of your mind?" Dave said when I told him my idea.

But I was on fire with my idea and wouldn't give up. Eventually he agreed to give it a try. Our other sons were more or less open — they knew Robin's life was on the line. Robin was thrilled with the idea — his boys and his family all under one roof.

Robin's gang leader, in serious trouble on the street, needed a place to hide out. He jumped at the chance to live with us, and the rest of the gang followed his lead. I called every parent I could reach to inform them of our plan, and they all agreed to let their sons come to us.

Our house was a small one, hardly large enough for our original family. When fifteen more boys moved in, it felt as crowded as a sardine can. But we made it work. All the boys slept in sleeping bags on the living room floor, and at mealtime the sleeping bags were rolled and stowed and folding tables and chairs were set up.

The first few weeks were difficult. Many times I wondered if Dave had been right about me being out of my mind. The boys chafed at doing chores, wouldn't participate in our family meetings and didn't want to get the part-time jobs I insisted on. But I was determined. I looked at the situation as if it were a puzzle and knew we'd have to find the right pieces if we were going to save the lives of these kids.

Finally we asked the boys to devise rules we could all live by. We were a little nervous about this because if we didn't like their rules, it would be difficult to enforce our own. But I breathed a sigh of relief when they read out their four rules: 1) No fighting in the house, 2) No drugs or drinking, 3) No girls in their rooms, and 4) No gang warring.

Maybe, just maybe, this will work, I thought. We found that since the boys had made up the rules, they were very good about keeping them.

The biggest and most pressing challenge was getting enough food. Our small savings were soon exhausted, but I had the idea to sell back issues of the magazine, *Umoja*, that were stored in our basement. The boys took stacks and peddled them all over Philadelphia, bringing home money to buy food.

We also approached a local church and told them we needed food. They were very supportive and sent notices to affluent parishes asking for food donations. The response was overwhelming. Soon we were inundated. Trucks loaded with food began coming down our block, headed for "The House of Umoja."

Now we had more food than we could use. We decided to give some away to people in the area who could use it. The boys were excited about distributing food. For most of them, it was the first time they had ever found themselves in the position of benefactors—giving something to help others.

After that, things began to fall into place. The boys got jobs and began contributing money to cover our household expenses. This new "gang" organized yard sales, sold candy door-to-door, and escorted elderly people to the bank.

We faced our largest hurdle the day George, one of the old gang's bitterest rivals, showed up asking to join our family. He realized he needed to take this drastic step, or he would end up in jail or dead. The boys were silent, wrestling with their hatred for their former enemy. But something new had entered their hearts—commitment to family, compassion, kindness—squeezing out their old "turf mentality." The tension broke as the boys accepted George into our new family.

As the weeks went by, I found myself falling in love with the boys; they became like my own children. Some of them even started calling me Mom. When the gang had first arrived, they'd all had street names like Killer, Snake Eyes, Bird, Crow and Peewee. I began to give them African names with special meanings. These were names that acknowledged their bravery or discipline or strength. Although it was never stated, the boys knew they had to earn those names.

Stories about our family spread all over the city. More and more boys came wanting to live with us. Finally, the state of Pennsylvania offered us a contract to officially care for these boys under the banner of foster care. We became "House of Umoja-Boystown," and with our new funds, we were able to expand, buying more houses on our street and hiring staff. The flow of boys kept coming... and we just kept opening our arms to gather them in.

It wasn't always easy living with these street kids. Most people had given up on them, and for good reason. Everyone else told these boys what to do, but I decided to listen to them instead. I tried always to see them through a mother's eyes, focusing on the good in them. It didn't always work, but enough of the time, it did.

It didn't work with one boy named Spike. From the first moment he arrived, he was a troublemaker—picking fights, refusing to work, disrupting meetings. When he left, I shook my head in despair. I had tried so hard to show him what it felt like to be a member of a loving family. I hated to lose any of the boys.

Some years later, a man came bursting into my office with a baby in his arms. It was Spike! "Mom," he said, placing his tiny daughter in my arms, "I want you to give her a name."

I was speechless with surprise, but as I looked at the beautiful child in my arms, her name came to me: "Fatima," I said softly, "it means 'Shining One.'"

Spike took Fatima from me and said, "I want to raise her like you showed me. I want her to be part of our family." Spike had heard me after all.

There have been other boys, too, who have surprised me by the depth of their dedication and commitment to our family. Two years after we started our experiment, we decided to have a gang conference. We asked the kids who lived with us, as well as the young men who had gone on to careers and their own homes, to go back to their old gangs and ask the new leaders to come to the conference to discuss ending gang deaths citywide. When one boy approached his old gang, they beat him up so badly he ended up in the hospital for a few days. But the minute he was released, that boy went straight back and again asked the gang leader if he would come to our house for the conference. Out of respect for his bravery, the gang leader attended.

Those were the first boys. In the thirty years since, over three thousand have followed. They are all my sons. Though some are now middle-aged men, they still come back to the house for advice or just to visit, play basketball and talk to the current group of young men who make up the family at the House of Umoja. They often bring their wives and children to celebrate birthdays and anniversaries.

I began with only the intention to save my son's life, but that simple act of motherly love grew, blossoming into a full-time service that has saved thousands of lives. While no one person can do everything, anyone can start something.

Unity, love, family—these are the things that saved my sons and will save many more sons to come. There is no limit to this love. My own name, Falaka, means "new day." Every day for me is another opportunity to be a mother to these boys who, more than anything, simply need love.

~Falaka Fattah
Chicken Soup for the Mother's Soul 2

84

Chicken Soup for the Soul

Terrorist Brownies

In helping others, we shall help ourselves, for whatever good we give out
completes the circle and comes back to us.
~Flora Edwards

My husband and I lived in Twentynine Palms, California, until he received orders for an unaccompanied year tour in Okinawa. Housing approved our request to remain, so we stayed in Twentynine Palms while he was away.

I decided to start my own little business of cake-and-goodie baking. I had several connections online through Marine support groups, and soon I was baking and delivering cakes to Marines stationed here. Shortly after 9/11, I received a call from a mom whose stepson was really stationed at Camp Lejeune in temperate North Carolina, but was out here in the hot desert taking part in a combined-arms exercise. She explained that it was his birthday soon, he loved brownies, and she wanted to do something very special for him. Was there any way I could find him and deliver a birthday treat of brownies to him? I said I would try.

After calling several people and being transferred from one office to another, I was finally patched into a field phone and was able to get a message to the Marine that he should call me about a birthday surprise. Later that night, he called me and of course was extremely suspicious. He asked me his mother's name, which I of course had to look up. After a mini-interrogation, he agreed to meet at the bowling alley when he had liberty the next day. His mother was unable to reach me that day, so I just went ahead and delivered the brownies, milk, napkins and a homemade card that said, "Love, Mom," to the bowling alley. He had not been able to make it, but his sergeant assured me the Marine would get the brownies. Mission accomplished—only better than I had ever imagined.

The next day, I received a phone call from his mother. It seemed this Marine finally got his brownies and called his mother at two in the morning. He asked her if she had sent him brownies. She said no, since she was half-asleep. At this point, her son began yelling, "There's been a freaking act of terrorism! You're not going to believe this, but someone sent me poison brownies saying they were from you. And I almost ate them!" He was in an absolute panic.

Then it dawned on her. "Wait, wait," she said, "Are they from an Amie Clark? I was half-asleep when you asked me. I did ask her to find you if she could, but didn't get back to her and had no idea that she found you and delivered the brownies!" They talked for a while longer. He was amazed that she had found him out there.

She later explained to me that their relationship had always been strained, to the point where, if she walked into a room, he would walk out. She had tried several times to reach out to him, but nothing had worked. She told me that the brownies finally opened a door for them. Her gesture made him realize that she loved him, not because she had to but because she wanted to. He now calls the house to talk to her and they sometimes talk for over an hour. The effort she made to send him a birthday treat touched more than his stomach; it touched his soul.

~Amie Clark
Chicken Soup for the Military Wife's Soul

85

Sweet Petunia

here it was—the advertisement that kept reappearing in her local newspaper, calling out to her. She could no longer resist. Much to the amazement of her family and friends, this rather dignified seventy-year-old woman followed her heart and enrolled in clown school.

Not surprisingly, she was the oldest in her class. She painstakingly mastered face painting and struggled to create recognizable balloon animals. But persist she did, graduating with top clown honors, and Sweet Petunia was born!

Most folks would find it rather strange that a woman of her age—and particularly someone so shy—would long to be a clown. But Sweet Petunia saw this as the perfect opportunity to unleash her long pent-up playful side without fear of disapproving eyes.

The transformation began. Chalk-white face, vivid blue widely-arched brows, cherry red nose and smiling, brilliant red mouth. She chose a baggy blue shirt and a pair of voluminous white trousers which puddled over red floppy shoes. Next came a bright yellow mop of hair topped by a white pork pie hat. In the hat, her signature—two purple petunias.

Out the door she would go, volunteering her services at hospitals, community fairs, store openings or a myriad of other places needing a good clown. "Don't you feel like a fool at your age?" snapped her older sister as they drove to a granddaughter's birthday party. These words served only to make Sweet Petunia more jubilant about her new pursuit. "What? Look at these faces! Smiling, laughing, having a good time. After all, everyone loves a clown!"

One particular afternoon, Sweet Petunia slapped her red floppy feet down the corridor of the downtown hospital. As she turned the corner of the east wing, her ears were assailed by a string of horrible curses and a clanking of metal hitting concrete. She hesitated and started to turn around. But just then a young sobbing nurse darted out of the room and nearly collided with her. Startled to see a clown, the nurse crumpled into Sweet Petunia's arms. Words shot from the young woman's mouth like staccato bullets, "He is awful! He's the meanest patient I've ever met! Sure, he's very ill, but that's not my fault!"

The young nurse was clinging so tightly to Sweet Petunia she could hardly breathe. "Let me see him," Sweet Petunia said.

The two moved slowly through the doorway. A waxen-faced man glared at them. As soon as his mind registered the fact that he was looking at a clown, his mouth fell open and he sucked in a great breath. "What? What is this? You look ridiculous!"

Sweet Petunia's red mouth smiled her brightest. "I look ridiculous? You look and sound ridiculous!"

"Get out! I'm dying, and I don't want to look at either one of you!"

The nurse moved to leave, but Sweet Petunia held her arm and stepped closer to the bed. "If you are dying, is this how you want to be remembered?" She pointed to the metal bedpan lying upside down between them where he had thrown it. "Some legacy!"

That was the first visit Sweet Petunia made to Room 226. "This unhappy man is going to be my special project," she resolved. In the following months she stopped by at least once a week. Never daunted by the patient's outbursts, Sweet Petunia was determined to reach that tender side she was convinced all people have no matter how tough the exterior.

Sometimes she would visit as Sweet Petunia and sometimes without the costume. Yet, something of Sweet Petunia remained even after the makeup was washed away and the clown suit was hanging in her closet. She always brought her supply of balloons. Patient 226 became very good at purple giraffes and green poodles. In spite of being very near death, this man's last weeks of life were brightened by Sweet Petunia. As for the young frightened nurse who introduced Sweet Petunia to Patient 226, she said, "Sweet Petunia gave me new perspective on how to help patients!"

Not only did Sweet Petunia change the life of the "meanest patient" and the young nurse, she also changed the lives of many others. But one of the most remarkable transformations took place in her. Once a reticent, shy individual who retreated from the limelight, she easily and happily became the focus of the room as Sweet Petunia. The affirmation she experienced as Sweet Petunia enhanced her ability to experience her "real" life. By the time Sweet Petunia had her five grandchildren, that radiant personality was full-blown and genuine. She was an absolute delight to Kevin, Victoria, Drew, Gabrielle and Gavin. One of their grandmother's favorite antics earned her the name "Grandma Whistle." Whenever she came for a visit, she wore a whistle around her neck and blew it, to the kids' delight.

Sweet Petunia has always been special to me, but one unexpected encounter was especially endearing. It had been one of the worst days at the company where I worked. Budgets were shrinking, files were vaporizing, impossible deadlines were looming. What next? The receptionist announced the arrival of my 4:30 appointment. I was unaware of any scheduled visitor for that time. Reviewing my calendar, I asked, "Are you sure this person has an appointment with me?"

"I think you need to see this one for yourself," replied our receptionist. Noting the wide grins of my associates, I headed down the hallway. Standing in our lobby, in all her clown glory, was Sweet Petunia! If I ever needed some love and laughter, it was now. She smiled and hugged me, squeezing out my stored-up misery.

When the onlookers knew it was safe to laugh, one of them asked, "Who is she?" With heartfelt love and admiration, I answered, "This is Sweet Petunia. Her grandchildren call her Grandma Whistle. I call her Mom."

~Leon J. Rawitz
Chicken Soup for the Golden Soul

Moms & Sons

Gratitude

All that I am, or ever hope to be,
I owe to my mother.
~Abraham Lincoln

86

Motherhood 101

The mother's heart is in the child's schoolroom.
~H. W. Beecher

At a recent neighborhood get-together, I was easily the oldest female there. Every other woman had young kids who were racing around, playing, laughing, occasionally generating shrill sounds that made their mothers cringe with embarrassment. One mom ordered her son to settle down, then quickly apologized. I assured her that he was just being a normal kid and that I was actually enjoying all the commotion. She didn't buy it. I said that children grow up way too fast, and suddenly they are gone. I explained that my husband and I had an empty nest: Our "baby" is twenty-seven, our oldest is thirty-one.

She asked, and I told her a little about my job and a lot about my four children. I shared that all four of our fledglings had tested their wings and moved to other parts of the country, that it was really hard to have them so far away, but that it made us feel good to know they were happily living in places that they had chosen for school, career or other unique opportunities. Fortunately, we manage to see all of them, plus our granddaughters, about three times a year.

I asked my neighbor how she spends her days. Almost apologetically, she stated that before she had children, she had an exciting professional career that kept her traveling all over North America, but that she was now a full-time homemaker, a "domestic engineer." She acknowledged that some days were tiring and monotonous, but stressed that it was mostly challenging and fun. She "couldn't imagine" not being home with her kids every day. I told her that I couldn't think of anything more important than raising a family. She seemed relieved that I didn't judge her negatively for being a stay-at-home mom. The truth is that I envied her immensely.

I had to fight off guilt over having had "latch-key kids." In fact, I felt like crying. Sometimes I miss our children terribly, and I'd give anything to recapture those wasted hours I spent working late in the office or those hours I spent in class instead of being at home with them.

That night I phoned "my baby." My voice cracked the second I heard him say hello. "Mom! What's the matter?" he asked.

"Nothing, honey," I lied. "I just miss you, I guess."

"I miss you, too, Mom," David answered, "but something else is going on. What's the matter?"

"I'm being silly," I confessed. "It's just that I saw all these young kids next door, and I wanted to tell you how sorry I am that I wasn't there when you got home from school every day. I'm sorry that I was gone at night sometimes too, when I had classes. I'd give anything to do it all over again and spend more time with you guys."

"Darn it, Mom. We never felt neglected! Quality of time is what counts. Some of my best memories are stuff we did together, even just sitting around talking. I can't think of any better mom I could have had, working or not! Never feel guilty! You did exactly what you needed to do."

Dave certainly let me have it. How glad I am that my kids feel comfortable enough to chew me out when I deserve it! I felt a million times better after we hung up. Dave's scolding would have been enough, but he obviously called his sister. Three days later, I received a priceless gift from Alyson in the mail. It was a typed paper that read:

Just a few of the wonderful things my mom taught me:
Support your kids' dreams, even if that means they move away
Rescue baby birds and squirrels
Love hearts, Ziggy, and teddy bears

Sing aloud, dance for joy, laugh with delight, smile big
Write
Learn to play music
Value fairness, kindness, honesty, and equality
Keep things in perspective
Surprise your kids with notes in their lunch boxes
Appreciate the simple things and know what really matters
Believe in yourself
You can achieve anything, no matter what the barriers
Help others less fortunate
Make pancakes in funny shapes
Grow and learn
Take family walks in the moonlight
Be sentimental
Drop everything to race outside and see a sunset
Be strong and independent
Look for the good in people and circumstances
Never feel guilty
Teach by example
Work to make a difference
Root for the underdog
Forgive
Siblings can be your best friends
Be loyal
Be silly
Take care of yourself
Be healthy
Treasure friends
Don't give up easily on commitments you make
Stay up late at night to talk with your kids even if you are tired
Feel lucky buying groceries
Stop to watch flocks
Cherish life — it is precious
Thank God for everything you have
Count and recount your blessings

Hug and say "I love you" a lot to the people you love
Put your family first

WOW! Did I teach my kids all that?

~Karen L. Waldman with Alyson Powers
Chicken Soup for Every Mom's Soul

87

She Has Always Been There

*S*hortly after graduating with my MBA from Brigham Young University, I read Dr. Raymond Moody's amazing book, *Life After Life*. The book is about Dr. Moody's research involving people of all ages, nationalities and religions who had survived near-death experiences (NDEs). Their stories shared many similar elements—these people had passed through a tunnel at death, had been greeted by a being of light and had experienced an instantaneous life review during which their life flashed before their eyes. Without exception, when they returned from the brink of death, their lives were forever altered—often dramatically.

The stories fascinated me. I bought and devoured every book I could find on NDEs. I shared the stories I had read with my Sunday school classes and even in my professional seminars. I couldn't figure out why I was so fascinated by the subject—and it would be almost thirty years before I found out. But I'm getting ahead of myself.

I'll never forget the day someone shared her personal NDE with me. In the late 1980s, I briefly mentioned my fascination with NDEs at a real-estate seminar in Cherry Hill, New Jersey. Following my presentation, a young woman in the audience approached me. She explained that she had been pronounced clinically dead after suffering a serious illness. The medical staff had actually zipped her up in a body bag to transport her body to the morgue. Then something shocking happened—the body bag began to move, and the "dead" person began pounding the inside of the bag. When they unzipped it, they realized the young woman was most definitely alive.

After her recovery, she didn't tell anyone what had happened during the few minutes while she had been "gone." She was afraid people wouldn't believe her—that they would think her crazy. Several years later, she finally told her mother what had happened.

Upon "dying," she told her mother, she saw her body lying "down there" as the medical staff was zipping up the body bag. She remembered being greeted "on the other side" by a beautiful woman who exuded so much love. This "angel lady" told the young woman that her "time" was not yet up, and that she needed to return to life. That's when she awoke to find herself zipped inside the body bag.

Her mother began to ask details about the "angel lady" who greeted her daughter. As the details came, the mother sensed that her daughter was describing a deceased relative. They rushed to the attic and began leafing through a pile of dusty old family albums. Suddenly, the young woman saw a photo that shocked her.

"That's her!" she exclaimed with excitement. "That's the angel lady!" Both mother and daughter stared at the photo in silence. Finally her mother spoke.

"I've never shown you these photos, because they are too painful for me to look at," she said softly. "The woman in the photo is my mother—your grandmother. She died when I was pregnant with you."

As the young woman shared her story, I felt warm goose bumps sweep over me. Perhaps her story touched me so deeply because, just as this grandmother had not lived to see the birth of her granddaughter, my own mother had not lived to see me.

Amy Judd Allen died in childbirth on May 20, 1948—the day I was born. Because of several disappointing miscarriages, she had laid in bed for months, determined that this pregnancy would be successful. I can only imagine how much she wanted to hold me in her arms after having carried me for nine long and painful months. And then, on that most joyous day, she didn't make it through the valley of death. As I came into the world, she passed out of it.

My forty-five-year-old father, sixteen-year-old sister, and ten-year-old brother did a wonderful job raising me, but I missed the warm, tender nurturing that most other babies enjoy. I still do. Mother's Day is always such a strange day for me. Fathers, sons and daughters stand up in church and praise their wives and mothers — then honor them with flowers and gifts. As I watch these ceremonies, I think how fortunate those people are who have had mothers to watch over them, care for them, correct them, nurture them, instruct them and love them. For most of my life, I've felt that I missed something very special.

And then, I had my own NDE.

It was March 15, 2003. I was returning from giving a speech to a thousand people at the Anaheim Convention Center. It was about 9 P.M. on a dark, rainy night, and as I drove home, I listened to the news of dozens of accidents on the California freeways caused by the heavy rain. I don't remember anything about "my" accident. A driver in the sole car behind me on that dark night witnessed my car veer off the road at full speed and smash into a large tree in the heavy brush just a few feet off the freeway. This "Good Samaritan" stopped, immediately called 911 from his cell phone and waited until the ambulance arrived. My car was so demolished that they had to cut me out with the Jaws of Life. If it hadn't been for this single witness, I most certainly would have bled to death in the darkness. I remember none of it.

I was rushed to the hospital with massive injuries. I was put on life support in a medically induced coma as they assessed the damage. I don't remember a thing. When I came to my senses a few days later, with my wife and two of my children at my bedside, I was shocked to learn how close I had come to dying.

I experienced only a few of the elements of a "classic" NDE. I don't remember seeing my body through spirit eyes. I don't remember a tunnel or a being of light or a life review. But, without doubt, my life has been forever altered. And the strangest thing happened as I came "back to life." I knew that my "angel mother" had been there that night — that she had been watching, letting me know that it wasn't my time. In ways that are hard to explain, I now realize that she has always been there—watching over me, caring for me, correcting me, nurturing me, instructing me and loving me, even though I couldn't see her.

It's been two years since my NDE, and I still feel her presence. I often find myself driving down the freeway, whispering under my breath, "Thanks, Mom—for the life you gave me and the life you gave for me. Thank you, thank you, thank you, thank you...."

~Robert Allen
Chicken Soup for the Latter-Day Saint Soul

88

Mom's Special Day

*I*n the early eighties, when my two sons were toddlers, I put them in day care when I went to work. Like thousands of other working moms, I, too, was plagued by the articles and news stories about the negative impact of children growing up in day care. Despite the growing ranks of women in the workplace, society's message still seemed to be: "Mothers belong at home with their children." Period! End of discussion.

Although I was doing my best to balance wholesome family life with an aggressive career track, I was filled with guilt and self-doubt. Am I ruining my kids for life by sending them to day care? Will they resent me? Should I be a stay-at-home mom?

On Mother's Day 1993, at the traditional eighth-grade Mother's Day Tea, the answers to my questions came in a very unexpected way. To celebrate this day, the children had written poems about their mothers. I sat there, listening to poems describing cookie-baking, Halloween-costume-making, birthday-party-giving and car-pool-driving moms. There was laughter and plenty of tears as we all heard how our teenage children saw us.

Then it was Justin's turn. As he walked to the front of the room, I held my breath, and my stomach did a flip-flop. How would his poem describe me?

My Mom
How will you be remembered?

A woman who owned her own business and became very successful,
You will be remembered by the way you fulfilled all your dreams,
How you spent time looking after kids while you reached the top —
Two young boys, rowdy as monkeys.
You were a great mom, a great wife, a great person —
Mom, how on earth did you do it?
Legends will be told about you, Mom.
When I needed help, you were there.
Your shoulder was a place where I could rest my head.
What would I do without you?
How would I survive?
What I'm trying to tell you is, I love you, Mom.

~Justin

In those few glorious moments, as I heard his words, all my doubts and fears about being a working mom were put to rest. Then and there, I knew, after years of babysitters, camps and daycare, that my son did not resent me. To the contrary, he let me know that through it all, I was always there when he needed me. He let me know that he was proud of me.

When he finished reading his poem, he looked over at me, sitting in the front row of the audience. He smiled that wide glimmering, silvery smile that only kids with braces are capable of. My first impulse was to race up and wrap my arms around him—like you would a small child—yet I resisted. Justin was a thirteen-year-old young man, and the process of "letting go" had begun. A thumbs-up from one proud mom said it all.

~Connie Hill
Chicken Soup for the Working Mom's Soul

89

Speaking

Each day comes bearing its own gifts. Untie the ribbons.
~Ruth Ann Schabacker

I was no different from any other mother.

When my little boy, Skyler, was born, I longed for the day he would talk to me. My husband and I dreamed about the first sweet "Mama" or "Dada." Every cry or coo was a small glimpse into my son's mind.

My baby's noises were even more precious to me because Skyler had been born with several health problems. At first, the problems had delayed his development, but once they were safely behind us, I looked forward to my son's first words. They didn't come.

At age three, Skyler was diagnosed autistic, a developmental disability destined to affect his social and emotional well-being his entire life. Skyler couldn't talk—wouldn't talk. I would probably never hear any words from him at all. In a store, I would hear a child calling "Mommy," and I would wonder if that were what my little boy might sound like. I wondered how it would feel to hear my child call out for me.

But I could have learned to live with his silence if it weren't for another hallmark characteristic of autism: Skyler formed no attachments. He didn't want to be held, much preferring to lie in his bed or sit in his car seat. He wouldn't look at me; sometimes, he even looked through me.

Once, when I took him to the doctor, we talked to a specialist who was my size, age and who had the same hair color. When it was time to go, Skyler went to her instead of me — he couldn't tell us apart. When Skyler was three, he spent three days at Camp Courageous for disabled children in Iowa, and when he returned he didn't even recognize me.

This pain was almost unbearable. My own son didn't even know I was his mother.

I hid the pain, and we did the best we could for Skyler. We enrolled him in our local area educational agency pre-school, where the teachers and speech pathologist worked hard to help Skyler connect with the world around him. They used pictures and computer voice-machines that spoke for him, and sign language. These devices gave me little glimpses of who Skyler was, even if he didn't understand who I was. "He will talk," the speech pathologist insisted, but inside, I had given up hope.

The one dream I couldn't let go was to have Skyler understand that I was his mom. Even if I never heard him say, "Mom," I wanted to see the recognition in his eyes.

The summer of Skyler's fourth year was when it started. A smoldering ember of understanding in him sparked, and fanned by our efforts, steadily flamed. His first words were hardly recognizable, often out of context, never spontaneous. Then, slowly, he could point to an item and say a word. Then two words together as a request. Then spontaneous words. Each day, he added more and more recognizable words, using them to identify pictures and ask questions. We could see his understanding increase, till his eyes would seek out mine, wanting to comprehend.

"You Mom?" he said one day.

"Yes, Skyler, I'm Mom."

He asked his teachers and caregivers: "You Mom?"

"No, Skyler, not Mom."

"You my Mom?" he said back to me.

"Yes, Skyler. I'm your Mom."

And finally, a rush of understanding in his eyes: "You my Mom."

"Yes, Skyler, I'm your Mom."

If those had been Skyler's only words ever, they would have been enough for me: My son knew I was his mother.

But Skyler wasn't done.

One evening I leaned against the headboard on Skyler's bed, my arms wrapped around him. He was cozily tucked between my legs, our bodies warm and snug as I read to him from one of his favorite books—a typical affectionate scene between mother and son, but because of Skyler's autism, one that I could never take for granted.

I stopped reading. Skyler had interrupted me, leaning back his head so he could look me in the eye.

"Yes, Skyler?"

And then the voice of an angel, the voice of my son: "I love you, Mom."

~Cynthia Laughlin
Chicken Soup for the Mother's Soul 2

90

The Beach Trip

The manner of giving is worth more than the gift.
~Pierre Corneille

It wasn't a typical trip to Carolina Beach. Oh, I had the cooler, beach chair and towel, but it still wasn't the same. I wasn't going to the beach to relax—I was going to remember my son, Cameron, who died of leukemia in March 1998. You see, on this day Cameron would have turned twenty-one.

I decided to go to a favorite part of Carolina Beach—the one within walking distance of a McDonald's (in case you get bored of the beach and want some fries).

Now, it's typical that little kids are drawn to me. Maybe it's the fact that I smile at them, maybe it's the fries, but it does happen. So I was not surprised to have one small child covering my feet with sand and another playing with his toys right by my beach chair. Their parents were seated behind me, and the two boys spent about an hour running back and forth from my chair to their parents'.

"What's your name?" I asked the oldest.

"Alex. I'm five."

"Oh, I have a son named Alex. He's twelve."

He continued covering my feet with sand until his parents walked by on their way to the water's edge.

"I'm going in with my parents."

"Okay."

"My little brother HATES the water—he doesn't go in ever."

"That's okay. I'll watch him while you go into the ocean with your mom and dad."

The smallest boy, about one-and-a-half, watched his brother run off, turned to me and reached up. Of course I picked him up, sat him on my lap and offered him some fries. We waved to the family down in the water, ate chips and just chilled out.

Suddenly, he slipped off my lap, took my hand and pulled me toward the water. I walked him to the edge, and he giggled when the water lapped over his feet. When a bigger wave came and hit his legs even harder, he started laughing. I scooped him up, swung him around, put him on my hip and walked over to his mom and dad.

"What a cutie he is," I said.

"Oh, he's very afraid of the water. I can't believe he's in the water at all."

I told them that he had taken my hand and pulled me in. "I told your son Alex that I have a son named Alex at home. Your little one is so cute. What's his name?"

"Cameron."

And my heart stopped. I looked into that little boy's eyes, and he looked right back and touched my face.

Thank you, Cameron.

~Dawn Holt
Chicken Soup for the Grieving Soul

91

Mother's Day

Sitting on one of the most beautiful tropical beaches on earth, I had every reason to be happy. For the past three years, my husband and I had been living on the private island of Lana'i, Hawaii. The calm blue Pacific stretched endlessly before me. The white sand felt warm beneath me, and the palm trees above swayed gently in the trade winds. Most people considered this to be paradise.

So why in the world was I crying?

It was my fortieth birthday, and I found myself battling with the same demons I had struggled with for the past twenty years: my fears of becoming a mother.

I'm sure it started with my own childhood. Though my parents loved me the best way they knew how, life dealt them some tough blows. My father, a Jewish soldier fighting on the front lines of World War II, experienced horrors that no human being should have to endure, including cleaning the ovens where his own people were slaughtered. He returned home a broken man, unable to give me the kind of love a child hungers for. My mother, a talented writer, gave up that life to marry and work jobs she hated. She spent the rest of her life bitterly disappointed. Somehow, between the two of them, I got lost. As a result, the idea of becoming a parent left me confused. I held two completely opposite images of motherhood: the harsh reality of my mother's despair versus the Betty Crocker television mom who baked perfect cookies, raised perfect children and handled life with a perfect smile. Becoming a mom myself, with all of my own real-life wounds and inadequacies, left me terrified.

As the years passed, I convinced myself I didn't want children. I, too, was a writer, and set my sights on birthing bestselling novels. There was no room for motherhood in my life.

I continued avoiding the whole issue, until I met Dennis. We met in a big city on the East Coast and fell head over heels in love. Within the year, we were engaged. Shortly after, work took him to Hawaii. We married there. Through a quirk of fate we ended up living on the tiny, rural island of Lana'i. Coming from a big crowded city myself, Lana'i was like a fairytale. There were no stoplights, no fast-food restaurants and virtually no crime. The entire population of 2,700 people lived in Lana'i City. It was a charming village with hundreds of giant pine trees, colorful wooden plantation houses with tin roofs and free-roaming roosters.

On Lana'i, people knew each other by the car they drove. In fact, the only "traffic jam" that existed on this island was when a car or an old Jeep suddenly stopped because the driver wanted to "talk story" with a friend strolling down the dirt road.

A tremendous sense of community, or 'ohana as it's called in Hawaii, existed on Lana'i. Slowly and almost magically, Lana'i melted away my urban crustiness. I began to slow down and truly connect to people for the first time. My heart began to open up more and more. I believe this was Lana'i's special gift to me.

As my relationship with Dennis deepened, I found myself wanting to give him a baby. It was a spontaneous feeling that I couldn't control. But when I admitted it out loud, all I could do was cry. Over and over, Dennis reassured me that we didn't need to have a child. He already had a grown son from a previous marriage. Yet he had spoken of his sadness about missing the day-to-day raising of his son. He would have loved to be "a true dad."

This all brings me back to what happened on my fortieth birthday. The night before, I came home feeling very upset. I knew my biological clock was ticking and winding down. I realized I had to face this fear and make a decision. But everything in me screamed, "No!" If I decided not to be a mother, I was afraid I would regret it in my final hours. If I chose to have a child, I was afraid my inadequacies would hurt my son or daughter the way I had been hurt.

Finally, late in the night, I crawled out of bed and got down on my knees. Tears flowing, my prayer was short but heartfelt: "Help me with this decision, God. Please. All I ask for is peace."

The next morning, I drove to the beach to be alone. Sitting by myself on the sand, staring blankly at the horizon, I felt exhausted. How would I ever make this life-altering decision?

Every once in a while I focused on the ocean, searching for my friends, the dolphins. On Lana'i, we were blessed with a group, or pod, of Pacific Spinner dolphins who have made this bay their home. Sometimes as many as 500 would come here to rest and play.

Over the past three years, my husband and I frequently swam with these dolphins. In the morning, we'd search for distant splashes that only a trained eye could see. When we spotted them, we'd don our masks and slowly swim out. The trick to getting the dolphins' attention, we discovered, was singing into our snorkels. We'd sing and splash around like kids, and minutes later the dolphins would show up. There are only two ways wild dolphins will approach you. Either the entire pod arrives, sometimes in the hundreds, or a few of their largest males will swim close by. These scouts then return to the group, letting them know you're okay. Dolphins are an intelligent, close-knit community. They would never send their most vulnerable members to investigate.

This particular morning, I thought I saw the telltale splashes offshore. I slipped on my mask and entered the water. My eyes were still puffy from crying all night from obsessing about this challenging decision. I swam out, weakly humming into my snorkel. Floating face down, looking into the clear water, I waited. About ten minutes later I glimpsed a ghostly shadow in the distance. Assuming this was the scout, I stayed perfectly still, never expecting what was about to happen. Through the turquoise mist a single dolphin emerged. What I didn't see immediately was the baby by her side.

They swam closer and closer, coming within a few feet of me. It was mesmerizing, and I was witnessing a miracle. Mother and baby began circling me. I could easily make out the stripes on the baby—proof it was truly a newborn. I felt a powerful connection with the mother. The instant our eyes met, I heard a gentle voice in my head. It was as crystal clear as the water surrounding me. Relax, the voice whispered. Motherhood is beautiful.

For almost an hour, the mother and baby dolphin circled around me. The whole experience was like a dream: the shimmering Pacific, the gentle dolphins so close. It was as if they were there to comfort me. Guests from the nearby hotel began gathering on the shore. They couldn't believe their eyes.

Eventually, some people swam out to investigate, which sent mom and baby back into the protection of the distant pod. I left the water in a trance.

Though my despair about the decision lifted, three years passed and still I didn't conceive. By my forty-third birthday I assumed that the dolphin encounter was just a coincidence, and that perhaps God had made a mistake. Others, who were less troubled than I, might have somehow seen the episode as an answer to my prayer for peace. I could only assume that if I hadn't gotten pregnant by now, I obviously wasn't meant—or fit—to be a mother.

A few weeks after my forty-third birthday, I found myself praying again. Something was missing in my life. With all my heart, I asked God for a fundamental change. Something so basic, it would permanently alter everything.

Only days later, I discovered I was pregnant. That was over nine months ago. Today, as I write this story, my newborn son, Reyn, lies sweetly and peacefully at my breast. A perfect little boy, as beautiful as any angel I could imagine.

So why in the world am I crying now?

Because I'm overwhelmed with gratitude and joy. Overwhelmed with the sheer miracle of his birth. Overwhelmed with such deep love that sometimes all I can do is weep.

I can see now, as clearly as I saw mama and baby dolphin

swimming beside me, that God was utterly and absolutely right. Relax, motherhood is beautiful.

~Marcia Zina Mager
Chicken Soup from the Soul of Hawaii

Gains and Losses

Most of us have experienced unforgettable moments in our lives. The moment that I will never forget happened in my family.

For the first fifteen years of my life, I was the only child in my family. I didn't have any siblings. Fortunately, I've always had my parents, who love and care about me a lot. They help solve any problem and they will do anything for me. What I'd never really thought about is that, someday, one of them could no longer be there for me.

One day, I found out that my mother was pregnant, which was big news in my family. Everyone was excited and happy, especially me. I imagined that I would have a baby brother, and I thought about playing and having fun with him. He would have a cute face and look at me with his naive eyes, begging me to play with him. I was expecting that day to come soon. I kept asking my mother questions about what my brother was going to look like, what he would eat and when he was going to be born.

Finally one morning, my mother went into labor and she and my father went to the hospital, while I went to school. Of course, I thought everything would be fine. After all, women have babies every day. Thus, I was hoping to see my baby brother as soon as I got to the hospital.

After school, when I went to the hospital, my brother had already been born. But my mother was still inside the operating room, while my father waited anxiously outside. After waiting for a long time, the doctor came out and told us that after my mother had given birth to my brother, they had trouble stopping the bleeding. He told us not to worry; my mother would be fine. Then, he went back into the operating room. Seconds later, lots of doctors and nurses rushed inside. My father and I were growing more anxious by the minute. Waiting was very painful for us, because we had finally realized that anything could happen and all we could do was wait.

At 7 P.M., my mother came out of surgery. She lay on the bed with an oxygen mask and an IV. Her skin was ghastly pale, and her eyes were closed.

"Mom, Mom...," I called to her, but she didn't react. The doctor told us that if my mother survived this night, she would be fine. Then the doctors sent my mother to the intensive care unit.

Inside the room were many instruments for checking blood pressure, pulse rate and heart rate. Standing next to the bed, I tried to talk to my mother, whether she could hear me or not.

"You have to wake up, you have things that you have not done yet.... You have me, my father and your newborn son. You cannot just leave us... and you will be fine... trust me...."

I was scared to death. At that moment, I felt that I would lose my mother forever—that she was never going to come back.

Many thoughts flashed through my mind. What would life be like if the unthinkable happened—life without my mother? I could only imagine that my life would be full of darkness, sadness and hopelessness. I would lose my closest relative, my dearest friend, and I would never again have the chance to enjoy the love of my mother. Remember, during these fifteen years, my mother was always around, watching over me, no matter what. I could not imagine how I was possibly going to survive without her.

Of course, I told myself that it would not happen, that she might leave me after thirty, forty, fifty or more years, but definitely not now, not yet. It was too early. I wasn't ready to let her go.

After I slowly came back to reality, I noticed that a flood of tears was running down my cheeks.

My mother survived that night. You can imagine my great relief when she woke up the next morning. I was so excited. I gave her a big hug as I cried tears of happiness.

My mother told me that she had actually heard the words that I had said to her when she was unconscious. Three times she had almost stopped breathing, but she told herself to stay alive, for us, her family.

Later, many nurses said my mother was incredibly lucky to survive because she had lost a lot of blood. Of course, I gave them the most glorious smile, which said it all.

Today, my brother is almost two years old. On the day of his birthday, I always remember this unforgettable event in my life. I remember that I'm a really lucky person, with great parents and a wonderful little brother.

~Xiao Xi Zhang
Chicken Soup for the Preteen Soul

93

Mom Taught Me to Play Baseball

On June 1, 1995, I was standing on the pitcher's mound at Rosenblatt Stadium in Omaha, Nebraska, about to pitch the first game of the College World Series. I had completed my warm-up tosses, and I was ready to make the first pitch. It was a perfect Midwestern Saturday afternoon. The sky was a deep blue with a handful of clouds. Though it was humid, a light breeze kept it from being too hot. Twenty-five thousand fans were in the stands, three times more than had ever watched me pitch. The pregame crowd noise I was used to was louder here, more intense than anything I had ever experienced. I could feel the crowd's excitement and anticipation. The game was being televised nationally. Ten million people would be watching; I could feel the pressure. I paced around the back of the pitcher's mound, my mind racing, my mouth dry, my heart pounding. I was having a hard time catching my breath.

We were playing Cal State Fullerton, the number-one-ranked team in the country. In my three years at Stanford University, this was the first time we had advanced to the College World Series.

As I stood behind the mound doing my final stretches, I was trying to focus. Instead, I found myself caught up in the moment. I looked into the stands, something I rarely did from out on the mound. The crowd was an awesome and daunting sight. Right above our dugout was the Stanford cheering section, where all the family, friends and people associated with the university were sitting. In that sea of cardinal-red shirts, hats and signs, I saw my mom, Lois Dempsey Robbins.

I wouldn't be here without her, I thought. My mom taught me how to play baseball, sitting on our living room floor, rolling a ball back and forth even before I could walk. When I was bigger, after the divorce from my dad, she'd take me onto the front lawn to play catch. She got me started in T-ball, and I'd been playing ever since. She was my biggest fan and my first coach.

I gripped the ball in my left hand, sweat already dripping down both my arms. I thought about how quickly Mom had learned to fend for herself and her two kids, my sister Lori and me. Dad got sick after the divorce and had stopped paying child support. In the midst of this, she took the risk of starting her own business, something in which she had no experience, because she wanted the flexibility to be with her kids when we needed her. Years later, she told me, "I was not going to have some boss tell me when I could or could not see my kids." That's my mom: strong, determined and willing to do whatever it takes to be there for Lori and me.

The announcer's voice boomed in the background: "Now, batting for the Cal State Fullerton Titans, left fielder Tony Miranda." The game was about to begin, but my thoughts were still focused on the stands and on my mom.

I could count on one hand the number of my games that Mom had missed while I was growing up. In high school and college, she came to every local game and even some of the games on the road. It wasn't surprising to look up now and see her sitting proudly in the stands. She'd been doing that my entire career. She never flinched or wavered in her support of me. I could always feel her love and her commitment; I could always hear her voice cheering loudly as I ran off the field, "Way to go, Mike!" No matter what was going on in her life, she was there.

As Miranda stepped into the batter's box, I realized I was pitching in the College World Series because of the support Mom had given me throughout my life. She'd shown me what determination, loyalty and power meant. She'd demonstrated through her life everything that I needed to succeed in mine. I stepped up onto the pitching rubber and gathered my thoughts. I took the sign from my catcher, wound up and fired my first pitch, forever and gratefully my mother's son.

~Mike Robbins
Chicken Soup for the Single Parent's Soul

Moms & Sons

Learning from Each Other

Love doesn't make the world go 'round.
Love is what makes the ride worthwhile.
~Franklin P. Jones

94

My Son, the Street Person

*L*et me start right off by confessing: my son lives on the streets. Of course, in response to casual inquiry about him, I usually say, "He's doing great." If pressed further I say, "He's traveling." No one can fault that. After all, many restless young men spend a year roaming before they settle down and go to college. Get it out of their systems, sow their wild oats, find themselves... you know. But questioners may remember that this is his second year out of high school. How many wild oats has he got?

Most of the interrogators let it drop. They are too busy with their own lives, and perhaps they sense some great darkness lurking behind my answers. But some people are tenacious. "Where is he?" they want to know. A tale of fictional intrigue is on the tip of my tongue, but for some reason I am compelled to tell the truth, so I answer, "New York City." I hear the wheels turning—how long can you be traveling in New York City? There are a lot of sights, a few good day trips, but hey, two weeks ought to do it. A writhing can of worms gapes open: "What's he doing? Where's he living?"

"My son is a street person," I must respond.

I glimpse the shocked response before it is politely stuffed away. "She's a failure as a parent," they're thinking.

The sociological data on street kids says that they come from divorced, alcoholic, abusive, unloving and often uneducated families. While that's the classic profile, it's no portrait of my son.

My husband, Lee, and I have, amazingly enough, been married for twenty-one years. Despite attempts to cultivate the pleasure of a glass of wine now and then, I must admit the stuff puts me to sleep. We did scold our son and send him to his room on occasion, even grounded him once or twice. But he was an easy child and, in our family, yelling is something you do on the sidelines of a hockey game. We tend to talk things out.

Unloved? This child has been adored, admired and cherished since he was conceived. To this day, he lights up a room when he walks in. There is an energy, a zest for life that can't be missed. So, please, don't say it's lack of love. I did not do everything right. But love him? Yes, that I did.

This kid's so smart his high school teachers still talk about him. Education runs on both sides of the family. Our family tree is practically sprouting with doctors, lawyers and MBAs.

Having eliminated all the usual criteria of homelessness, "mentally unbalanced" is the only one left. He must be crazy, right? Wrong. He's the most rational, practical person you could hope to meet.

My son has lived on the streets for almost a year now. He is not homeless or living out of a cardboard box. He is a squatter, living with a group of people in an abandoned building that is city-owned. There are many cities where street people take up residency, begin repairs and avoid authorities. Others link in, and soon there is a community of sorts, with rules, guidelines for joining and extended support.

In the beginning, I actually imagined that he was planning to write a book, make a documentary or organize assistance for the homeless. I had it all worked out. My son the social activist, the do-gooder. But it turns out that he did not go to New York City to help those "poor people." He claims that would be a form of manipulation, taking advantage of street people, standing apart and observing. This is his life. Though he comes home for occasional visits, he does not ask us for any money or help.

My son has chosen this life. He is not a failure. It is not a last resort, a desperate attempt to survive or a dead end. He wants to be exactly where he is. Nor did he do this out of a romanticized notion of what it would be like. He knows the hunger, the fear, the violence, the disease.

Day after day, I ask myself, why? Why did he end up in this place? I am not able to fully understand or accept it. I cannot change it, or approve it, or even explain it. Yet it doesn't go away. That is my child out there. I have talked to many of my son's friends. After overcoming my initial reaction to body piercing, multiple tattoos, ripped clothes, and dyed hair, I find them to be kind, intelligent, thoughtful people. They are searching for something.

After my initial horror, I began to comprehend some of the appeal of the life he has chosen. It is a day-to-day existence in which there is no worry about career goals, or what the neighbors will think, or making your mark in the world. My son and his friends focus on the basics of survival. How are you going to eat today? Where will you sleep? Will you keep warm? Where will you relieve yourself? These are questions that inspire considerable passion and take up a major portion of each day. Then you are free to pursue your own daydreams. There is, in fact, a freedom in the squats. The price is danger, discomfort, bugs and ill health; the street beats you up and ages you quickly. But the freedom is there. It is not pretty or pastel or romantic, but beneath the dirt and desperation, I can sometimes see freedom shining through my son's eyes.

A strong sense of community exists among his friends. There are a few subgroups: the down-and-out families; the drug dealers and users; the desperate runaways; and the cases, like my son, who are there by choice. Some are old timers, others are new to the life. The group my son is part of has organized their places of shelter into a network of communication that could be a model for any revolutionary group. There is an excitement and purpose in their rejection of a world order they consider decadent and off-target. They are not abusing the earth or taking advantage of people or accumulating wealth. They may be more sure of what they do not want than what they do, but their intention is to do no harm.

They live in the buildings abandoned by society, eat the vast quantities of food society throws out, and scrounge for clothing and comforts of life from the discarded piles on the curbstone. Books on revolution and philosophy are passed around and discussed late into the night. They offer each other protection and help, often giving their only dollar to one whose need is greater. They are proud of their ability to survive. Sometimes I think they are telling us something about the dysfunction of our nation of unhappy, out-of-control consumers.

I know the dangers of his life. On those long nights when fear grabs hold of me and will not let go, the fears parade beneath my closed eyes. I imagine all the guns in New York City. I see berserk crackheads pursuing my son. I picture him caught in crossfire, or poking his head in the wrong Dumpster, or simply ticking off some hothead. I see him cold and shivering, dirty and lice covered, his immune system weakened, disease ready to ambush him. I see him falling in love and wanting to settle down but unprepared for a "normal" life. I see these things, and for all my attempts at understanding, I am simply a frightened mother.

All this pensive philosophy falls away and is replaced by excited anticipation when he returns for a visit. The one form of assistance that he accepts other than spare building supplies, is a round-trip bus ticket home. We cook a big meal, stock up on a supply of his favorite foods, and expect a late night filled with descriptions of the people in his life: the local hotdog vendor, the Puerto Rican brothers who own the corner bodega, the hovering drug dealer, the young squatter couple from Ohio, the artist with AIDS, the old communist who has been living like this for twenty-five years, the guy who taught him plumbing. There are so many stories.

In the daylight, I surreptitiously examine his skin sores, listen to his cough, and check out his cuts and bruises. He plays with his little brother, rests, showers and takes his sisters out for coffee. Soon the local grapevine carries word of his arrival in town. By the second evening, a jam session is underway in the back room, the pulsating bass notes lull me into a contented sleep.

What is the price he will pay for this lifestyle? I don't know; I can try to guess. I know that he is young, and he will change. I know that the college graduate we once imagined is a dream deferred. I am much more clear about my cost: the endless days of worry, the incessant wondering about what we could have done differently, the hesitant greeting I give him while I look at the sores on his face with a growing dread. Yet, is this so different from any parent? Maybe my case is more dramatic and extreme than many, but in the end, we mothers all worry and pray for our children whatever their age or whereabouts. Our inability to ensure safety and happiness never changes the longing.

Yes, I feel embarrassed when I am questioned, and sometimes I believe I am the failed parent others perceive me to be. Yet I am also proud. This handsome, vibrant young man to whom I gave birth has courage. He is on a quest, even if his goal is not the Holy Grail. He is learning, seeking and questioning everything. What will be his future? In the old days he might have gone west or searched for a river's source; today the cities have become our wilderness. Perhaps he, more than I in my frenetic, practical life, has found what it is all about. Who can say for sure?

So now you will better understand my request. If you pass a strange, grungy kid on the street, wherever you may be, don't look away or grimace in disgust. Look him in the eyes, talk to him, at least give him a greeting—he might be my son, or he could be yours.

~Eva Nagel
Chicken Soup for Every Mom's Soul

95

Good News on the Paper Route

Good fortune shies away from gloom. Keep your spirits up. Good things will come to you and you will come to good things.

~Glorie Abelhas

Once upon a time our four sons had paper routes. Their entrepreneurial dad and I were grateful for the opportunity to help them learn about keeping commitments, working for wages and handling accounts.

We were also grateful the local paper was only a weekly.

On Wednesdays, they'd fold the papers in thirds, slide a rubber band around (on rainy days a plastic bag), and load them in their carrier bags. I'd drop the boys off one by one at their start points, then pick them up at the end of their routes. I'll never forget the dedication and determination on the face of my eight-year-old, Zach, staggering beneath the weight of his bag. His route consisted of two very long blocks of mostly retired people, who anxiously awaited their Wednesday paper. When I picked him up, no matter how exhausted he was, he glowed.

Things like this brought out the glow in me as well. Over my years of mothering, I've found no matter what I set out to teach my kids or how, God never fails to send a few lessons my way too.

Another part of delivering papers was collections. This was critical because each boy was billed for all the papers dropped on our driveway that month. To break even, each needed to collect from at least two-thirds of his customers. So collecting involved lessons in record keeping, courtesy and, most of all, perseverance.

It also took a little extra ooomph to get out the door on winter nights, when dark had fallen early and cold whipped through the hills of suburban California like a most unpopular party crasher.

On one such night, I packed the boys in the van after dinner and we headed out to do collections together. Each boy was loaded with change in his pocket, pen and clipboard in hand.

Ben's route was closest. Heater blasting, we wound our way to the first address. I stopped the car, turned off the ignition and turned to shoo my third son out the door.

The porch light was on, assuring us Ben would not stumble in the dark. But it also illuminated something special for me — a radiant smile spreading over my son's face.

"The nicest people in the world," Ben said before he stepped out into the cold. With the engine off, his brothers and I blew on our hands to keep them warm. Ben came back with dimples flashing.

We drove up four doors to Ben's next customer. As I turned off the engine, Ben beamed again. "The nicest people in the world!"

"I thought the first house was the nicest people in the world," I said.

"Yeah, but these people are too," Ben said, sincere as sunshine. Another big smile, another big tip.

We replayed this scene again and again. Soon Ben's brothers and I forgot the cold, warmed by Ben's infectious love of the people he served. Soon we were all chanting, "The nicest people in the world," in front of each customer's house.

For our family, this became a defining moment. Though our newspaper days are long gone, the lessons we learned stayed with us. Even now, "The nicest people in the world" remains part of our family's idiom — a reminder of the gladness of heart when we forget ourselves and think more highly of those we serve.

~Barbara Curtis
Chicken Soup for the Christian Soul 2

Kiss

Children spell love: "T-I-M-E."
~Dr. Anthony P. Whitman

I'm in the military, and being on time is always an issue. I woke up late that morning, left late... the day was going horribly. My six-year-old son wasn't speedy enough for me, which increased my frustration. We finally left for school and I was in no mood for chit-chat. Halfway there I felt bad for all my grumblings that morning. It wasn't his fault I got up late. He's only six, I thought, but didn't relent. We got to school, gave a quick hug and kiss and then I left. While thinking about what lay ahead for the day, still worrying about being late, I backed out of the school parking lot. Something told me to look up. There he was, my sweet precious child blowing a kiss in the window. It stopped me in my tracks. For all the grumbling I had done that morning, all the yelling to hurry up, that one blown kiss made me stop. Who cared if I was late? I certainly didn't, not by then at least. My boss and my job would wait. What really mattered here? It was a simple reminder to slow down, lighten up, keep it simple. My six-year-old reminded me time really didn't matter, only love. I'll try harder not to forget that lesson, Son—I love you, too.

~Katherine Pepin
Chicken Soup for the Working Mom's Soul

Recipe for Life

Son, you outgrew my lap, but never my heart.
~Author Unknown

I stood at the departure gate in Boston, preparing to cross the Atlantic. Although I had made the journey countless times before, it never really got much easier to leave my home and family, and this time was no different. I looked at my mother, our eyes full of emotion, and as we wondered when we would see each other again she handed me a package, saying it might help me feel better. Typical Mom. Little did I know that it would not only help me feel better, but would also teach me one of life's greatest lessons.

Through the airplane window I watched the last lonely lights slowly disappear off the North American coast and thought about the fateful day years before that had changed my life forever. I had wanted to see Britain, the land of my family's ancestors, and there I was fatally smitten with a young Swiss girl, whom I later married and with whom I had started a family. Now, back in Switzerland after visiting my parents in Massachusetts, I opened my mother's package. It was a book of recipes; I laughed out loud as I thumbed through it. All the sections like vegetables, soups and breads were empty but the one section on desserts was chock full. Typical Mom. Here were handwritten cards bearing names like "Seven Layer Squares" or "Double Chocolate Fudge," many of which my mother had created or named. Then my heart skipped as I noticed that she had written this on the inside front cover:

To my dear son: Make some fudge. Think about us. Remember all the wonderful times we have had together, and have them now with your family.

Love, Mom.

It's okay, she was telling me; we must grow up and lead our own lives, even when it sometimes hurts. But there was more. Recipes in hand, I remembered snowy winter mornings with no school and hot chocolate; Christmases of joy and special homemade treats; afternoons when my mother was always there, consoling me after a rough time with the school bullies by saying, "Let's make cookies!" Now, years later, Mom was telling me about what really matters in life: the only real gifts we can leave behind for our children or loved ones are the appreciation of a full life and the beautiful memories of our time together. Other things will rust or decay or get lost. The things that really matter never will. It is never too late or too early to create beautiful memories and it is now my job to give them to my children.

I sincerely hope that my Swiss-American girls will not do what I did; with luck they will marry the boy next door and stay on this side of the Atlantic. But wherever they may be, I hope that they, too, will one day open my mother's recipes and read her words. And like me, they will find a recipe for life. Typical Mom.

~Arthur Bowler
Chicken Soup for Every Mom's Soul

98

Wasting Water

*I*t was a Friday evening, and I had just settled into bed with a new novel when I heard it: The kitchen faucet had been turned on. Evidently someone in my family was getting a drink of water before bed. Normally, this action would immediately go in one ear and out the other, but tonight was different. Having just spent several weeks educating our two children about conservation, specifically electricity and water, I was overly attuned to every fan blade turning, every drop of water, every flush.

Anyone who has ever paid the household bills will agree that the humid, unrelenting heat of summer can be especially brutal on the pocketbook. Family funds designated for monthly water usage are flushed down the toilet—literally. Electric bills can fry even the most generous of budgets.

So, it was with a large amount of righteous determination that I laid out the rules: Lights and ceiling fans must be turned off when you leave the room. Don't waste the water. Keep the air conditioner on eighty degrees. Turn off the television when you aren't watching. Such simple ideas! I thought. Of course we can do this!

On this particular Friday night, perched in bed reading, I turned my attention away from the running faucet and was temporarily lost in the pages of my paperback. One chapter later, I came out of fantasyland long enough to hear the distinct sound of the kitchen faucet still cascading at full speed.

It couldn't be! At least five full minutes had elapsed since the faucet was first turned on, and it hadn't stopped flowing yet! I was mortified, angry and desperately wanted to punish whoever was blatantly ignoring Rule #2, "Don't Waste the Water."

I leaped out of bed, ready to blast into the kitchen and reprimand the evil-doer, realizing nearly too late that my scantily clad self would not get the respect I needed for this particular lecture. So I stuck my head around the corner, saw my ten-year-old son, Christopher, and exploded, "What in the world are you doing? That water's been running for over five minutes. Are you trying to put our last penny down the drain?"

I stomped back to bed and pulled up the covers, satisfied that my point had been made, but it wasn't long before I heard another noise coming from the kitchen. It wasn't the water running. The faucet had been turned off immediately after my verbal assault.

No, the sound was much worse. It was the unmistakable echo of a muffled sob.

Quickly slipping on a pair of shorts, I ran out into the kitchen. What I saw sent my heart into that tiny place in your throat where it sticks and threatens to make camp. I couldn't swallow. I could only cry.

There was my son, carefully wiping down the stove top, his silent tears mixing with window cleaner as they dropped softly onto the range. I looked around the kitchen that I had been too tired to clean before bed. It was spotless. Dishes were put away, the countertops sparkled, and my sink was once again white. Even the microwave was fingerprint-free.

Stunned that Christopher would take such an initiative, on his own, and thoroughly disgusted with myself I slowly walked up behind my son, and gently encircled him with my arms.

"I'm so sorry, Son. I was wrong. Terribly wrong," I whispered, my hot tears now dropping onto his back.

"It's okay, Mom," he replied faintly. "I understand."

My son's decency and forgiving nature prevailed over my unfortunate behavior.

So who is the adult here? I wondered, as I turned him around to face me.

"Please forgive me," I half-stated, half-asked, mostly begged. "I shouldn't have flown off the handle without checking first. I should have taken the time to see what was happening. I should have trusted you more. I was wrong."

His hug was strong. We held on to each other as he struggled with forgiveness and I suffered with regret and guilt.

"Christopher," I finally said, "you have taught me to take my time and be cautious when accusing anyone of wrongdoing. You've taught me never to assume anything. You've taught me a great deal about your character and about trust."

He was silent, taking in the apology.

"It's awfully hot tonight, isn't it?" I asked, attempting to establish some positive communication. Then, acting on impulse, I blurted out, "Go get your bathing suit on."

Christopher gave me a questioning look but did as I requested, even though the hands on the kitchen clock were approaching midnight. In two minutes we were both outside in the yard with the sprinklers running hard at full tilt. We raced around in circles, laughing, cooling our bodies and acting silly until finally, Christopher asked the inevitable.

"What about the water bill, Mom? It's going to be huge."

"Water, schmater," I replied, letting a shot of spray hit me directly on the rear end. "It's only money, Honey, and you are much more important than any stack of green paper."

The moonlight cast a strange glow upon his face, and I saw what appeared to be a single teardrop falling from one eye. Or maybe it was just the water dripping from his wet head. It really didn't matter because he walked over to me, gave me a high five and whispered, "I love you, Mom."

We romped and played outside that night for nearly an hour. The water ran continuously, but not once did I envision currency being sucked down the drain. And when the bill came later that month, I paid it, with contentment in my soul and joy in my heart, for now I know the simple truth: To err is human, but to be forgiven by your child is truly divine.

~Susan H. Hubbs
Chicken Soup for the Mother's Soul 2

The Purse

*M*y mother always has the Purse with her. The Purse contains a receipt for everything she has purchased that cost more than twenty-five cents since around 1980. The Purse also contains at least one dose of every conceivable over-the-counter medication, all expired.

If you need something, more likely than not, it can be found in the Purse. Tissues? In the Purse. Breath mint? But, of course. Tweezers, nail polish remover, nail clippers, needle and thread, pens, pencils, calendar, calculator, paper clips, tiny stapler—all in the Purse.

The Purse started out a relatively normal size, but over the years it has expanded to what seems like two feet in width. It is hopelessly, permanently open and overflowing. If you need something, virtually everything in the Purse has to be removed and examined in order to locate it, usually onto the nearest park bench or desktop. Many great discoveries are often found during such expeditions into the Purse, like pieces of paper containing long-forgotten locker combinations or telephone messages that should have been returned three or four weeks ago.

My mom just can't bear to not know what I am up to at any given moment. For example, when I get home from school, I have to download everything that happened during the day. Over the years, she has developed expert interrogation techniques that enable her to remove every tiny detail of a day's events from my brain. No detail is too small or too insignificant or too boring for her. And the same applies when she is telling you a story about something that happened to her.

I think my mother's mind is kind of like the Purse inside — all jumbled up with tiny artifacts and useless items. Most of them have to come out and be spread around before you get to something good or what you were looking for, but when she does get to that one valuable thing, it is as if you have just won the lottery.

When I first started hanging out with Heather, it was mostly at school or on the weekends. I don't know why I didn't tell my mom about her. I guess I just wanted to keep something private, or maybe I didn't want her to make a big deal about it, or maybe I was afraid my mom, with the Purse, would want to meet Heather. I think it was mostly that.

And so, every day I would come home from school and proceed to tell my mom what happened in each class, between each class, at lunch and after school. I would be urged to disclose what happened on the way to school and on the way home from school and up until the very second that I walked into the house. But every day I would conveniently leave out all details about Heather.

This went on for a few months and I knew my mom was starting to get suspicious, but I just couldn't tell her about Heather. I didn't want to admit it to myself, but I was ashamed of my mother. It made it worse that she prided herself on the honesty we shared, telling her friends that I could tell her anything and it would be okay.

Since I mostly saw Heather in groups, I would tell my mom that I was going to the movies with Katrina and Steve and Trevor and Julian, but conveniently leaving out Heather. But one Saturday night I decided I wanted to see Heather alone. I wanted to go out on a real date with her. I had two choices: Either come clean and tell my mom about Heather, or lie. So I told my mom I was going to the movies with "some friends." I don't know why I thought this would work. She wanted to know which friends, what movie, what theater, who was driving, what time, if it was an R-rated movie, where I was going afterward, what time I would be home and whether or not I planned on buying popcorn. She left me no choice. I lied to her, and once I got started, I couldn't stop. I lied about things that didn't matter. I told her I was going to buy Red Vines when I knew I wanted

Raisinets, and I told her the wrong movie at the wrong theater. I told her I was going with Katrina and Trevor. I told her Katrina's mom was driving.

And so I left the house with a pit in my stomach. I wasn't good at this lying thing, and I felt guilty. I walked to Heather's house, and we caught the bus to the movies. I don't even remember what movie we saw, but the whole time I could only think about the fact that I had lied to my mom. We came out of the movie holding hands and, to my complete horror, my mom was standing there with the Purse. She had decided to take my sister to a movie and since she didn't want to intrude on me with my friends, she had chosen a different theater than the one I had told her, which of course was the wrong one because I had lied.

She didn't say anything, but if I had been paying attention, I would have been able to read the look of disappointment on her face. I was too busy worrying about her embarrassing me in front of Heather. All I could see was the Purse. I couldn't lie anymore, so I introduced my mom to Heather. My mom just stood there. She was in shock. I was in shock. And then I saw the look.

I guess I should have been relieved when she smiled at me, and then Heather, and invited us to dinner. It seems she had a coupon for Sizzler; they were having some sort of family dinner special for four, and my mom thought it was just perfect that we had run into each other. A coupon? What were we, homeless? I couldn't believe she suggested a coupon in front of Heather. And just when I thought things couldn't get worse, she started looking for the coupon. Oh no! Not the Purse!

At first I tried to stop her as she started to open the Purse. Then I realized there was no stopping her, so I tried to help. The Purse had to be completely unloaded onto a bench outside the theater. I was shuffling through the papers, trying to find the prized coupon, and I guess I was moving my hands too fast and I knocked the Purse. It flipped up in the air and as it did, I saw my life flash before my eyes, as if in slow motion, each one of those million receipts representing an important event. They ended up on the ground, spread about the theater, just as the movie next door was letting out. Crowds of people were stepping on all those papers.

That's when I lost it. The words came out in torrents, and I was powerless to stop them. "I can't believe you!" I yelled. "You are totally embarrassing me! Why do you have to carry all this crap with you all the time? Who cares about all these stupid receipts?" I picked up a Target receipt from the early 1990s. "Look at this," I said. "You bought T-shirts for Dad, and you got them on sale. Isn't that special?"

Heather looked on in shock. She grabbed me by the arm and pulled me to the side. "It's no big deal," she said.

"Yes, it is. I can't believe she's embarrassing me like that. She's so lame."

"Calm down," Heather replied. "It's okay. She was just trying to take us out to a nice dinner. I like Sizzler."

I couldn't calm down. Heather and I just stared at each other.

My mom and my sister were on their hands and knees picking up all those little pieces of paper and bits of string and lint-covered pills. I got down there and helped them. We left the theater and drove Heather home in silence. Other than hello and goodbye, my mom didn't speak to me for the rest of the weekend. I went to school on Monday, and Heather acted weird. I came home from school and walked in as usual. My mom was there, but she didn't say anything to me. Not even, "How was your day?" She just had that look of disappointment on her face. As long as I live, I will never forget that look.

I went up to my room to do some homework and play around on the computer. It was eerily silent. Hey, this isn't so bad, I thought. I have a lot more time to myself. But after a few hours, I began thinking about my day. I had gotten an A on an algebra test. It didn't seem to have any value until I could tell my mom about it. And I wanted to go down there and tell her about Heather. I wanted her to know how bad I felt. Worst of all, I had disappointed her. We had a good relationship and an honest one until I blew it. I lied. I was so disappointed in myself.

I finally got up the courage to go down there. She was sitting at the kitchen table with the Purse, sorting through all those receipts.

Next to her was a new purse. A nice, flat, closable purse. She was transferring things into the new one. Just a few things. I sat there silently for a few minutes watching her sort. I noticed a restaurant receipt from Pizza Hut. I picked it up from the discard pile and noticed the date: August 26. My birthday.

"Hey, remember my birthday party last year?" My mom just looked at me. "You know, when I got the new skateboard?" Silence. More sorting. "I got an A on my algebra test." Silence. It was unbearable. I couldn't take it.

"I'm sorry. I'm really sorry. I didn't mean any of the stuff I said. I... I... miss you." She looked up from the sorting. There was a long pause. I was waiting for her to yell at me. I expected her to tell me how mad she was. I was ready for the worst, but all she said was, "How was your day?"

It's a few months later now, and that new purse, the one my mom was sorting, has become the Purse. And the next time Heather and I run into my mom and the Purse, I hope she has dinner plans in there somewhere.

~Tal Vigderson
Chicken Soup for the Teenage Soul on Tough Stuff

Seven Days to Live

I don't think of all the misery but of the beauty that still remains.
~Anne Frank

I once thought of a midlife crisis as questioning whether to pluck out the gray hairs or to let them grow in haphazardly, to get a divorce or stay in a nowhere marriage, to deal with the hormones or lack thereof. Maybe, better yet, it consisted of changing careers in midstream. At no time did I think it would consist of a phone call stating that my son has taken a turn for the worse, and if I want to see him, I'd better get there now.

That was the way my midlife crisis became defined. He went from having a stomach infection to a total nonfunctioning liver in a matter of hours. I scrambled to make connections from Idaho Falls to Phoenix to arrive at the Mayo Clinic to find my normally muscular son looking like "marshmallow man." His hands were swollen beyond belief, as was the rest of his body. The life support was pumping away, and the tubes seemed to be coming from all parts of his body. The ICU nurse was monitoring him constantly. His only response was the single tear that rolled down his cheek when I grabbed his monstrous hand and told him that I was there and that I loved him so very much.

It seemed as if I went through everything on autopilot or, maybe I should say, with God as the pilot. The prognosis was not good. They were giving him seven days to live, and without a new liver, he would surely die. How does one grasp the fact that someone has to die in order for your son to live? How do you pray that way? The doctor said not to think of it as someone needing to die, but rather that someone is going to die and that those organs could be used rather than having the death serve no purpose whatsoever. Prayers were said all around the world. The love and support was overwhelming.

Jeremiah was put on a transplant list and the waiting seemed like an eternity but in seven days, a young man whose life was cut short by an auto accident breathed new life into my nineteen-year-old son. A new liver, so graciously and selflessly given in grief, gave him the miracle he so desperately needed.

A new chapter was added to the crisis when Jeremiah began to have a toxic reaction to the antirejection medication. Once again, I watched him slide into a near-death mode, first losing his speech and then having seizures and then being placed back on life support. The vigil began all over again. The bedside watch for any indication that he was going to come out of it whole was long and agonizing. Hours turned into days, but finally the life support was removed, and he once again was on the arduous path of a long, uphill climb.

He slowly started to come out of his toxic state, but the doctors had no idea how long it would take to flush the poisons from his brain or if he would ever regain total function. A month had gone by, and I had to return to my job and to register my younger son in school. I had to leave Jeremiah in the hands of the wonderful staff at the Mayo Clinic and his father. The hardest thing I ever had to do in my entire life was to walk out of that hospital room and get on an airplane. I could not say goodbye to him. All I could say were the words that I had repeated over and over to him: "I love you, Jeremiah!"

He was just starting to support himself with a walker and could barely walk without the help of a therapist. He was unable to speak. He could give thumbs up but it was more of thumbs sideways. I went back to work and somehow went through the motions to get through each day. The nurse with the transplant team gave me a daily report on his slow but steady progress.

Then I received a phone call that seemed to take an eternity. I heard from a very slow and very forced voice, "Hi, Mom," a very long pause and then a forced and slurred, "I love you, Mom!" Tears were streaming down my cheeks because they were the very words I had repeated over and over to him, "I love you!" "I love you, Jeremiah!" "I love you!" They were words that every mother longs to hear and wants to hear but probably doesn't get to hear often enough. They were words that only a mother could recognize and decipher. On October 8, 2001, Jeremiah celebrated his twenty-first birthday. My son survived because someone was able to see beyond their own grief and loss to grant my son the gift of life.

As for gray hair and hormones, let's just say I'm keeping everything in perspective because I've learned what a crisis really is. The important part of midlife is life — life and love are all that matters.

~Mary Anne Fox
Chicken Soup to Inspire a Woman's Soul

Tears and Laughter

Through misted eyes I gazed at my little son as if for the first time — and perhaps for the last time. He lay sedated, fighting for his life, with two holes in his heart and pneumonia. Doctors questioned whether my two-month-old baby with Down syndrome would live.

I wanted to remember what it felt like to be his mother. I wanted to savor my inability to distinguish where my flesh ended and his began. As I softly pressed my cheek against his, our connection calmed my fears. I wanted to remember the wisp of curls that twirled behind his ears, and the feeling of life fulfilled when his almond-shaped eyes drifted to look into mine. Mostly, I wanted to remember the inexplicable warmth that filled my heart when I held him.

I had dreamed of days when we might build sand castles at the beach together; when Eric would swing so high in the park that he'd feel like he was flying; when he would play catch with his daddy and cuddle with me. I begged the doctors to keep him alive. I pleaded with the nurses to feed him more. And I prayed to a God that I didn't know well to let me keep my baby.

After one special conversation with my husband, Bob, I came to realize that Eric's soul would choose whether to stay with us or let his body go. We stood on either side of his cold metal hospital crib and told him we would stay with him, love him and nurture him if he chose to stay with us. My mind trusted whatever his soul chose, but my heart ached with the hope that he would choose to stay.

Meanwhile, desperate to remember what it was like to hold my baby when it might last only these two precious months — to remember every moment — I decided to write it all down so I could never forget anything. From that moment of resolve, words flooded my thoughts. I formulated chapters in my mind between conversations; phrases appeared as I slipped off to sleep; and whole pages might appear to me upon waking, while driving or at Eric's bedside.

During his second week on life support, I strode into the hospital, past the reception desk to the bank of elevators, all the while transmuting emotions into words, mixing hopes and prayers. I stood before the elevator doors and stared up at numbers blinking all too slowly — 5... 4... 3... 2... — until the soft bell rang and the doors parted to reveal smiling grandparents, nurses and orderlies from the pediatric ward. They passed within a few feet of me, but we were worlds apart. I entered and leaned against the cold wall, returning to my sanctuary of words as the elevator rose, and then I walked slowly down the long hallway to the children's ward.

Before Bob arrived, I whispered to my baby about plans for our book; it would be our secret. Then I remembered that I don't keep secrets, especially when opening up is essential, so I told my husband and some close friends as we gathered near Eric. I began writing that very evening at my kitchen table, occasionally turning to gaze upon the empty cradle in the living room, a reminder of my baby still in the hospital. It felt like a part of me had been pulled away.

Eric triumphed through those six weeks of life support, but over the next two years, he had numerous bouts of pneumonia, respiratory viruses and digestive problems. He was dependent on a breathing tank for his oxygen. We always knew where our little guy crawled to by following the fifty-foot oxygen tube that trailed from the breathing tank at the end of the hall, wound around the kitchen table and into the living room, and ended attached to Eric's face, allowing the prongs to let purified air flow into his nasal passages.

When he was seventeen months old, the doctors told us it was time for Eric to have his heart repaired. They said, "He's as healthy as he can be under such conditions. If you wait much longer, it will be too late." But they couldn't guarantee that his fragile heart and weak lungs would make it through the grueling surgery.

Forty-eight hours later, I stood by his crib and gazed past the tubes and wires to his angelic face, looked down and watched as he opened his eyes and focused on me. His smile illuminated the room. I let out a cry of relief. I knew Eric was here to stay.

Through it all, the writing has carried us through the recurring life-support crises as Eric's legs dangled again and again off death's pier. I recorded every experience, every emergency and breakthrough, every painful moment and every miracle as love carried us deeper into ourselves, peeling away our resistance, teaching us to rely on faith.

Our son needed cardiologists, pediatric nurses, therapists and specialists to repair his heart; we needed Eric to repair ours. Our lives were opened up to a degree I never knew existed. In the midst of these past years, I found myself sitting at the large table in the corner room of the Unity Center, where we held our Up with Down meetings. I sat across from a brand-new mom and dad. She held her one-month-old, blond-haired, baby with Down syndrome protectively against her chest, while her husband wrung his hands in his lap. "We haven't told our parents yet," she said. My eyes fixed on the young father's face as she spoke. His tears never stopped.

Then it came to me that my book should not be a secret from anyone, because we have known great pain and found miraculous healing. It comes from Eric's heart and mine. After more than four years, his valiant little heart beats stronger with each passing day we are given.

Today, we can't keep our son out of the playground. It's either monkey bars or basketball, soccer or T-ball. We've since built many a sand castle together, discovered new parks and playgrounds, have taken turns reading and rereading his books—yes, he is reading now! We have pretended to be manatees in our swimming pool and have eaten too much popcorn at the circus. We have a special boy who lives a joyful life.

Eric has his heart checked once a year, but his laughter washes away my fears. When I look into his bright eyes and feel the warmth of his bear hugs, I know his loving heart is going to be just fine. And so is mine.

~Kimberly Thompson
Chicken Soup to Inspire the Body & Soul

Chicken Soup for the Soul

Share with Us

*W*e would like to know how these stories affected you and which ones were your favorites. Please e-mail us and let us know.

We also would like to share your stories with future readers. You may be able to help another reader, and become a published author at the same time. Please send us your own stories and poems for our future books. Some of our past contributors have launched writing and speaking careers from the publication of their stories in our books!

Your stories have the best chance of being used if you submit them through our web site, at:

www.chickensoup.com

If you do not have access to the Internet, you may submit your stories by mail or by facsimile. Please do not send us any book manuscripts, unless through a literary agent, as these will be automatically discarded.

Chicken Soup for the Soul
P.O. Box 700
Cos Cob, CT 06807-0700
Fax 203-861-7194

Chicken Soup for the Soul®

Like Mother, Like Daughter

Our **101** BEST STORIES

Stories about the Special Bond between Mothers and Daughters

Jack Canfield
& Mark Victor Hansen
edited by Amy Newmark

How often have you seen a teenage girl pretend to be perturbed, but secretly smile, when she is told that she acts or looks just like her mother? Fathers, brothers, and friends shake their head in wonder as girls "turn into their mothers." This book contains the 101 best stories from Chicken Soup's library on the mother-daughter bond. Mothers and daughters will laugh, cry, and find inspiration in these stories that remind them of their mutual appreciation.

978-1-935096-07-8

Just for Mothers and Daughters

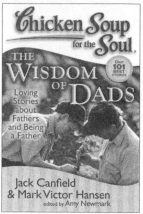

The Wisdom of Dads

Children view their fathers with awe from the day they are born. Fathers are big and strong and seem to know everything, except for a few teenage years when fathers are perceived to know nothing! This book represents a new theme for Chicken Soup – 101 stories selected from 35 past books, all stories focusing on the wisdom of dads. Stories are written by sons and daughters about their fathers, and by fathers relating stories about their children.

Dads & Daughters

Whether she is ten years old or fifty – she will always be his little girl. And daughters take care of their dads too, whether it is a tea party for two at age five or loving care fifty years later. This wide-ranging exploration of the relationship between fathers and daughters provides an entirely new reading experience for Chicken Soup fans, with selections from forty past Chicken Soup books. Stories were written by fathers about their daughters and by daughters about their fathers, celebrating the special bond between fathers and daughters.

On Being a Parent

Parenting is the hardest and most rewarding job in the world. This upbeat and compelling new book includes the best selections on parenting from Chicken Soup's rich history, with 101 stories carefully selected to appeal to both mothers and fathers. This is a great book for couples to share, whether they are just embarking on their new adventure as parents or reflecting on their lifetime experience.

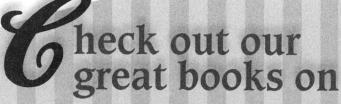

Check out our great books on

Moms Know Best

"Mom will know where it is…what to say…how to fix it." This Chicken Soup book focuses on the pervasive wisdom of mothers everywhere, and includes the best 101 stories from Chicken Soup's library on our perceptive, understanding, and insightful mothers. These stories celebrate the special bond between mothers and children, our mothers' unerring wisdom about everything from the mundane to the life-changing, and the hard work that goes into being a mother every day.

Grand and Great

A parent becomes a new person the day the first grandchild is born. Formerly serious adults become grandparents who dote on their grandchildren. This new book includes the best stories on being a grandparent from past Chicken soup books, representing a new reading experience for even the most devoted Chicken Soup fan. Everyone can understand the special ties between grandparents and grandchildren -- the unlimited love, the mutual admiration and unqualified acceptance.

Teens Talk Growing Up

Being a teenager is hard — school is challenging, college and career are looming on the horizon, family issues arise, friends and love come and go, bodies and emotions go through major changes, and many teens experience the loss of a loved one for the first time. This book reminds teenagers that they are not alone, as they read stories written by other teens about the problems and issues they all face every day.

Family

Our 101 BEST STORIES

Books for Teens

Chicken Soup for the Soul: Preteens Talk
Inspiration and Support for Preteens from Kids Just Like Them
978-1-935096-00-9

Chicken Soup for the Soul: Teens Talk Growing Up
Stories about Growing Up, Meeting Challenges, and
Learning from Life 978-1-935096-01-6

Chicken Soup for the Soul: Teens Talk Tough Times
Stories about the Hardest Parts of Being a Teenager
978-1-935096-03-0

Chicken Soup for the Soul: Teens Talk Relationships
Stories about Family, Friends, and Love
978-1-935096-06-1

Chicken Soup for the Soul: Christian Teen Talk
Christian Teens Share Their Stories of Support, Inspiration and
Growing Up 978-1-935096-12-2

Chicken Soup for the Soul: Christian Kids
Stories to Inspire, Amuse, and Warm the Hearts of Christian
Kids and Their Parents
978-1-935096-13-9

Books for Pet Lovers

Loving Our Cats

Heartwarming and Humorous Stories about
Our Feline Family Members

978-1-935096-08-5

We are all crazy about our mysterious cats. Sometimes they are our best friends; sometimes they are aloof. They are fun to watch and often surprise us. These true stories, the best from Chicken Soup's library, will make readers appreciate their own cats and see them with a new eye. Readers will revel in the heartwarming, amusing, inspirational, and occasionally tearful stories about our best friends and faithful companions — our cats.

Loving Our Dogs

Heartwarming and Humorous Stories about
Our Companions and Best Friends

978-1-935096-05-4

We are all crazy about our dogs and can't read enough about them, whether they're misbehaving and giving us big, innocent looks, or loyally standing by us in times of need. This new book from Chicken Soup for the Soul contains the 101 best dog stories from the company's extensive library. Readers will revel in the heartwarming, amusing, inspirational, and occasionally tearful stories about our best friends and faithful companions — our dogs.

Chicken Soup for the Soul

Who Is
Jack Canfield?

*J*ack Canfield is the co-creator and editor of the *Chicken Soup for the Soul* series, which *Time* magazine has called "the publishing phenomenon of the decade." Jack is also the co-author of eight other bestselling books including *The Success Principles™: How to Get from Where You Are to Where You Want to Be, Dare to Win, The Aladdin Factor, You've Got to Read This Book,* and *The Power of Focus: How to Hit Your Business and Personal and Financial Targets with Absolute Certainty.*

Jack has recently developed a telephone coaching program and an online coaching program based on his most recent book *The Success Principles*. He also offers a seven-day *Breakthrough to Success* seminar every summer, which attracts 400 people from fifteen countries around the world.

Jack is the CEO of the Canfield Training Group in Santa Barbara, California, and founder of the Foundation for Self-Esteem in Culver City, California. He has conducted intensive personal and professional development seminars on the principles of success for over a million people in twenty-three countries. Jack is a dynamic keynote speaker and he has spoken to hundreds of thousands of others at more than 1,000 corporations, universities, professional conferences and conventions, and has been seen by millions more on national television shows such as *The Today Show, Fox and Friends, Inside Edition, Hard Copy, CNN's Talk Back Live, 20/20, Eye to Eye,* and the *NBC Nightly News* and the *CBS Evening News.*

Jack is the recipient of many awards and honors, including three honorary doctorates and a *Guinness World Records Certificate* for having seven books from the *Chicken Soup for the Soul* series appearing on the *New York Times* bestseller list on May 24, 1998.

To write to Jack or for inquiries about Jack as a speaker, his coaching programs, trainings or seminars, use the following contact information:

Jack Canfield
The Canfield Companies
P.O. Box 30880 • Santa Barbara, CA 93130
phone: 805-563-2935 • fax: 805-563-2945
E-mail: info@jackcanfield.com
www.jackcanfield.com

Who Is
Mark Victor Hansen?

*M*ark Victor Hansen is the co-founder of *Chicken Soup for the Soul*, along with Jack Canfield. He is also a sought-after keynote speaker, bestselling author, and marketing maven.

For more than thirty years, Mark has focused solely on helping people from all walks of life reshape their personal vision of what's possible. His powerful messages of possibility, opportunity, and action have created powerful change in thousands of organizations and millions of individuals worldwide.

Mark's credentials include a lifetime of entrepreneurial success. He is a prolific writer with many bestselling books, such as *The One Minute Millionaire, Cracking the Millionaire Code, How to Make the Rest of Your Life the Best of Your Life, The Power of Focus, The Aladdin Factor,* and *Dare to Win,* in addition to the *Chicken Soup for the Soul* series. Mark has had a profound influence in the field of human potential through his library of audios, videos, and articles in the areas of big thinking, sales achievement, wealth building, publishing success, and personal and professional development.

Mark is the founder of the *MEGA Seminar Series. MEGA Book Marketing University* and *Building Your MEGA Speaking Empire* are annual conferences where Mark coaches and teaches new and aspiring authors, speakers, and experts on building lucrative publishing and speaking careers. Other MEGA events include *MEGA Info-Marketing* and *My MEGA Life*.

He has appeared on *Oprah*, *CNN*, and *The Today Show*. He has been quoted in *Time*, *U.S. News & World Report*, *USA Today*, *New York Times*, and *Entrepreneur* and has had countless radio interviews, assuring our planet's people that "You can easily create the life you deserve."

As a philanthropist and humanitarian, Mark works tirelessly for organizations such as Habitat for Humanity, American Red Cross, March of Dimes, Childhelp USA, and many others. He is the recipient of numerous awards that honor his entrepreneurial spirit, philanthropic heart, and business acumen. He is a lifetime member of the Horatio Alger Association of Distinguished Americans, an organization that honored Mark with the prestigious Horatio Alger Award for his extraordinary life achievements.

Mark Victor Hansen is an enthusiastic crusader of what's possible and is driven to make the world a better place.

Mark Victor Hansen & Associates, Inc.
P.O. Box 7665 • Newport Beach, CA 92658
phone: 949-764-2640 • fax: 949-722-6912
www.markvictorhansen.com

Who Is
Amy Newmark?

*A*my Newmark was recently named publisher of Chicken Soup for the Soul, after a thirty-year career as a writer, speaker, financial analyst, and business executive in the worlds of finance and telecommunications.

Amy is a graduate of Harvard College, where she majored in Portuguese, minored in French, and traveled extensively. She is also the mother of two children in college and has two grown stepchildren.

After a long career writing books on telecommunications, voluminous financial reports, business plans, and corporate press releases, Chicken Soup for the Soul is a breath of fresh air for Amy. She has fallen in love with Chicken Soup for the Soul and its life-changing books, and found it a true pleasure to conceptualize, compile, and edit the "101 Best Stories" books for our readers.

The best way to contact Chicken Soup for the Soul is through our web site, at www.chickensoup.com. This will always get the fastest attention.

If you do not have access to the Internet, please contact us by mail or by facsimile.

Chicken Soup for the Soul
P.O. Box 700
Cos Cob, CT 06807-0700
Fax 203-861-7194

Chicken Soup for the Soul

Thank You!

*W*e would like to thank the entire staff of Chicken Soup for the Soul for their help on this project and the 101 Best series in general. Among our California staff, we would especially like to single out D'ette Corona, who is the heart and soul of the Chicken Soup publishing operation, and who put together the first draft of this manuscript, Barbara LoMonaco for invaluable assistance in obtaining the fabulous quotations that add depth and meaning to this book, Patty Hansen for her extra special help with the permissions for these fabulous stories and for her amazing knowledge of the Chicken Soup library, and Patti Clement for her help with permissions and other organizational matters. In our Connecticut office, we would like to thank our able editorial assistants, Valerie Howlett and Madeline Clapps, for their assistance in setting up our new offices, editing, and helping us put together the best possible books. We would also like to thank our master of design, Brian Taylor at Pneuma Books, for his brilliant vision for our covers and interiors. Finally, none of this would be possible without the business and creative leadership of our CEO, Bill Rouhana, and our president, Bob Jacobs.

Chicken Soup for the Soul

www.chickensoup.com